Praise for *There's a Customer Born Every Minute*

"P.T. Barnum was quite an extraordinary human being, and this book is great. It's time someone wrote the truth about Barnum."
> —Evel Knievel

"A fascinating look at one of the greatest and most misunderstood promotional geniuses of all time. *There's a Customer Born Every Minute* is the next best thing to having P.T. Barnum himself personally reveal his money-making secrets to you."
> —David L. Deutsch, Advertising and Direct Mail Copywriter,
> author, *Million Dollar Marketing Secrets*

"This book will hold you spellbound. It is electrifying! It illuminates every creative impulse of Barnum and his timeless marketing genius. Joe Vitale has captured the power of Barnum's successes and has given us the tools to plug in! If you want to dramatically increase your ability to promote your business, then buy this book now!"
> —Allen D'Angelo, M.S., author, *Explosive Marketing:
> 2000 Ways to Release Creative Marketing Power into
> Your Business to Quadruple Your Income*

"Joe Vitale presents a three-ring circus of wise and profit-producing ideas in *There's a Customer Born Every Minute*. The book is as easy to read as it is enlightening. It's a must-read if you have even a vague interest in money."
> —Jay Conrad Levinson, author, *Guerrilla Marketing* series

"P.T. Barnum became rich and famous because he understood people. This made doing business with them simple. This book reveals the great showman's business secrets, including his little-known negotiation skills."
> —Gerard Nierenberg, President, The Negotiation Institute,
> author, *The Art of Negotiating* and *The Complete Negotiator*

"At a time when 43 percent of Americans cannot recall the name of the vice president of the United States (according to a 1994 Gallup Poll), Barnum's name remains a household word. Joe Vitale quickly dispels ignorantly conceived myths and rumors, and reveals Barnum for what he truly was (and still is)—a marketing titan whose genius *must* be reviewed and modeled after. Anyone who claims to be serious about business, marketing, and advertising needs to read, study, and keep a copy of this book handy."

> —Hector R. D. Baron, Marketing and
> Sales Strategies Consultant, Executive Project Coordinator
> of The Billionaire Power Summit in the Philippines

"It's a Barnum and Bailey world, so it's fitting that the best business book of the year is one about the most exciting and original businessman of them all—P.T. Barnum. Unlocking years-old secrets, Joe Vitale's fresh perspective on this legendary master is a joy to read, plus it's packed with up-to-date insights for today's entrepreneurs. There really is a customer born every minute, and this book is the best way to learn how to win in the clown-eat-clown circus world of business today."

> —John Martin, CEO, Bold Creative Services

"Definitely a mind-stretching read."

> —Lennie Grimaldi, Publicist, author of *Chased* and *Only in Bridgeport*

"Wow! I *really* couldn't put this down! This magnificent new book reveals the inner workings of a historic, inventive, and persistently positive man. Joe Vitale has taken the classic wisdom of P.T. Barnum and made it accessible to us all. Amazing!"

> —Ron Kaufman, President, Active Learning Sales Training, Singapore

"This book fired up my imagination, blasted me past my limits, and launched a zillion ideas for outrageous personal and professional success. It's fun, fast-paced, inspiring, and packed with powerful ideas!"

> —Rick Butts, President, The Safari Adventure Company

"What could be more fun to read than the business secrets of P.T. Barnum?! This book is filled with practical information I can use right now, and information I want to pass on to my clients and anyone else who wants to further their stretch and achieve more happiness and success."

> —William Wittmann, M.Ed., LMP, Seattle

THERE'S A CUSTOMER BORN EVERY MINUTE

P.T. BARNUM'S AMAZING 10 "RINGS OF POWER" FOR CREATING FAME, FORTUNE, AND A BUSINESS EMPIRE TODAY— GUARANTEED!

JOE VITALE

WILEY

John Wiley & Sons, Inc.

Published by John Wiley & Sons, Inc., Hoboken, New Jersey.
Published simultaneously in Canada.

For general information on our other products and services or for technical support, please contact
our Customer Care Department within the United States at (800) 762-2974, outside the United
States at (317) 572-3993 or fax (317) 572-4002.

Wiley also publishes its books in a variety of electronic formats. Some content that appears in print
may not be available in electronic books. For more information about Wiley products, visit our web
site at www.wiley.com.

Library of Congress Cataloging-in-Publication Data:

Vitale, Joe, 1953–
    There's a customer born every minute : P.T. Barnum's amazing 10 "rings of power" for creating
fame, fortune, and a business empire today—guaranteed! / Joe Vitale.
        p.   cm.
    Includes bibliographical references and index.
    ISBN-13: 978-0-471-78462-3 (cloth)
    ISBN-10: 0-471-78462-1 (cloth)
    1. Success in business.   2. Barnum, P.T. (Phineas Taylor), 1810–1891.   I. Title.
    HF5386.V58   2006
    658.4'09—dc22

                                                                    2005034030

Printed in the United States of America.

10 9 8 7 6 5 4 3 2 1

For Murray Rogow,
the world's second greatest press agent
(P.T. Barnum was the first)

I fully believe that if you faithfully follow my methods you cannot fail.

—P.T. Barnum, 1891, five days before he died

P.T. Barnum. (Used by permission, The Barnum Museum, Bridgeport, Connecticut.)

Contents

Introduction

I believe this world is in a great measure what we choose to make it, and I therefore propose to point out so far as I can, the methods that are best calculated to enable us to "get on" in it, and obtain comparative happiness.

P. T. Barnum.

Hotel Victoria
London January 19th 1890.

The handwritten introduction (on the previous page) by P.T. Barnum comes from *Dollars and Sense*, one of the many reissues of the famous showman's autobiography. The first time I saw this handwriting in a copy of the book on display in the Barnum Museum in Bridgeport, Connecticut, I assumed Barnum had personally signed the book. Apparently that's what Barnum wanted people to think. Dr. A. H. Saxon, author of *P.T. Barnum: The Legend and the Man*, told me the handwritten introduction was printed in *every* copy of *Dollars and Sense*. It was probably a clever marketing strategy on Barnum's part, knowing people would assume the book was a priceless autographed edition and more books would be sold. Hoping for the same thing, I include Barnum's introduction in this book.

(From author's private collection)

Foreword

Why is Joe Vitale writing about P.T. Barnum?
And how do you win as a result of it?

"There's a sucker born every minute" is a quote often attributed to P.T. Barnum. There's only one problem: Barnum never said it.

Barnum said lots of incredible things, and you're about to read them in a way that will make them applicable to your work because of one man: Joe Vitale, the P.T. Barnum of today.

Barnum was one of the most advanced thinkers of his time.
So is Joe Vitale.
Barnum was the consummate promoter.
So is Joe Vitale.
Barnum was a succinct and prolific writer.
So is Joe Vitale.
Barnum was a dynamic speaker.
So is Joe Vitale.
Barnum was hypnotic.
So is Joe Vitale—he even wrote the book on it.
Barnum was an idea person.
So is Joe Vitale.
And like all great men, Barnum was ahead of his time.
So is Joe Vitale.

Everyone is looking for the perfect mentor. Most people look for someone who is alive. As an advanced thinker, Dr. Joe had a hard time relating to present-day thinkers, so he turned to history to find his mentor, and found the perfect match. Vitale had the wisdom to study the master promoter and idea man of his time, P.T. Barnum, and through Joe's interpretations, P.T. can be your mentor, too.

If Barnum were still alive, he'd be vying with Joe Vitale for the title of Internet viral-marketing king. If Barnum were still alive, he'd be writing about Joe Vitale.

The first time I came across *There's a Customer Born Every Minute*, I was jealous. The book was so well done, so well written, I wished I had written it myself. I e-mailed Joe, ordered a case of copies (autographed, of course), and sent them to business friends.

Their response was the same as yours will be: Wow!

When you look at the chapter titles and scan some of the ideas contained on every page, you not only admire the years of study and research that went into creating this book, you also can't wait to devour it. Actually, you'll get excited.

Once you dig into Barnum's 10 rings of power, you will become empowered.

Once you dig into Barnum's incredible power to persuade, you will become a persuader.

Once you dig into Barnum's power to promote, you will become a promoter.

Once you dig into Barnum's success secrets, you will understand what it will take for you to become a success.

This book is loaded. It's loaded with thoughts, gems, and insights that you can use the minute you read them.

A word of caution: This is a thinking man's (okay, a thinking person's) book. It will give you pause. The good news is, it will give you hundreds of ideas of how you can follow in the successful footsteps of P.T. Barnum. Read it twice. Study it. You'll find, as I did, that it's a book you can carry with you and read for an instant inspiration.

There's a Customer Born Every Minute—and I'm one of them.

—JEFFREY GITOMER
Author of *The Little Red Book of Selling*

Preface

How P.T. Barnum Almost Killed Me Twice (and Why I Don't Really Mind)

I never knew P.T. Barnum, of course. The famous showman has been dead more than one hundred years. Still, his name, business, and influence are alive and well today, and will be well into the twenty-first century. There have been several movies about him, several plays, numerous books, and, as I pen these words, Elvis Costello is writing an opera about Barnum. As long as there will be a circus, the name Barnum will remain associated with it. And as long as I live, I'll never forget how Barnum inadvertently nearly killed me twice.

I was 16 years old the first time. I wanted to be Harry Excello, the world's most famous magician. I went to the circus when it came to my hometown in Niles, Ohio in the late 1960s with the idea of talking to the magician who worked with it. Young and bold, feeling a little Barnum and Houdini in my blood, I walked right into the tent and asked to see the magician.

He came out and we talked. He was friendly and charming, and

XV

seemed more like a used car salesman trapped inside a magician's role in a circus. As we spoke I learned that he loved magic, loved the circus, and loved his work. He introduced me to the sword swallower, another charming man, only he wore a Tarzan-like outfit to show his tan and his muscles. I remember thinking that he looked like a gypsy. I asked the sword swallower how he performed his tricks, but he laughed and said it was a family secret. For a 16-year-old boy in a small midwestern town, I felt as if I was walking among the legends of the earth.

The sword swallower and magician asked me if I wanted to work in the circus for the weekend. I couldn't believe it. I could help clean up the grounds, they said, and take down the tents when the show ended the next night. Wow, I would get to clean up animal dung! I would get to see the circus acts for free and they would pay me three dollars a day. The money meant nothing. The adventure meant everything. I jumped at the chance.

I was in for a surprise. I found the circus to be a business like any other. Events started and stopped on time. People had jobs to do and places to go. They worked, entertained, laughed, cried, and complained. They were paid like any other employee in any other business. I learned that even when something was fun—like being a clown, a magician, or a sword swallower—good business kept the jobs alive. It may have been show business, but it was still a *business*.

This is where Barnum almost killed me the first time.

On closing night, when things were being taken down and packed up, I somehow found myself walking through the entrance of the main tent just as several elephants were being directed out of the tent. One of the animal caretakers yelled for me to get out of the way. I'll always remember the look on his face. He looked angry as well as terrified. He knew a young man was about to be trampled to death. *Me.*

I froze. For a moment I felt as if I was standing in the wilds of Africa and killer elephants were coming to mindlessly crush me like a grape. I remember glancing to my left and then to my right, seeing the empty wooden bleachers on both sides of me, knowing they were too tall for me to reach from where I stood, and realizing I had nowhere to run.

My heart pounded like a wild drum. I could feel the throbbing in my ears. I can still see the elephants coming at me, their huge gray bellies swaying left and right as their feet thundered on the dirt. I quickly pushed my back against the bleacher on my left, sucked in my breath, tried to become one with the wood, and became very religious. I prayed that I would live. I prayed that I would not be flattened by a beast of the jungle. This was no way for the great Harry Excello to exit the world.

The first elephant passed without coming too close to me. So did the second. I can still smell them both, though. Even today. But the third elephant must have been related to Jumbo, because he was colossal in size and seemed destined to turn me into his next coat. He was so close to me that his canvas skin blocked out my view of the world, but he, too, missed me. All the elephants came, passed, and went on their way. I was safe.

I never forgot the experience. In a way, the near fatal trampling by a herd of circus elephants when I was a boy branded my soul with the name Barnum forever.

The second time Barnum almost killed me occurred while writing the first edition of this book.

I found Barnum to be an overwhelming character. For example, although everyone thinks of Barnum in connection with the circus, he actually didn't run a circus until he was a senior citizen. That was one of his *final* accomplishments. Before that he had been everything from a lottery salesman to an entertainer, bestselling author, mayor, manager, publisher, public speaker, crusader against alcohol, philanthropist, entrepreneur, practical joker, friend to presidents and royalty, and owner of one of America's biggest and most successful early museums.

Trying to follow Barnum's colorful and active career throughout his 80 years, trying to make sense of his exhibitions, working to understand the time he lived in, fighting to make sense of his tendency to pull jokes on the public, digging to unearth his secrets for making any business a success—all worked to make me one stressed out adult.

In addition, I spent every penny I had on old books by and about Barnum, and for traveling across the states to visit museums and historical collections concerning him. I was also pushing aside other projects in order to write this book. I was becoming obsessed. One day, during the writing of the first edition of this book back in 1995, I looked at my savings account and saw it was empty. So was my checking account. So was my business account. I was spending all my money on Barnum collectibles and all my time on this book. I was neglecting everything else. That's when I realized this Barnum book was literally taking its toll on me.

Many times I nearly gave up, thinking Barnum was far too big a character for me to wrestle to the ground. Many times I felt such tension that I wondered how my heart withstood the pressure. This has been the hardest book I've ever written. The statistics maintained on my word processing program say I've rewritten this book 438 times, and that was just the first edition of this book. I've since rewritten it and expanded it for this new edition. I spent hours, days, weeks, months, researching, writing, rewriting, polishing, testing, learning, understanding, and expressing Barnum's business secrets. This has not been an easy task. I really felt as if this book on Barnum would kill me.

Fortunately it—like the elephants—let me survive, and once I began *using* Barnum's techniques, I also began to prosper. I now live a life of luxury, with numerous books to my credit, and great wealth, as well.

That's why I have a special fondness for Barnum today. He took me to the edge of life and let me see the true joy of living. Nearly being creamed by an elephant was, well, hair raising. (I had hair then.) Researching this book has been—I admit it—inspiring. I've learned new ways to help my clients achieve breakthrough success in business. In short, Barnum gave me for free what he charged millions of people to receive during his lifetime: *Excitement.*

As a result of my invigorating research and writing, you now hold in your hands the first book ever written on the sales and marketing methods of the world's greatest showman—a man who in his day became rich beyond all measure and famous beyond all comprehension; a man who introduced the first superstars to the world and was never afraid of seeking publicity in some of the most audacious ways imaginable; a man so deeply religious that his friends called him Reverend Barnum; a man who survived our bloody Civil War, personal bankruptcy, and some of the worst economic panics in American history and *still* became a millionaire; a man who nearly inadvertently killed me twice—Phineas Taylor Barnum.

Let the show begin!

—JOE VITALE

Austin, Texas   www.mrfire.com

Acknowledgments

The million-dollar title for this book came from David Deutsch, brilliant copywriter and friend. Barbara Celitans showed extraordinary service by opening the doors of the San Antonio public library's Hertzberg Circus Museum before regular hours and allowing me to look through Barnum's original letters. Mary Witkowski, head of the historical collections at the Bridgeport Public Library, helped me locate rare books, letters, and ads by and about Barnum.

Dr. Arthur H. Saxon, biographer of Barnum, patiently answered my questions and gave me a personal tour of the Bridgeport Barnum would have known. Robert Pelton, past curator of the Barnum Museum in Bridgeport, personally guided me through the museum and photocopied special articles.

Allen D'Angelo donated his time and effort in conducting research and locating many rare articles for me. Penny Perez acted as my special assistant while researching Barnum in Bridgeport. Blair Warren helped me in San Antonio. Colleen of Houston's Colleen's Books and Linda Strike of Optical Insights located rare books about Barnum and his era. Ronnie Reno of Brockton Publishing scanned Barnum's introduction at the front of this book, and his famous talk on making money at the back of this book, so I didn't have to retype either.

Murray Raphel helped by lending me a few of his books to stimulate my thinking. Kare Anderson generously gave me leads, ideas, and advice. Paul Hartunian has been a source of inspiration. Win Wenger shared his techniques for inducing creativity. Paul Mattek, Rick Butts, and Linda Credeur let me test drive Project Phineas on their businesses. Nerissa, my love, was supportive of my investing more time in the rewriting of this book. She fed the cats and dog so I could get working.

I want to acknowledge my four primary sources for the information in this book: Bryan's edition of Barnum's autobiography, A. H. Saxon's biography of Barnum and his collection of Barnum's letters, and Kundardt's pictorial life history of the great showman. These as well as all other sources are listed in the bibliography.

Advance readers whose input helped shape the final book include Linda Credeur, Rick Butts, Connie Schmidt, Ron Kaye, Greg Manning, Ron Kaufman, Lennie Grimaldi, Robert Pelton, Penny Perez, Larry Weinstein, Mark Weisser, Blair Warren, John Martin, Allen D'Angelo, William Wittmann, Scott Hammaker, Debbie Zimmerman, Brocky Brown, David Deutsch, Hector Baron, Murray Rogow, and Jim King.

Upon my soul, I could not have completed this book without everyone's help. Thank you, one and all.

1

Presenting . . . the Greatest Marketeer of All Time—*P. T. Barnum!*

I know you will not consider a few words of advice from me as impertinence, but will heed them and treasure them up as a legacy.
—P.T. Barnum, 1891, five days before he died

"Y ou here on business?" asked the man beside me.

I was on a late afternoon flight from Dallas to Houston, where I lived at the time. Most of the people on the crowded airplane were coming from business meetings in the cowboy city. The fellow beside me wanted to make the short flight go even faster by speaking with somebody, anybody, and I happened to be sitting in the lucky (?) seat beside him.

"I'm flying home after doing some research in Connecticut for my next book," I said. "It's going to be about the business secrets of P.T. Barnum."

I said it with a certain pride. I knew this man beside me, whoever he was, was aware of Barnum's name. Everybody knows it. I also knew nobody had ever written a book on Barnum's business ingenuity. I was feeling smug, waiting for the applause. But it never came. The man beside me looked confused.

"It's a book about the circus guy?"

I cringed. I tried not to look insulted or impatient.

"Barnum operated a circus in the *last* part of his life," I explained, trying to point out that Barnum was far more than a "circus guy."

"Long before the circus he ran numerous businesses, made unknown people famous, started dirt poor, got rich, lost all his money, and got rich all over again," I said.

"He was the most recognized name in America and maybe in the world in the 1800s. He knew Presidents and was even considered as a Presidential nominee. He was a clever businessman and maybe the greatest marketing mind that ever existed. His techniques made his museum famous and helped make his circus something every child wants to attend today. The man was so famous you even know his name right now, yet he died more than one hundred years ago."

I caught my breath and let the businessman beside me consider the facts I expressed. Finally he spoke.

"Didn't Barnum say 'There's a sucker born every minute'?"

"*No*, Barnum never said that," I replied. "Barnum respected people and gave them more than their money's worth. He never said, wrote, and probably never even thought that stupid line. No researcher or historian has ever found evidence that he said it."

I counted to 10 and waited for my fellow passenger to say something else that would rile me. I didn't have long to wait.

"Barnum's methods might work for a big company or for some corporation with a huge general audience, but I don't see how I can use his ideas in my little business."

I realized here was an opportunity to expand this man's thinking. I asked him what he did for a living. He said he owned a small company that refurbished vans. When I asked him how he marketed his business, he said he went to trade shows.

"And how do you make yourself stand out at these trade shows?" I asked.

"We get a big table."

I had him now.

"How many other people get big tables?" I asked.

"I guess most of them do."

"Do you realize that if you pretended you were P.T. Barnum, and acted more flamboyantly, more brashly, more boldly, you could have a trade show booth that would be the talk of the entire trade show?"

He still didn't get it.

"Look," I began. "I wrote a book for the American Marketing Association on small business advertising. I know that it is no longer enough for you to just advertise your business or attend trade shows. There's just too much competition in today's world. You have to stand out in the crowd. You have to do something more daring to bring attention to your business."

"What do you mean?"

"You have to be like the businessman who hung from a towel that was tied to a flying helicopter to show his towels would not tear. You have to be as bold as the publisher who threw a media event announcing his new magazine by hiring the Beach Boys to sing.

"Look at Cal Worthington, the car dealer who ran television ads featuring 'his dog Spot.' Every week his dog was some animal, from a dog to a goat to a pig to a giraffe. That's Barnum-like thinking. These publicity stunts helped Worthington become the most successful auto dealer in history. And it's that kind of thinking that made Worthington a millionaire. A hundred years ago it made Barnum a millionaire. It can also make you a millionaire today."

I let the businessman consider my argument while I looked out the window at the Texas sky. If nothing else, the conversation made me more aware of the fact that people don't really comprehend just how phenomenal this character called P.T. Barnum really was. Not everyone realizes that the sales and marketing methods Barnum invented can be used today. But my daydreaming was soon interrupted.

"We use promotional gimmicks like pens with our name on it and calendars with our logo," my fellow passenger said. "We get stories done on us in the trade papers, too."

"And how's business?"

"It's good. We nearly went bankrupt at first, but we're moving along and growing."

"I'll be blunt with you," I announced, preparing this man for the radical honesty I was about to say. "Unless you do something with more guts, you will remain one of the little guys."

"How do you figure that?"

"Because you have competition and sooner or later that competition will rear its head and take a bite out of you. Whether you survive or not will depend on how stable you are, how smart you are, and how much outrageous marketing you do."

"Outrageous marketing?"

"Look at Robert Allen. He wrote an investment book called *Nothing Down*. Well, who cares about another money book? There are 2,000 books published every week. To separate his from the crowd, Allen issued a challenge."

"I think I remember it."

"He said, 'Take my wallet and all of my money, leave me with one hundred dollars in cash, drop me in any city, and within 72 hours I will have a piece of prime real estate.'"

"He did it, didn't he?"

"You know it. And that stunt got him front page coverage in the papers, brought him national publicity, helped make his book a bestseller, and made Allen a multimillionaire."

"Yeah, but—"

"And look at Tony Robbins. The man was so poor he used to wash his dishes in his bathtub. To make himself stand out in the crowd, he started conducting seminars on firewalking. That grabbed media attention. Now the man lives in the Fiji Islands and spends more money in one day than he used to make in a year."

"Yeah, but—"

"Or look at Ted Turner. The world thought he was nuts when he created a national cable network. Now CNN gets studied and copied by the other networks!"

"Yeah, but—"

"You can't be an also-ran in business and expect to survive and prosper," I continued. "You have to stick your neck out. You have to wedge your name into the minds of your prospects. Once you break into their awareness, they won't easily forget you. That's what Robert Allen did. And Tony Robbins. And Ted Turner. And P.T. Barnum. They forced themselves into our minds."

"Yeah, but—"

"If you want your business to rocket to Mars and back, you have to be willing to take the next step. And the next step just might be off the top of a tall building."

"Coffee or tea?" interrupted a smiling flight attendant.

Neither of us wanted anything.

"And let's not forget Houdini or Ali or Stanley Arnold or Edward Bernays," I said.

"Who?"

"I'm writing about them in my book, too," I answered.

"Yeah, but Barnum had it easy," my friend said. "He lived in a time when there wasn't much competition."

This guy was getting to me now.

"Barnum grew up with our country, that's true, but he had competition just like everyone else. And more importantly, he took people and places that others had *tried* to promote, used his own methods, and made his enterprises known around the world. The museum he bought had already been around when Barnum made it a colossal success. He brought Jenny Lind, the famous singer, to America and made crowds flock to see her. But when Lind tried to promote herself without Barnum, she flopped and soon returned to Europe. No one thought the midget Charles Stratton was special, until Barnum renamed him General Tom Thumb and started to publicize him."

My passenger just looked at me, his eyes blank.

"Barnum was the key," I explained. "His methods turned otherwise passable people and shows into money making—even historic—events. And you can use his methods today. That's why I'm writing this book. I've discovered his 10 Rings of Power for making any business into a money machine. I'm writing this book to convey these techniques to people just like you. You need it."

"I need it?"

"Don't you think there's an outside chance that Barnum knew something you didn't? Isn't there a remote possibility that there are sales and marketing techniques you haven't used or heard of yet—techniques that just might make you rich?"

"I never really thought about it."

"Look. The San Antonio public library's Hertzberg Circus Museum has courses where they teach children business skills, graphic arts, and advertising principles by letting them start and run their own little circus. That's pure Barnum. And if this information helps kids learn about business, don't you think it might help you, as well?"

"They're teaching your Rings of Power to kids?"

"No," I replied, smiling. "They're teaching kids how to run a business with the circus as their metaphor. They haven't studied Barnum like I have. Besides, Barnum wasn't involved in the circus until after he was sixty years old. *I'm* teaching adults how to create empires by telling them how to use Barnum's 10 Rings of Power. I call my program *Project Phineas.*"

"But I don't think my customers would enjoy seeing me do wild stunts."

"Do you think people enjoy seeing Sir Richard Branson fly around the world in a balloon?" I asked.

"Well, he's likeable."

"He's likeable because he's *daring,*" I said. "Besides, people won't care as long as you *deliver* what you promise. Barnum had few complaints from his customers. Tony Robbins, Robert Allen and Ted Turner also get few complaints. Why? Because they deliver. They give legendary service. Their customers leave feeling incredible. The idea behind publicity stunts is to get attention. It's no longer enough to advertise or hand out flyers or sit at a trade show. You have to think more outrageously and act more boldly, and you have to deliver what you promise, or else."

"Or else?"

"Or else you're history."

The World-Famous Matchstick Guitar

My neighbor looked away from me. I think he had had enough of my arguments in defense of Barnum. That's good, as I had had enough of him. I picked up the guitar magazine I had brought with me to pass the time and flipped to the back. I chuckled to myself as I read about a matchstick guitar made in 1937.

Seems a certain sailor named Jack Hall collected matchsticks and made musical instruments out of them. He first created a fiddle, then two mandolins, and then a guitar made up entirely of 14,000 used matchsticks which he painstakingly glued together. This particular matchstick guitar was finally played in public in 1991 on BBC television, two years before Hall died.

What a waste, I thought to myself. Barnum would have taken that unusual guitar and its creator and put them on a world tour. He might even have rented out the guitar to be placed on display at trade shows like the one my fellow passenger attended. The guitar would have brought attention to his booth, made people talk, and helped increase his business. Visitors would walk away and talk among themselves, asking each other, "Did you see that wild matchstick guitar over at the refurbished vans table?"

Instead, the people who knew of the matchstick guitar let an opportunity for fame and fortune slip through their fingers. And the man beside me was content to sit at trade show tables and struggle along in business. As I wondered why, I closed my eyes and tried to imagine what it must have been like to live in Barnum's time. . . .

How Will You Survive?

Imagine you are in business in the mid-1800s.

Four-fifths of all Americans are farmers. There are only three large cities in the country, and New York is the biggest with barely 400,000 people. Most of the wonderful tools of technology have not yet been invented. You cannot advertise on radio or television, because they don't exist. You cannot send out news releases by fax, use a computer to track results, sign on to the Internet, call prospects on a telephone, hail a cab or drive a car to present your case to a client. You can't even take a train to many places until after the Civil War.

You don't have electricity to light a sign or send a message. Most of your customers don't have indoor bathrooms, and bathing once a week is the norm. If your customers get sick, they probably die, as surgeons during this period washed their hands *after* surgery, not before it. Indian wars are still terrifying people. Gun fights still occur. When the Civil War hits, a large percentage of your customer base gets destroyed. And then you may be restricted to conducting safe business in only the Northern states.

Talk about living in stressful times!

How will you ever survive?

American Millionaire—*Twice*

Yet these were the conditions in which P.T. Barnum lived. And he managed to amass a fortune, lose it, and then create an even greater one.

He was probably America's second millionaire (after John Jacob Astor). He was incomparably famous. A letter mailed from New Zealand to "Mr. Barnum, America" made it without a hitch. General Grant said everywhere he went around the globe, people knew of Barnum. President Garfield called him "the Kris Kringle of America."

Barnum knew every important person of his time, from presidents and queens to celebrities and inventors. He went buffalo hunting with General Custer. He was friends with Mark Twain and Abe Lincoln. He took unknowns and made them international stars. He built the most unusual mansion in the country, watched it burn to the ground, and built yet another. A total of five huge fires wiped him out—temporarily. Yet he got back on his feet almost instantly. He was a famous speaker, a bestselling author, a politician, a showman, an investor, an entrepreneur, and a marketing genius.

In his youth he sold lottery tickets and ran a newspaper. In later years he became one of the world's first prohibitionists and spent much of his time lecturing about the evils of alcohol. He invented the beauty and baby contests. He made a large fortune in real estate, inventing a clever method of selling alternate lots, financing the purchasers so they could build homes, and then collecting profit from the enhanced value of the lots in between. He donated land to his favorite city and watched his own stock in land rise as a result.

In 1853 he started New York's first illustrated newspaper and helped it achieve a circulation of 500,000. He was a deeply religious man who was imprisoned for writing about his beliefs, and at the same time got his first taste of publicity. He was once in partnership with the tycoon Commodore Vanderbilt, acted as a bank president, and ran for Connecticut legislature, fighting to free slaves. He was on intimate terms with several U.S. Presidents, was named as a possible Presidential candidate in 1888, and was Mayor of Bridgeport, Connecticut. He made a fortune, lost it with a bad investment at the age of forty-six, and then succeeded in creating a still larger fortune before his death at the age of eighty in 1891.

How I Discovered Barnum's Secrets

So who was P.T. Barnum? And what were his Rings of Power? How was he able to bring international attention to his famous museum, his singers and side-shows, his still legendary circus, and even to himself? And more importantly, how can you use Barnum's methods to promote your own business today? Is his genius translatable and are his techniques transferable?

To answer these questions I studied books about Barnum, read stacks of his letters, listened to a rare Edison recording of his voice, watched the various movies and commentaries made of his life, visited with collectors of Barnum materials, went to Bridgeport, Connecticut and San Antonio, Texas to research the Barnum materials there, and reread his lively autobiography, titled *Struggles and Triumphs*, the primary source to read if you want to know about this fascinating man's life.

Barnum's classic book was first published in 1854 and revised and enlarged numerous times. Barnum sold over a million copies of his famous autobiography (further evidence of this amazing man's marketing skills). In the book, Barnum tells of discovering a tiny four-year-old boy by the name of Charles Stratton, how he named him Tom Thumb, taught him to sing and dance, gave him status by calling him "General," and promoted him to the world by personally introducing "General Tom Thumb" to editors of major newspapers in New York City.

Barnum also writes of discovering and presenting Joice Heth, a black slave said to be over 160 years old (Barnum said she looked much older) and alleged to have been George Washington's nurse. Other famous Barnum successes include his American Museum (the Disneyworld of the 1800s), his promotion of the famous Swedish soprano Jenny Lind, his infamous promotion of the bizarre (as Barnum spelled it) "Fejee mermaid," his creation of America's first superstar, and of course his still thriving "Greatest Show on Earth," the Barnum and Bailey Circus, which formed as a result of Barnum running into a businessman just as shrewd as himself.

While Barnum had more than his share of failures, his success rate as a marketing wizard has never been beaten. Why? What can we learn from him? How did he make people stampede to his place of business? What did he do that most of us in business today aren't doing? What were his sales and marketing secrets? That's what I will reveal in this book, the first ever written about the marketing methods of P.T. Barnum.

I don't know whatever happened to the businessman who sat beside me on my flight to Houston. I hope he's not just sitting at a big table at a trade show.

I hope he heard some of what I said to him that day in the Texas sky, and that he is now stretching his mind, lining his wallet, serving people, having fun, and seeing his business grow by starting to think just a little like the greatest marketeer of all time, P.T. Barnum.

2

P. T. Barnum's Amazing 10 Rings of Power for Creating an Empire

Every man's occupation should be beneficial to his fellow-man as well as profitable to himself. All else is vanity and folly.

—P.T. Barnum, *The Humbugs of the World*, 1866

When President Lincoln and his family entertained Tom Thumb and his wife at the White House during the Civil War, the sad eyed, weary Lincoln asked Tom if he had any suggestions about handling the war.

"Mr. President," Tom replied, "my friend Barnum could settle the whole thing in a month."

Barnum was never given the opportunity to solve that ugly war, but Tom's answer reflects the high esteem most of the country held for the talents of P.T. Barnum's creative powers. It makes you think: What would Barnum have done to stop the war?

And in our bloody shark eat shark current business environment today, what would Barnum do to leap-frog ahead of the competition? What were his essential keys to success—keys you can use right now to solve the expensive battle of getting and keeping new clients in a time when most people regard business as war?

I found 10 keys to Barnum's astonishing success as a businessman. Because so many people associate Barnum with his three ring circus, I decided to call these keys Barnum's "Rings of Power." In a nutshell, here they are:

1. *He believed there was a customer born every minute.* This man did not think small. His American Museum, one of the three great passions of Barnum's life, was so popular over four million people visited it during his lifetime. At twenty-five cents a head (children half price), Barnum made a tidy sum of money. But Barnum did not aim for a tiny segment of the market. He went for the world. And he captured it. He took Tom Thumb to Europe several times, and he brought Jenny Lind from Europe to America, both by *ship* (which took two weeks to make the journey in the 1800s). He was probably the most famous man—and one of the wealthiest—on the planet in the mid-1800s. Why? Because he didn't limit his target to his local neighborhood or even to the city where he lived. He aimed for the planet itself. In Chapter 4 you'll learn how to expand your customer base, and discover new ways to reach those customers quickly, easily, and inexpensively.

2. *He believed in using skyrockets.* Barnum strove to capture people's attention in whatever audacious ways he could devise. He was probably the father of the publicity stunt. At one point he had an elephant plowing the field on his property. Why? Because the field was near the railroad tracks that took passengers into New York City. While most people saw a bunch of people riding a train, Barnum saw a herd of potential customers. Barnum knew an elephant would grab their attention and act as an unforgettable publicity stunt. It worked. Barnum received so much nationwide publicity that agricultural societies wrote to him for advice on how to get elephants to do farming. "Newspaper reporters came from far and near, and wrote glowing accounts of the elephantine performances," Barnum wrote. "The six acres were plowed over at least sixty times before I thought the advertisement sufficiently circulated. . . ." In Chapter 5 you'll read many astonishing stories about getting attention, and discover new ways to use this proven technique in your own business.

3. *He believed in giving people more than their money's worth.* Barnum worked hard to find something people would enjoy. He wanted people to feel good spending money with him. He traveled the world in search of performers and products that had appeal. Tom Thumb, Jenny Lind, Siamese twins, questionable artifacts, all of these items were curiosities to the public, and vastly engaging. The public wanted what Barnum had to offer: unusual entertainment. Barnum used outlandish stunts and curiosities to call attention to his show, but once he had people in his door, he satisfied them. There are few records of anyone complaining. He recreated the sleazy circus and dime museums of his day into popular enterprises people felt great attending. In Chapter 6 you'll discover the one thing people want—no matter what business you are in—and how to deliver it to them.

4. *He fearlessly believed in the power of "printer's ink."* Barnum was unusually creative at generating publicity. Known worldwide as a showman, lecturer, politician, author, philanthropist, and marketing genius, Barnum became globally famous and incredibly wealthy by knowing how to befriend the media. In his last known letter, written five days before he died in 1891, he wrote, "I am indebted to the press of the United States for almost every dollar which I possess, ..." In Chapter 7 you'll get to see Barnum's clever methods for getting the media to promote his enterprises—methods anyone in business can implement today to edge out their competition.

5. *He believed in persistently advertising.* While Barnum believed in free publicity, he never overlooked paid advertising. He used posters, display ads, classified ads, window signs, and booklets to broadcast what he had for sale. Barnum believed with an almost evangelical zest in the power of advertising. (See Figure 2.1.) People called him the "Shakespeare of Advertising." He wrote, "When you get an article which you know is going to please your customers, and that when they have tried it they will feel they have got their money's worth, then let that fact be known that you have got it." In Chapter 8 you'll discover Barnum's surprising little known rules for creating ads that get results.

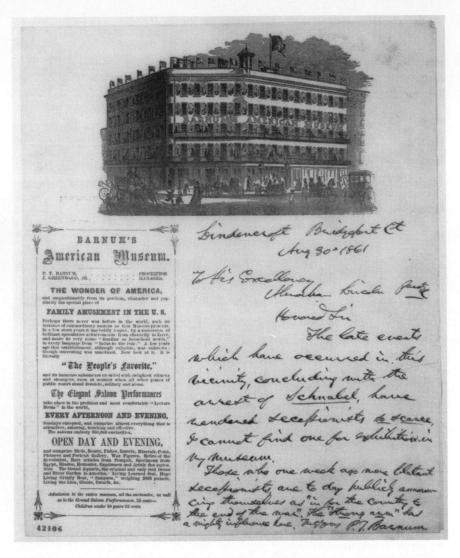

FIGURE 2.1   This is an 1861 letter from P.T. Barnum to President Abraham Lincoln. Note how Barnum even used his stationery to advertise his business. (From author's private collection.)

6. *He believed in people helping people to get results.* While *networking* lives as a buzzword in today's business world, Barnum practiced it more than one hundred years ago. When he wanted to see the Queen, he got a letter of introduction from a distinguished statesman. He got that letter from the famous newspaperman, Horace Greeley. That's networking. When he wanted publicity, he asked for favors from everyone from local influentials to even the President of the United States. Barnum knew people liked to help people with a good cause. He was a charming fellow and most people liked him. When Barnum wanted to buy what was to become his museum, and the owner wanted references, Barnum's testimonials were so enthusiastic that at first the owner didn't believe they were honest. Barnum treated people fairly, making asking for favors easier. In Chapter 9 you'll find out how to use this Ring of Power to meet anyone alive.

7. *He believed in negotiating creatively, treating employees and performers with respect.* His terms were fair. His staff loved him. He paid good wages, shared profits, and made many of his performers—Jenny Lind, Tom Thumb, Commodore Nutt, the Siamese Twins—rich. When Chang and Eng, the famous Siamese Twins, agreed to show themselves after the Civil War wiped out their fortune, Barnum again split all profits equally, allowing the twins to have wealth where they certainly otherwise would have had poverty. Barnum also made William Henry Johnson, a black dwarf in show business for over six decades, a full partner in their enterprises. And when Brigham Young jokingly asked Barnum what he would pay to show Young and all of his wives, Barnum said one-half of all ticket sales, an expected $200,000. Barnum negotiated fairly. In Chapter 10 you'll discover Barnum's clever approach to making deals—a technique you can use right now to achieve more of what you want in your own business.

8. *He believed all was well.* Mark Twain suffered business failures, personal bankruptcy, and family tragedy, and those experiences scarred him for the rest of his life, turning him into a brooding cynic with a pen "warmed up in hell." Barnum suffered the same events, and even many more, yet was not destroyed by the losses. His American Museum, which he so passionately loved, burned down twice. His Iranistan home, one of the first, biggest and most unusual palaces in America, burned to the ground. He also lost his wife, and two children. Yet Barnum never seemed to bat an eye. He quickly recovered, made new arrangements for new homes, new museums, and even remarried, to a woman forty years younger than himself. His inner strength came from an unshakable faith that everything happened for a good reason. The simple marker over his grave says, "Not my will, but thine, be done." His faith helped him survive and prosper in business. In Chapter 11 you'll read about my amazing experience at Barnum's grave, and discover how business can become a path of personal growth and self-discovery, giving you the strength to weather any storm.

9. *He believed in the power of the written word.* Barnum's second great love was his autobiography, which he updated right up to his death—and then had his wife complete by writing a chapter about his funeral. Barnum began writing when he was twenty-two years old, editing a religious newspaper and being arrested for it. He saw the power of the written word as a force to influence and mold public opinion. He used it throughout his life, whether by writing letters to Presidents or editors of newspapers, or by writing booklets that advertised his atrocious "Fejee" (as Barnum spelled it) mermaid or his beloved General Tom Thumb. Right till the end, Barnum would write, knowing that every word he wrote led him closer to fame, fortune, and immortality. In Chapter 12 you'll see why so many successful business people have written books, and learn how you can easily write one of your own.

10. *He believed in the power of speaking.* Barnum was not afraid to address a crowd, whether to convince them to stop drinking, to get them to free slaves, or to persuade them that his shows were moral, cultural, and safe for children and animals. He knew the spoken word could move mountains. He held his own with the best speakers of his day. He was a lecturer when Mark Twain and Charles Dickens were popular, and he drew just as much praise as his colleagues. Speaking led to more publicity and more business. Even his running for political office, while an opportunity to do good for his third great passion (the city of Bridgeport), was also a chance to conduct what he called "Profitable Philanthropy." He knew being public made him famous and brought further attention to his enterprises. In Chapter 14 you'll learn unique ways to become a more powerful, persuasive, and charismatic speaker.

There are more chapters in this book, more surprises waiting for you, and more keys to Barnum's success.

The great showman himself revealed what he regarded as his most important secrets in a lecture he gave hundreds of times called, "The Art of Money Getting." Many said this talk changed their lives. At least one man, the father of Barnum's second wife, said the secrets made him rich. So you have a complete picture of Barnum and his ideas for business success, I've included his famous talk at the end of this book.

But for now you might want to start thinking about how you can use Barnum's Rings of Power in your own business. Most people in business use only one, two, or three of the Rings of Power. If you implement all ten, astonishing success can be yours. But how will you do it? We'll explore each Ring of Power in the chapters ahead.

To help stimulate your imagination, let's hear from Barnum himself right now. . . .

3 | Bonus

Barnum's Rules for Success in Business

by P.T. Barnum

What did Barnum feel were the laws for success in business? When Edwin T. Freedley wrote Barnum in 1852 and said he was working on a book about business, he asked Barnum to offer his thoughts on the subject. Barnum sat down and wrote the following article, which he later reprinted in the 1855 edition of his autobiography (see Figure 3.1).

1. *Select the KIND of business that suits your natural inclinations and temperament.* Some men are naturally mechanics; others have a strong aversion to anything like machinery, and so on; one man has a natural taste for one occupation, and another for another. "I am glad that we do not all feel and think alike," said Dick Homespun, "for if we did, everybody would think my gal, Sukey Snipes, the sweetest creature in all creation, and they would all be trying to court her at once."

I never could succeed as a merchant. I have tried it unsuccessfully several times.

I never could be content with a fixed salary, for mine is a purely speculative disposition, while others are just the reverse; and therefore all should be careful to select those occupations that suit them best.

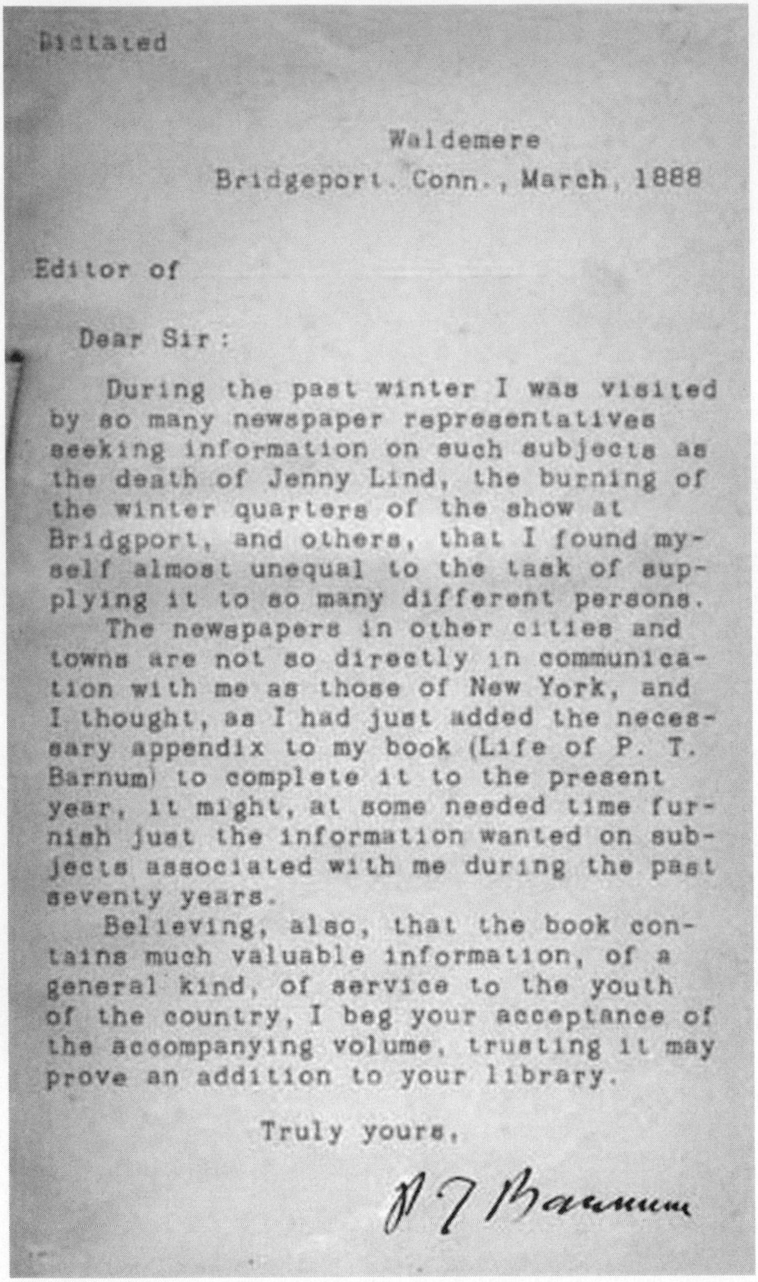

Waldemere
Bridgeport. Conn., March, 1888

Editor of

Dear Sir:

During the past winter I was visited
by so many newspaper representatives
seeking information on such subjects as
the death of Jenny Lind, the burning of
the winter quarters of the show at
Bridgport, and others, that I found myself almost unequal to the task of sup-
plying it to so many different persons.

The newspapers in other cities and
towns are not so directly in communication with me as those of New York, and
I thought, as I had just added the necessary appendix to my book (Life of P. T.
Barnum) to complete it to the present
year, it might, at some needed time fur-
nish just the information wanted on subjects associated with me during the past
seventy years.

Believing, also, that the book con-
tains much valuable information, of a
general kind, of service to the youth
of the country, I beg your acceptance of
the accompanying volume, trusting it may
prove an addition to your library.

Truly yours,

P T Barnum

FIGURE 3.1   This is a very rare "news release" by Barnum. It is a dictated and signed
letter from Barnum, stuck inside a copy of his autobiography, and sent to editors of
newspapers. It was Barnum's way of sending out news and promoting himself. (From
author's private collection.)

2. *Let your pledged word ever be sacred.* Never promise to do a thing without performing it with the most rigid promptness. Nothing is more valuable to a man in business than the name of always doing as he agrees, and that to the moment. A strict adherence to this rule gives a man the command of half the spare funds within the range of his acquaintances, and always encircles him with a host of friends who may be depended upon in almost any conceivable emergency.

3. *Whatever you do, do with all your might.* Work at it if necessary early and late, in season and out of season, not leaving a stone unturned, and never deferring for a single hour that which can be done just as well now. The old proverb is full of truth and meaning, "Whatever is worth doing at all, is worth doing well." Many a man acquires a fortune by doing his business *thoroughly*, while his neighbor remains poor for life because he only *half* does his business. Ambition, energy, industry, perseverance, are indispensable requisites for success in business.

4. *Sobriety. Use no description of intoxicating drinks.* As no man can succeed in business unless he has a *brain* to enable him to lay his plans, and *reason* to guide him in their execution, so, no matter how bountifully a man may be blessed with intelligence, if his brain is muddled, and his judgment warped by intoxicating drinks, it is impossible for him to carry on business successfully. How many good opportunities have passed never to return, while a man was sipping a "social glass" with his friend! How many foolish bargains have been made under the influence of the *nervine* which temporarily makes its victim so rich! How many important chances have been put off until to-morrow, and thence forever, because the wine-cup has thrown the system into a state of lassitude, neutralizing the energies so essential to success in business. The use of intoxicating drinks as a beverage is as much an infatuation as is the smoking of opium by the Chinese, and the former is quite as destructive to the success of the business man as the latter.

5. *Let hope predominate, but be not too visionary.* Many persons are always kept poor, because they are too *visionary.* Every project looks to them like certain success, and therefore they keep changing from one business to another, always in hot water, always "under the harrow." The plan of "counting the chickens before they are hatched" is an error of ancient date, but it does not seem to improve by age.

6. *Do not scatter your powers.* Engage in one kind of business only, and stick to it faithfully until you succeed, or until you conclude to abandon it. A constant hammering on one nail will generally drive it home at last, so that it can be clinched. When a man's undivided attention is centered on one object, his mind will constantly be suggesting improvements of value which would escape him if his brain were occupied by a dozen different subjects at once. Many a fortune has slipped through men's fingers by engaging in too many occupations at once.

7. *Engage proper employees.* Never employ a man of bad habits, when one whose habits are good can be found to fill his situation. I have generally been extremely fortunate in having faithful and competent persons to fill the responsible situations in my business, and a man can scarcely be too grateful for such a blessing. When you find a man unfit to fill his station, either from incapacity or peculiarity of character or disposition, dispense with his services, and do not drag out a miserable existence in the vain attempt to change his nature. It is utterly impossible to do so. "You cannot make a silk purse," etc. He was created for some other sphere. Let him find and fill it.

8. *Advertise your business. Do not hide your light under a bushel.* Whatever your occupation or calling may be, if it needs support from the public, *advertise* it thoroughly and efficiently, in some shape or other that will arrest public attention. I freely confess that what success I have had in my life may fairly be attributed more to the public press than to nearly all other causes combined. There *may* possibly be occupations that do not require advertising, but I cannot well conceive what they are.

Men in business will sometimes tell you that they have tried advertising, and that it did not pay. This is only when advertising is done sparingly and grudgingly. Homeopathic doses of advertising will not pay perhaps—it is like half a potion of physic, making the patient sick, but effecting nothing. Administer liberally, and the cure will be sure and permanent.

Some say they cannot afford to advertise; they mistake—they cannot afford *not* to advertise. In this country, where everybody reads the newspapers, the man must have a thick skull who does not see that these are the cheapest and best medium through which he can speak to the public, where he is to find his customers. Put on the *appearance* of business, and generally the *reality* will follow. The farmer plants his seed, and while he is sleeping, his corn and potatoes are growing. So with advertising. While you are sleeping, or eating, or conversing with one set of customers, your advertisement is being read by hundreds and thousands of persons who never saw you, nor heard of your business, and never would, had it not been for your advertisement appearing in the newspapers.

The business men of this country do not, as a general thing, appreciate the advantages of advertising thoroughly. Occasionally the public are aroused at witnessing the success of a Swaim, a Brandreth, a Townsend, a Genin, or a Root, and express astonishment at the rapidity with which these gentlemen acquire fortunes, not reflecting that the same path is open to all who *dare* pursue it. But it needs *nerve* and *faith.* The former, to enable you to launch out thousands on the uncertain waters of the future; the latter, to teach you that after many days it shall surely return, bringing an hundred or a thousand fold to him who appreciates the advantages of "printer's ink" properly applied.

9. *Avoid extravagance; and always live considerably within your income, if you can do so without absolute starvation!* It needs no prophet to tell us that those who live fully up to their means, without any thought of a reverse in life, can never attain to a pecuniary independence.

Men and women accustomed to gratify every whim and caprice, will find it hard at first to cut down their various unnecessary expenses, and will feel it a great self-denial to live in a smaller house than they have been accustomed to, with less expensive furniture, less company, less costly clothing, a less number of balls, parties, theater-goings, carriage ridings, pleasure excursions, cigar smokings, liquor-drinkings, etc., etc., etc.; but, after all, if they will try the plan of laying by a "nest-egg," or in other words, a small sum of money, after paying all expenses, they will be surprised at the pleasure to be derived from constantly adding to their little "pile," as well as from all the economical habits which follow in the pursuit of this peculiar pleasure.

The old suit of clothes, and the old bonnet and dress, will answer for another season; the Croton or spring water will taste better than champagne; a brisk walk will prove more exhilarating than a ride in the finest coach; a social family chat, an evening's reading in the family circle, or an hour's play of "hunt the slipper" and "blind man's buff," will be far more pleasant than a fifty or a five-hundred-dollar party, when the reflection on the *difference in cost* is indulged in by those who begin to know the *pleasures of saving.*

Thousands of men are kept poor, and tens of thousands are made so after they have acquired quite sufficient to support them well through life, in consequence of laying their plans of living on too expensive a platform. Some families in this country expend twenty thousand dollars per annum, and some much more, and would scarcely know how to live on a less sum.

Prosperity is a more severe ordeal than adversity, especially sudden prosperity. "Easy come, easy go" is an old and true proverb. Pride, when permitted full sway, is the great undying cankerworm which gnaws the very vitals of a man's worldly possessions, let them be small or great, hundreds or millions. Many persons, as they begin to prosper, immediately commence expending for luxuries, until in a short time their expenses swallow up their income, and they become ruined in their ridiculous attempts to keep up appearances, and make a "sensation."

I know a gentleman of fortune, who says, that when he first began to prosper, his wife *would have* a new and elegant sofa. "That sofa," he says, "cost me thirty thousand dollars!" The riddle is thus explained:

When the sofa reached the house, it was found necessary to get chairs to "match," then sideboards, carpets, and tables, "to correspond" with them, and so on through the entire stock of furniture, when at last it was found that the house itself was quite too small and old-fashioned for the furniture, and a new one was built to correspond with the sofa and *et ceteras*; "thus," added my friend, "running up an outlay of thirty thousand dollars caused by that single sofa, and saddling on me, in the shape of servants, equipage, and the necessary expenses attendant upon keeping up a fine 'establishment,' a yearly outlay of eleven thousand dollars, and a tight pinch at that; whereas, ten years ago, we lived with much more real comfort, because much less care, on as many hundreds. The truth is," he continued, "that sofa would have brought me to inevitable bankruptcy, had not a most unexampled tide of prosperity kept me above it."

10. *Do not depend upon others.* Your success must depend upon your own individual exertions. Trust not to the assistance of friends; but learn that every man must be the architect of his own fortune.

With proper attention to the foregoing rules, and such observations as a man of sense will pick up in his own experience, the road to competence will not, I think, usually be found a difficult one.

—P.T. Barnum, 1852

4

P.T. Barnum's Amazing Mind-Set for Success

The Mermaid, Woolly Horse, Ploughing Elephants, etc., were merely used by me as skyrockets or advertisements, to attract attention and give notoriety to the Museum and such other really valuable attractions as I provided for the public. I believe hugely in advertising and blowing my own trumpet, beating the gongs, drums, etc., to attract attention to a show; but I never believed that any amount of advertising or energy would make a spurious article permanently successful.

—P.T. Barnum, private letter, 1860

To fully grasp P.T. Barnum's first ring of power, you have to know the surprising truth about Barnum, and a little about the odd nature of the people who lived in the 1800s.

Ask anyone what they know about Barnum and they will probably say, "He's the guy who said 'There's a sucker born every minute.' " However, Barnum never made that statement. He never wrote it, either. That shouldn't be too surprising. Many famous statements were never written or spoken by the people they were attributed to.

Take "He who hesitates is lost." The line itself is a misquote from a 1713 play by Joseph Addison. The actual sentence reads, "The woman that deliberates is lost."

Or consider "You dirty rat!," the famous quote attributed to early film star James Cagney. According to *They Never Said It: A Book of Fake Quotes, Misquotes and Misleading Attributions*, Cagney never said the line in any of his seventy movies.

You no doubt heard that George Washington said, "I cannot tell a lie." Actually, Washington never said it.

What about Abe Lincoln's famous quote, "You can fool all of the people some of the time and some of the people all the time, but you cannot fool all the people all the time"? Lincoln never said it.

And remember Willie Sutton's famous reply when he was asked why he robbed banks?: "I rob banks because that's where the money is." Sutton never said it. The reporter who interviewed him made it up.

Barnum never said the infamous line attributed to him, either. No one can locate where the quote came from with much certainty. One story says Adam Forepaugh, a rival of Barnum's, said it. Another version says Joseph Bessimer, a con man, uttered it.

Another explanation is that from the 1840s on, many Barnum imposters surfaced to capitalize on the showman's name. One of these other "Barnum's" may have delivered the notorious line.

And according to information I found online, written by R. J. Brown and posted on the Newspaper Collectors Society of America's web page on the Internet—which admittedly is subject to further investigation—the line may have originated this way:

The Amazing Story of the Cardiff Giant

In the 1860s, George Hull, a cigar manufacturer, decided to profit by the country's love for a good hoax. He was a student of archeology, he desired money, and he knew at least one evangelist of the time was preaching that giants once roamed the earth. Hull saw an opportunity.

He hired stone cutters to carve a ten-foot tall giant out of some unusual gypsum quarry he had found. Hull then buried the fake giant on his property in Cardiff, New York and waited for the right moment to discover it. He didn't have to wait more than six months. In 1869 fossil bones were unearthed and newspapers covered the story. Hull leaped into action. He hired two laborers to dig a well on his property, where the giant had been buried earlier. It didn't take long for the diggers to hit the statue and run to tell Hull the news of their discovery.

Because the public was already enthusiastic about fossils, curious about evolution, and mesmerized by the idea that giants once walked the land, wagons loaded with people started coming to see Hull's giant. By midday Hull had set up a tent and was charging visitors 25 cents each to see the curiosity. After the newspapers covered the story, Hull raised his price of admission to 50 cents. Thousands of people came every day.

Barnum of course heard of this event and sent one of his agents to buy Hull's giant for $50,000. Hull refused. As you know by now, nothing stopped P.T. Barnum. He sensed that the Cardiff giant was a fake and hired a crew of workers to build a giant of his own. They did, and Barnum immediately started displaying it. Thousands of people came to see Barnum's giant, as well. Barnum even made more news by proclaiming that Hull's giant was fake whereas his own was authentic. The papers gave the two promoters plenty of free advertising.

By this point Hull had sold two-thirds of his interest in the Cardiff giant to a banker by the name of David Hannum. It was Hannum who complained about all the people paying to see Barnum's fake giant when they could be paying to see his "real" one. Hannum summed up his feelings by saying, "There's a sucker born every minute."

Hannum brought Barnum to trial, accusing him of calling his giant a fake. During the trial, Hannum confessed that the Cardiff giant was indeed a hoax. The judge ruled that Barnum could not be sued for calling Hannum's giant a fake because it really was a fake.

Although Hannum's name has dropped out of most of the history books, his famous line remains. Unfortunately, people attached it to the only name they could remember: P.T. Barnum.

Barnum, of course, never complained.

Poe and Twain Pull Fast Ones

Although Barnum respected people and enjoyed making money, he had an even greater fondness for practical jokes. That shouldn't be too surprising.

Barnum was born in Bethel, Connecticut on July 5, 1810, a period in American history when hijinks, hoaxes, and "humbugs" were becoming popular. It was a Yankee form of recreation that helped people break from their strict Puritan past. The Cardiff Giant was just one in a long list of hoaxes.

- Edgar Allan Poe promoted a famous Balloon Hoax, where he wrote journalistic reports about a manned balloon flight across the Atlantic.
- Walt Whitman wrote fictitious fan letters and reviews to promote his poetry.
- Mark Twain wrote an ad in 1874 selling passenger seats on the tail of the comet Coy Coggia—and encouraged people to contact Barnum for tickets.

Hoaxes were in the air. Usually these hoaxes were created to drum up new business. For example:

- In 1855 a daring hotel operator created a "Silver Lake Serpent" to encourage people to visit Perry, New York. They did, too. Everyone wanted to see the monstrous tourist attraction.
- In the 1870s the city of Palisade, Nevada increased their number of tourists by becoming "the toughest town west of Chicago." People would visit Palisade to witness exciting gun fights and street brawls. What the visitors never knew was that the fights were staged. It was a hoax to increase tourist revenues.

This Hoax Started a War

According to Carl Sifakis' *The Big Book of Hoaxes* and Robert McBride's *Great Hoaxes of All Time*, some hoaxes changed the course of history.

When four Denver reporters wanted to increase newspaper sales in 1898, they contrived a story about the Great Wall of China coming down to open the Orient to world trade. Other papers, fearing they were being scooped out of a good story, invented their own news about the Great Wall. That news finally made it to China, where the people became so angry they began to kill each other to protest and prevent the Great Wall's dismantling. The result was the Boxer Rebellion.

And, some believe, it all started as a hoax in Denver to increase newspaper sales!

Clearly hoaxes were being used in an attempt to bring in customers. They just weren't being used with much respect for those customers. Barnum, of course, couldn't help being influenced by this madness.

The Irina Hoax of 1997

Don't be too hard on our cousins of the 1800s. They were fascinated by animals, evolution, and human "curiosities" (midgets, giants, etc.). We are fascinated by space aliens, life after death, and alternative medicine. People never change; only our focus of interest does.

And don't think for a minute that hoaxes don't happen today.

In 1993 a crop circle was found in South Africa. Think what you like of these unexplained symbols cut in someone's field, they usually get media attention. This one did, as well, until someone noticed it was in the shape of the famous BMW logo. According to Alex Boese, author of *The Museum of Hoaxes*, the crop circle turned out to be the work of the Hunt Lascaris Agency, working on behalf of BMW.

Let's not stop there. According to the March 1997 issue of *The Net*, Penguin Books' publicist Guy Gadney sent out e-mail from a fictional Professor Prideaux warning people of a computer virus called "Irina." This brought global free publicity to Penguin Books' new publication, titled *Irina*.

Business people create most hoaxes, then and now, because they know there exists a bigger audience for their product or service than what they currently have. Their hoaxes act like fishing lure designed to get free publicity and catch a whale—the public.

I've done this myself, with an Elvis Mermaid, but I'll tell you that story a little later.

The Joke's on Barnum!

Barnum's grandfather influenced him the most when it came to hoaxes, humbugs, and practical jokes.

"He would go farther, wait longer, work harder, and contrive deeper, to carry out a practical joke, than for anything else under heaven," Barnum wrote in his autobiography.

One popular story was how his grandfather once tricked a group of sailors into shaving off half of their beards. You have to remember that this joke took place before radio, television, computers, film, photography, lights, cameras and much else that we take for granted today. People entertained themselves with their stories and pranks. Barnum's grandfather somehow convinced the passengers to take turns using the only razor on board the ship. After each man had shaved off half of his beard, the razor went back to Barnum's grandfather, who carefully shaved his own face clean. He then "accidentally" dropped the razor into the ocean. When the crew landed and they marched into town, the only clean shaven one in the group was Barnum's grandfather.

Stories like this taught Barnum that people loved a good joke. However, the defining moment for Barnum came when he was 12 years old.

Barnum's grandfather gave him a tract of land called Ivy Island. Though Barnum did not see his grand gift for most of his childhood, he was proud of his inheritance. "My mother often reminded me of my immense possessions, and my father occasionally asked me if I would not support the family when I came in possession of my property." The entire city encouraged the young Barnum, asking him if he would still play with their children after he claimed his immense wealth.

When Barnum turned 12, he finally saw his famous island. It was pure swamp and virtually worthless.

"The truth rushed upon me," wrote Barnum. "I had been made a fool of by all our neighborhood for more than half a dozen years."

He never forgot the experience, but he also benefited from it. Years later he shrewdly offered his Ivy Island as collateral when purchasing his first museum.

The Story of the Ugly Fejee Mermaid

Barnum gave people an Ivy Island of one sort or another throughout his 80 years. "The American people like to be humbugged," he said. It was his way of getting attention for his business while entertaining people. His Fejee Mermaid, for example—made of half monkey and half fish—was a humbug to publicize Barnum's museum.

Mermaids have been on display throughout history. There's a record of one shown in 1565 at a busy port on the Red Sea. There was one hanging in a church in Holland in 1660. The first mermaid to tour England was in 1737. The manufacture of mermaids was actually a nineteenth century Japanese craft. According to Jan Bondeson, in *The Feejee Mermaid*, there have even been mermaids in the 1990s, including one on display at the British Museum in London. Even I found a mermaid, in 1997, which I'll tell you about shortly, but no mermaid has ever been better promoted than the one Barnum rented and advertised—the Fejee mermaid.

A ship captain bought the Fejee mermaid in Calcutta for $6,000—a jolting amount of money in 1817. However, the captain did not know how to advertise his unusual product and died without making a dime from his curiosity. His son sold it to Moses Kimball, owner of the Boston Museum and a friend of Barnum's. Kimball also didn't know how to promote the curiosity. In 1842 Barnum examined the mermaid. Here's how Barnum described it in his autobiography:

. . . the monkey and fish were so nicely conjoined that no human eye could detect the point where the junction was formed. The spine of the fish proceeded in a straight and apparently unbroken line to the base of the skull—the hair of the animal was found growing several inches down on the shoulders of the fish, and the application of a microscope absolutely revealed what seemed to be minute fish scales lying in myriads amidst the hair. The teeth and formation of the fingers and hands differed materially from those of any monkey or ourang-outang ever discovered, while the location of the fins was different from those of any species of the fish tribe known to naturalists. The animal was an ugly, dried-up, black-looking, and diminutive specimen, about three feet long. Its mouth was open, its tail turned over, and its arms thrown up, giving it the appearance of having died in great agony.

Barnum leased the Fejee Mermaid from Kimball and began a publicity campaign that made people line up to see the monstrosity. He sent anonymous letters to the New York newspapers about the mermaid, in order to stir up interest. He had an assistant pose as a naturalist and answer questions about mermaids. He created ". . . wood-cuts and transparencies, as well as a pamphlet, proving the authenticity of mermaids. . . ." He printed 10,000 copies of his booklet and stored them for just the right moment.

Barnum then went to the three major New York newspapers and let each editor have an exclusive feature story on the mermaid. On the morning of Sunday, July 17, 1842, all three newspapers ran stories on the mermaid. When the editors found out Barnum had humbugged them, they ". . . pronounced it a *scaly* trick."

By now everyone in the city had heard of the Fejee Mermaid. Barnum then hired boys to distribute and sell—for a penny each—his 10,000 mermaid pamphlets. The public eagerly bought them up. He then had his assistant pose as a professor and display the mermaid at Concert Hall, in order to give the show an air of respectability. After two weeks there, Barnum printed ads announcing that the Fejee Mermaid could now be seen at his American Museum—"without extra charge."

Clearly, the Fejee Mermaid was a preposterous joke that Barnum used to increase business at his museum. Although thousands of people had been tricked by Barnum, few complained about the ruse. Remember, this was the age of humbugs. People enjoyed the entertainment.

Barnum wrote, "I have yet to learn of a single instance where a visitor went away from the Museum complaining that he had been defrauded of his money."

Why didn't anyone complain? Once they were inside Barnum's house of curiosities, they had more than *half a million* other objects to gawk at. Consequently, they didn't mind the joke.

And the ugly lady fish *tripled* Barnum's ticket sales.

The Elvis Mermaid

I once bought a mermaid on eBay, the famous auction site. It was half fish and half wax, and smelled terrible. It probably began life as a sea horse, but someone with a Barnum touch turned it into a mermaid and sold it online—to me.

Truth is, I was embarrassed to show it to anyone. Sometimes I brought it with me to my speaking engagements. (Barnum had done the same thing at one point in his career.) I would tell people they could see my mermaid by going to my booth in the back, where I had my books and recordings for sale. The mermaid always drew a crowd, but once they saw it, they were disappointed and rarely bought much. So I hid the mermaid from the world.

Until one day I got a Barnum-inspired idea.

I knew eBay got millions of people visiting it. And everyone going there is a buyer, looking to spend money. I wanted to capture some of that traffic. I thought about what drives traffic there, and realized that celebrities do. Britney Spears this, Elvis that, Tom Cruise this, will always get hits.

I wondered how I could connect my mermaid to a celebrity. I went and spoke to my lady, Nerissa, who is a graphic and video wizard. She thought and said she could create a celebrity mermaid by taking a picture of my mermaid and then shaping it into something else. I loved the idea. We decided on an Elvis mermaid (see Figure 4.1).

Nerissa created it and I posted it on eBay, saying we were selling an original print. Instantly—within *seconds*—traffic was going to the listing, and then jumping over to my web site, at www.MrFire.com. Every-

FIGURE 4.1   The Elvis mermaid, created by Nerissa Oden.

one wanted to know who the nut was selling the mermaid. Well, that
nut was me.

    As it turned out, people bid on the print, but what was truly won-
derful is that a radio station did three interviews with me, and ended up
bidding and winning the print of the Elvis mermaid. They never complained, and this hoax brought me and my work a lot of attention.

The Fire Extinguisher That Caused a Fire

Barnum learned that people in the 1800s often *expected* jokes. The public's desire to see hoaxes often interfered with their ability to recognize a good thing when it stood right in front of them.

Barnum invested in a newly patented English fire extinguisher in 1851, but at the demonstration to prove it could really put out a fire, the crowd assumed the invention was a hoax, got rowdy, and ended up causing a fire so big that it burned down a building.

Barnum later wrote, "My experiences in life have convinced me that real merit does not always succeed as well as 'humbug.'"

Barnum's Definition of *Humbug*

You can't cheat anyone, of course. Barnum felt you were misleading the public if you did something outlandish to get their attention but then didn't serve them when they lined up at your door.

Most people define a *humbug* as "a swindle." The *American Heritage Dictionary* defines a humbug as "Something intended to deceive; a hoax; an imposture." Barnum would not agree. He felt a humbug was a good natured joke, and the people of the 1800s would probably agree with him. He explained it this way in his 1866 book, *Humbugs of the World*:

> Two physicians reside in one of our fashionable avenues. They were both educated in the best medical colleges; each has passed an examination, received his diploma, and been dubbed an M.D. They are equally skilled in the healing art. One rides quietly about the city in his gig or brougham, visiting his patients without noise or clamor—the other sallies out in his coach and four, preceded by a band of music, and his carriage and horses are covered with handbills and placards, announcing his "wonderful cures." This man is properly called . . . a humbug. Why? Not because he cheats or imposes upon the public, for he does not, but because, as generally understood, "humbug" consists in putting on glittering appearances—outside show—novel expedients, by which to suddenly arrest public attention, and attract the public eye and ear.

If you deliver a good product or service, few should complain about how you got their attention. It's when your business disappoints people that the problems arise. Barnum added:

> If, however, after attracting crowds of customers by his unique displays, a man foolishly fails to give them a full equivalent for their money, they never patronize him a second time, but they very properly denounce him as a swindler, a cheat, and impostor. . . .

In short, be sure your business satisfies what people want. Your advertising and publicity methods may be courageous and audacious to get attention, but you still must serve people. You still must help them to feel good.

"Do not try to get money without giving fair value for it," Barnum warned.

Wise words indeed.

Create Alliances for Profit

Barnum enjoyed harmless humbugs because they helped him reel in more prospects. He knew that his target audience was bigger than his local area. He believed "There was a customer born every minute." This belief was one of his rings of power.

He went after those customers with a zest and a religious zeal that few business people have ever exhibited. He used every means of advertising, publicity, and technology available. He invented ways to help him achieve the goals he wanted, and he never stopped. He even managed to get his obituary published two days before he died, knowing the obituary of such a famous man would get front page news—and help publicize his circus.

Barnum did all of this because he knew there was a customer born every minute and he wanted to reach those customers. Although you should always target your market, you also don't want to limit your scope. Your market may be bigger than you ever imagined. Barnum wore no blinders. He went after planet earth. And I really believe that were he alive today, he would be building a show on the moon and finding ways to get people there. If we found life on Mars, Barnum would be selling the Martians something and promoting a trio of singing Martians.

Keep in mind you don't have to go after the world all by yourself. Barnum was famous for what we now call cross-promotion. When he advised John Genin, the hatter who had a store next door to Barnum's museum in New York City, to make the highest bid for a Jenny Lind ticket, he was promoting his own enterprise as well as Genin's. Genin ended up paying $225 for a one dollar ticket. But he and Barnum achieved priceless media attention. Barnum's concert for Jenny Lind became the talk of the city. And Genin's hats became prized possessions overnight. Both won.

Here are a few modern day examples of businesses working together for mutual profit:

- A gas station owner put flyers at eye level on his fuel pumps asking "Getting Hungry?" The flyer also had a map to three nearby restaurants. This served the restaurants. How did the gas station owner benefit? Besides generating goodwill, the restaurants had flyers at their locations asking "Need Gas?" The flyers of course had maps leading to the gas station. Win win.
- A lawyer, a doctor, and an accountant team up and present a speech entitled, "When You Hit 35: Know Your Money, Know Your Health, Know Your Rights." This event attracted more prospects and helped all three businesses grow faster. Win-win-win.
- Paul's Therapeutic Furniture sent letters to prospective customers saying that if they would visit his showroom, they could have a coupon for a free dinner at Luby's restaurant. In exchange, Luby's carried coupons for discounts on Paul's furniture. Win-win.
- Many Exxon gas stations now have Subway sandwich shops in them. Subway reaches more customers this way and gets to slash their advertising costs; Exxon gives people another reason to stop at their pumps. Again, win-win.

- I have used this win-win-win approach numerous times to make my books best sellers online. I work with other list owners to create a package of freebies, which people get when they buy my books. The list owners get free promotion, I get list owners telling their fans about my books, and the customers get dozens of bonuses as well as my books. It's a beautiful system. In 2005 it helped one of my latest books, *The Attractor Factor*, to actually outsell the latest Harry Potter book—which no other book had done!

Find businesses who are already serving your market and create an alliance with them. In the simplest form, this may be asking them to display your brochures while you agree to display theirs. In a more advanced arrangement, you might offer a business discount coupons to their customers while they do the same for yours.

For example, if you sell paint and the business on the corner sells groceries, you might print coupons that say, "$5 off paint—Compliments of Joe's Groceries." Joe will obviously offer your coupons to his customers because it makes him look good and gives extra benefit to his clientele. In return, he might print coupons that say, "$5 off groceries—Compliments of Pete's Paints." Pete would of course be glad to offer these coupons to his customers. You are not competing with each other, but working together for mutual benefit. Win-win again.

How to Do It

You create a successful cross-promotion by asking yourself three questions:

1. Who are my potential customers?
2. Who else wants to reach these same people?
3. How can we reach our potential customers more effectively?

Barnum's primary colleague throughout his life was Moses Kimball, owner of a museum in Boston. Barnum wrote countless letters to Kimball suggesting ideas for shows and trading curiosities. Barnum actually rented the Fejee mermaid from Kimball, and then let Kimball show it. Deals like these successfully answer the three key questions:

1. Who were Barnum's potential customers? Anyone who had twenty-five cents.
2. Who else wanted to reach these same people? Moses Kimball.
3. How could they reach these potential customers more effectively? By swapping ideas, techniques, and curiosities.

Barnum negotiated cross-promotion arrangements like this in the 1800s, before the phrase "cross-promotion" was coined. When he worked in a tiny store in Bethel, Connecticut, bartering and negotiation were common. "Ours was a cash, credit, and barter store," he wrote. Barnum once traded a whole wagon of worthless scrap at his store for a whole wagon of worthless green bottles. "Some bargain," you say? Barnum then held a lottery (legal then) where virtually every ticket holder won something: a green bottle. But this win-win made everyone feel they got a deal.

In later years, when Barnum advised his hat-making neighbor, Genin, to bid on the Lind ticket, he knew an auction would get attention. He knew the high bid would get Genin attention. And he knew even more customers would line up at Lind's concert as a result. He was right. Lind's concert sold out, and Genin became famous in a day.

Here's how their arrangement looks using our three guidelines:

1. *Who were Barnum's potential customers?* The population of New York City, where his museum was located.
2. *Who else wanted to reach these same people?* John Genin, who had a hat store next door to the museum.
3. *How could they reach their potential customers more effectively?* Barnum's idea for an auction, where the highest bidder would receive the most publicity, would bring attention to both businessmen, as well as to what they sold.

This strategy was so effective that Barnum used it several times. He encouraged an unknown singer by the name of Ossian Dodge to buy the highest selling Lind ticket. The singer paid $625 and his career took off. He was suddenly famous and in demand. Later still a businessman paid $650 for an auctioned ticket. He, too, got the fame he wanted for his business, and to prove that that was all he wanted, he never even bothered to attend the Jenny Lind concert.

Who Else Can Benefit?

One day I sat down with Paul Mattek, CEO of Paul's Therapeutic Furniture, and began to walk him through "Project Phineas," my new sales training program based on Barnum's rings of power. We began the process by discovering a larger customer base for his business.

"Who have you been trying to reach?" I asked him.

"Senior citizens," he said.

"Why?"

"Because they are old and their bones are aching. They obviously need therapeutic furniture to help them and even heal them."

"That's good, but your audience is bigger than that," I explained. "Who else might benefit from what you offer?"

"I don't know."

"What about athletes? Don't they have aches and pains? Aren't many of them so big that they can't find comfortable beds to sleep in?"

"I never thought of that before," Paul replied. "I even know Bob Lilly, who used to play for the Dallas Cowboys. I might talk to him about our beds."

"Good! And who else might benefit from your products?"

"People who have been in accidents might," Paul answered. "They are in pain and could use relief."

"That's good, too, and I still think your market is bigger than that," I said. "I think anyone who feels stress in today's chaotic world could use your furniture. Fifteen minutes in one of your massage chairs might give them two hours of relaxation."

"Come to think of it, anyone who wants a good night's rest and can afford an adjustable bed is a prospect," Paul told me, his eyes large with excitement. "That means my potential customers are virtually every adult with a job."

Within a few minutes of brainstorming Paul saw that his customer base was actually much bigger than he ever previously imagined. All I did was encourage him to think that "There's a customer born every minute."

Later he called Bob Lilly and ended up selling him a bed and three massage chairs. After that, Paul got Lilly to okay a direct mail campaign to other NFL athletes who might be interested in Paul's therapeutic furniture.

Paul's not done, of course. The next step for him is to create cross-promotion arrangements with businesses who serve the same people he does. For example, he might work out deals with massage therapists, chiropractors, housing apartments for seniors, or even with attorneys who serve personal-injury victims. Creating win-win arrangements with these other businesses will help him reach his new world of prospects.

Go after your market, don't limit your target, and work with other businesses to enrich what you offer these people while getting rich in the process. That's how you Barnumize your business in today's world. It's one of Barnum's rings of power. It's how you profit on the fact that "There's a customer born every minute."

Start considering that you have an untapped customer base out there in the world. Although you are wise to research your market and target your customers, you would also be wise to start casting a bigger net. In other words, limited thinking might stop you from cashing in on the level you want. To discover who else might be interested in your product or service—and not miss any potential customers in the process—you have to capture the attention of the world. And you'll discover how to accomplish just that in the next chapter.

For now, ask yourself, "Where are my prospects, and who can I work with to turn more of them into customers?"

5 | Attention!
What P.T. Barnum Learned When He Was Almost Hanged

It has been my universal plan, as you know, to make the public aware of what I was about to offer, to get the best of everything and the most of it, and then to advertise freely and without fear. Never attempt to catch a whale with a minnow.

—P.T. Barnum, 1891, five days before he died

A 26-year-old P.T. Barnum discovered the value of getting attention for his business when he was nearly hanged by an angry mob.

Barnum helped operate a circus for six months in 1836, many decades before he was to be involved in the now famous Barnum and Bailey circus. During those early years he learned a valuable lesson through a terrifying experience.

One day he had just bought a new suit of clothes that he wore with pride. He left his hotel in Annapolis, Maryland and noticed a dozen men following him, quickly gaining on him. At first Barnum thought the men

43

were admiring his suit. However, he quickly learned the men wanted his life. They roughed him up, ruined his new suit, and led him to a rail where they prepared to hang the young showman.

Barnum protested, finally realizing that the men about to hang him thought he was a minister who had killed a local woman. Barnum spoke as quickly as he could but could not get the men to listen. They had been informed by Barnum's partner—by his *partner*, mind you—that he was indeed the minister who committed the murder.

Barnum couldn't believe it. He begged for a chance to talk to his partner and clear up the error. The men finally agreed. They pushed and shoved him all the way back into town. By the time the mob reached the hotel, there were now fifty men ready to hang Barnum. They walked right to the hotel where his partner was waiting, laughing so hard he had to hold his belly. Barnum's partner explained that the whole thing was a joke on Barnum. The mob laughed and dispersed. However, Barnum was fuming. Finally his partner explained:

> My dear Barnum, it was all for our good. Remember, all we need to insure success is *notoriety*. You will see that this will be noised all about town as a trick played by one of the circus managers upon the other, and our pavilion will be crammed tomorrow night.

Barnum's partner was right. The cruel joke made the circus the talk of the town, and business boomed. Barnum had learned another ring of power: the magic of getting attention.

Mangin's Great Secret of Success

P.T. Barnum somehow intuitively knew the first law of advertising, and he knew it before it was ever expressed as a law: Get attention.

Barnum had a knack for knowing how to provoke public attention, a knack that can help you in business today. Without capturing the attention of the public, you won't have a chance to tell the public what you have for sale. Barnum wrote, "The great secret of success in anything is to get a hearing. Half the object is gained when the audience is assembled."

One of the people who reminded Barnum of this secret was Monsieur Mangin, a famous French businessman who sold the best pencils in all of Europe. Mangin would appear on a street corner dressed in unusual royal garb, riding a team of large horses. He would park, open his wagon with a great deal of pomp and circumstance, and slowly begin to put on a theatrical performance. A crowd would always form, wondering what was happening. The French entrepreneur would then demonstrate his pencils, involve members of his audience, entertain them, and end by selling his product to nearly everyone present.

Years later Barnum met Mangin and complimented him on ". . . your manner of attracting the public. Your costume is elegant, your chariot is superb, and your valet and music are sure to draw."

"Aha! You never saw better pencils," Mangin replied. "You know I could never maintain my reputation if I sold poor pencils. But *sacre bleu*, my miserable would-be imitators do not know our grand secret. First, attract the public by din and tinsel, by brilliant sky-rockets and Bengola lights, then give them as much as possible for their money."

Mangin ended their meeting by saying he was planning "a grand humbug," which "shall double the sale of my pencils."

Within four months of their meeting, Barnum read in the Paris newspapers that Mangin had died. The news was published in every newspaper in Europe because, as Barnum explained, ". . . almost everybody had seen or heard of the eccentric pencil maker." Barnum felt sad that he would never know the great humbug Mangin had been planning.

What Barnum did not realize at the time was that Mangin's death was a humbug designed to get attention. After being "dead" for half a year, Mangin suddenly surfaced, began giving his pencil demonstrations, and was selling more product than ever before. In a second meeting with Barnum, Mangin explained:

> Did I not tell you I had a new humbug that would double the sales of my pencils? I assure you my sales are more than quadrupled, and it is sometimes impossible to have them manufactured fast enough to supply the demand. You Yankees are very clever, but by gar, none of you have discovered you should live all the better if you would die for six months.

Although Barnum considered Mangin too conceited to be pleasurable company, he had to admit that the man knew one of the secrets for increasing business: Get attention.

Attention-Getting Tricks

Barnum learned well. When he took over the Scudder Museum, and renamed it Barnum's American Museum, he immediately made changes that no one in New York City could overlook:

- He put flags across the roof of the museum, so that their flapping was visible for a mile.
- He put a wraparound balcony around the second floor for customers to step out and get air—while making people on the ground below curious.
- He installed a huge revolving lighthouse lamp on the roof, making it the city's first spotlight.
- He hung huge color paintings of animals on the outside of the building, between every window on every floor, making the building itself a curiosity.
- He hung oversized banners on the outside of the building to advertise what was inside.
- At night he hung large illuminated transparencies that projected eerie images on the museum's walls.

Imagine walking down the streets of New York City in the 1840s and seeing such a display. No wonder Barnum's museum became the talk of the city and the center of activities, and no wonder Barnum's success there helped make him rich. Within the first year of his operating the museum, ticket sales nearly tripled.

Build Attention—with Bricks?

In the 1860s a merchant might hire a man to stand and stare at his store so others walking by would get curious and go into his shop.

In the 1890s you could find an Italian organ grinder standing on a downtown street madly turning the handle of his music box—but without a sound coming from it. When you bent over and looked at his musical instrument, wondering what was wrong with it, you would see an advertisement, such as, "Buy Pease's candy today."

One man kept a live bear in his store window to bring attention to the "bear grease" he sold that supposedly grew hair. (It didn't.) The bear wore a sign saying "To be slaughtered next." (It wasn't.)

All of these business people were creatively striving to bring attention to whatever they sold. Barnum showed much more originality in his attention-getting tactics.

At one point a fellow came to Barnum looking for work. Barnum gave the man several bricks and said:

> Now go and lay a brick on the sidewalk at the corner of Broadway and Ann street; another close by the Museum; a third diagonally across the way at the corner of Broadway and Vesey street, by the Astor House; put down the fourth on the sidewalk in front of St. Paul's Church, opposite; then, with the fifth brick in hand, take up a rapid march from one point to the other, making the circuit, exchanging your brick at every point, and say nothing to no one.

The unemployed man asked why in the world Barnum wanted him to carry out this bizarre routine. Barnum said:

> No matter. All you need to know is that it brings you fifteen cents wages per hour. It is a bit of my fun. And to assist me properly you must seem to be as deaf as a post; wear a serious countenance; answer no questions; pay no attention to any one; but attend faithfully to the work and at the end of every hour by St. Paul's clock show this ticket at the Museum door; enter, walking solemnly through every hall in the building; pass out, and resume your work.

The confused but now employed man did as he was told. Within 30 minutes over 500 people were gathered in front of Barnum's museum watching the mysterious silent man move the bricks. Then, when the man went into the museum, people bought tickets and went in after him.

This unusual stunt was so successful that the police had to stop it. The crowds in front of the museum were blocking traffic.

Why Iranistan?

Don't forget that Barnum's colossal mansion—called Iranistan—was designed to help bring attention to Barnum's various businesses.

Barnum modeled his extraordinary palace after the Royal Pavilion of King George IV of Wales. Barnum wrote:

> I cared little for style, and my wife cared still less; but as we meant to have a good house, it might as well, at the same time, be unique. In this, I confess, I had "an eye to business," for I thought that a pile of buildings of a novel order might indirectly serve as an advertisement of my Museum.

After two years of construction, Barnum opened the doors of his oriental villa on November 14, 1848, to more than 1,000 guests. Barnum's home became the talk of the country.

The Violinist Who Played—Upside Down!

Another time, Barnum had posters placed all over his museum showing a black man playing a violin. Not many people were coming to the show, so Barnum told his crew to turn all the posters upside down. Crowds flocked. Why? People saw the ads and assumed the performer was going to play his violin upside down.

In 1883, when the Brooklyn Bridge was completed, Barnum offered $5,000 if he could walk Jumbo across it for the grand opening. The offer was declined, but later, in 1888, Barnum got attention when he led a dozen elephants over the new bridge across the Pequonnock River. The existing photo of the event shows the elephants standing, dozens of men wearing hats to keep their heads warm in the chilly December air, but with one man—

knowing the photographer's camera was on him—posing, hat in hand, white hair visible to all: P.T. Barnum.

Barnum Finds More Ways to Grab Attention

Barnum always looked for ways to grab the public eye. For example:

- He studied ballooning when it became the rage and was one of the first people to have a man in a balloon attempt to cross the Atlantic.
- He brought the first live hippopotamuses to America.
- To help publicize the midget Commodore Nutt, he ordered the making of a magnificent carriage, hand carved out of wood in the shape of an English walnut. Nutt would ride inside this unusual carriage, no doubt stopping people in their tracks wherever he was seen.
- When the transatlantic cable was completed, Barnum offered $5,000 for the right to send the first 20 words by telegraph across the ocean. He said, ". . . not that there was any merit in the words, but that I fancied there was more than $5,000 worth of notoriety in the operation."

Barnum Turns an Embarrassment into an Empire

Only once did a publicity stunt of Barnum's backfire, and even then Barnum benefited from it.

When Hebe the circus elephant gave birth to the first elephant in captivity in 1880, Barnum sent a telegram offering the owners $200,000 for the mother and child. The circus owners declined but cleverly turned Barnum's offer into an advertisement for their own show. They enlarged Barnum's telegram, put it on posters, and added the headline, "What Barnum Thinks of the Baby Elephant."

Barnum winced, but decided he had met foes "worthy of my steel," and joined forces with them. The result was the Barnum and Bailey circus.

Barnum's famous humbugs, from the Fejee mermaid to the great buffalo hunt (which I'll describe later), were tools to get attention for his more worthwhile items. These stunts were never overlooked by the public or the press. The additional press coverage always helped Barnum, his associates, and his cause. He regarded it as free advertising.

How can you do the same for your business? Let's see.

Houdini!!!

Publicity can bring you enough attention to last generations. P.T. Barnum's name lives today. So does Houdini's, who was a disciple of Barnum's methods and a collector of Barnum's writings. That famous escape artist was such a master at harnessing media attention that he was often asked to speak at advertising clubs.

Although many magicians can make doves and rabbits appear, Houdini produced an eagle. He once shot a gun and made an elephant disappear. He challenged the police to lock him up in their finest restraints—and he always escaped. The press loved it. Barnum had a museum and a circus to promote, but Houdini was the greatest one-man show of his era.

What if you're not Barnum or Houdini? Consider the modern business people who grab the public eye:

- The president of the Original New York Seltzer beverage company plunged 10 stories off a building and into an air bag with his company name on it. He lived, and his business got plenty of free publicity.
- Jack LaLanne promoted his physical fitness business by swimming across a lake in Japan while towing 65 boats full of 6,500 pounds of pulp—and he was 65 years old at the time.
- When Robert Allen, author of *Creating Wealth*, wanted to promote his work he issued this challenge: "Send me to any unemployment line. Let me select someone who is broke, out of work, discouraged. Let me teach him in two days time the secrets of wealth. And in 90 days he'll be back on his feet, with $5,000 cash in the bank, never to set foot in an unemployment line again." The media, of course, ate it up.

- And when Robert Allen wanted to promote his book, *Nothing Down*, he told the world, "Send me to any city, take away my wallet, and in 72 hours I'll buy an excellent piece of property using none of my own money." He received reams of newspaper coverage as a result. When the *Los Angeles Times* actually took him up on the challenge and even said, "You do it or we will fry you on the front page," Allen took a deep breath. He had issued a challenge that took courage. Having someone take him up on the challenge was terrifying, but he accepted and he did it.

- T. Harv Eker, author of the number-one *New York Times* bestseller, *Secrets of the Millionaire Mind*, boldly stated, "Give me five minutes, and I can predict your financial future for the rest of your life!" This got him enormous publicity.

- I did something similar when Nightingale-Conant released my first audioprogram, *The Power of Outrageous Marketing*. I declared, "I can make anyone famous in only 90 days!" People would buy my program, listen to it, and then call and e-mail me, begging me to take them on as a client. I was flooded with replies. I took one client, for example, and made him a Las Vegas headliner. He's still performing and has been for over two years straight on the Vegas strip. He's Dr. Scott Lewis, author, hypnotist, celebrity, and Vegas superstar. How did I do it? I simply Barnumized him!

- Red Baron Pizza flew vintage World War I planes in 13 key markets and watched pizza sales jump 100 percent whenever a fly-by took place.

- Mark Joyner, author of *The Irresistible Offer*, retired from Internet marketing after a long and prosperous career, only to return a year later, reinvented, and promoting himself to the world he had left behind. The online buzz for his coming and going caused international attention for his businesses.

- Joe Weider took unknown bodybuilders and turned them into superstars. One of his greatest and biggest creations was Arnold Schwarzenegger. Weider would then put the superstar in his magazines, to help sell the nutritional products advertised there. It was all a well crafted strategy to turn publicity into wealth.

- Mark Levy promoted his book, *Accidental Genius*, by sending out a news release with the headline, "Man Prepares to Stop Midtown Traffic With His Mind." He sat in a Barnes & Noble store window across from Lincoln Center in New York, on a Saturday night (the biggest store in the country, at the time, during their busiest time and day of week). The store ended up selling over 800 copies, and his book was at one point the third best-selling business book at the Wall Street Borders. He also got on CNN-FN.

- And let's not overlook Evel Knievel, a former life-insurance salesman who made history—and tons of money—by risking his life with daredevil stunts. As he began to promote his famous Snake River Canyon jump of 1974, Knievel merchandise began to sell. One executive claimed the products brought in more than $200 million, with $5 million going to Knievel. You may not want to leap trucks or canyons in a motorcycle, but you have to admire anyone who makes a reported $50 million in a 16-year career, basically from getting attention.

According to Aaron Cushman, author of *A Passion for Winning: Fifty Years of Promoting Legendary People and Products*, a good stunt might turn into a long-lasting business in itself or even make history. For example:

- The Rose Bowl started out strictly as a business stunt, and once involved a bizarre race between a camel and an elephant.
- The Miss America pageant began in 1921 as a shameless publicity stunt.
- The Academy Awards started out in 1927 as nothing more than a publicity stunt for the fledgling movie industry.
- The first modern Olympic Games, held in Athens in 1896, was actually created as a way to promote peace among nations.

Again, you never know where these events can lead. Not only might they improve your bottom line, but they also might make you and your business famous.

The Power of a Challenge

A common theme throughout many publicity stunts or staged events is a challenge. Houdini challenged the world by saying, "I can escape from any confinement anyone can create." The challenge brought him international fame. Houdini actually refused some of the challenges that came his way because they seemed guaranteed to kill him, but people paid attention to the challenge. Houdini accepted enough of the challenges to secure his standing as the greatest escape artist the world had ever seen.

It's important to understand that Houdini was aware of the risks. He issued the challenge to get attention for his business. Many of the challenges left him exhausted and in pain. At least one caused him permanent liver damage, but he was willing to take the risk to receive the benefits.

It's also worth noting that other businesses benefited from Houdini's challenge.

- A Chicago envelope company put him in the world's largest envelope. This helped promote the company as well as Houdini.
- Houdini also escaped a giant football manufactured by A. J. Reach, which also promoted that company.
- He was often stuffed into a U.S. Postal Service canvas mailbag, which helped promote the postal service.

Houdini was definitely a disciple of Barnum. He once offered $2,500 to anyone who could duplicate his escapes. No one accepted the challenge. At another point he hired seven bald men for an unusual publicity event: Each man had a letter of Houdini's name etched on his head. The seven would go to dinner at a busy time of day, take off their hats, and lower their heads so the public could see the name "H-O-U-D-I-N-I" spelled out. Without question, Houdini's escape stunts brought him much notoriety.

The Real Secret

Your own challenges don't have to be so radical or risky. Barnum promoted Jenny Lind with song contests. Although the submissions were uniformly bad, the contest brought much publicity to Lind. It was a low cost, low risk way to generate attention.

When Barnum was promoting a juggler, he issued a challenge saying he would give one thousand dollars to anyone who could reproduce all of his juggler's act. You can do the same for your own business. All it takes is some creative thinking and a little courage.

Lack of courage may actually be what stops most business people from doing something challenging to grab attention. Knowing you are about to stand out in the crowd because of your stunts may make you feel ridiculous, but Houdini, Allen, Knievel, and Barnum not only did it, they grew rich and famous as a result of it.

Sometimes you simply have to take a deep breath and go for it. For example:

- Muhammad Ali was not afraid to yell "I am the greatest!" into the faces of reporters.
- Babe Ruth pointed into stands, signaling where he was going to knock the baseball.
- Joe Namath said, "We will win—I guarantee it."
- Tom Monaghan said we'd get pizza in 30 minutes or it's free—and he rules the Domino's empire today.

Courage and audacity can quickly bring attention to your business.

Barnum Shocks His Staff

Courage can lead to wealth beyond all expectations. In 1872 several of Barnum's assistants tried to talk him out of taking his show across the country. They had facts and figures to prove the enterprise would lose money. They presented a very logical case. Barnum politely listened, but then said he planned even more expenses, a bigger show, and *more* stops in *more* cities. His assistants were stunned.

Barnum explained that he planned to put the show itself on railroad cars, not on wagons, and bring it to the people by rail. Railroad cars were new and certain to get attention, while also making transportation easier.

Despite expenses of $780,000, at the end of six months Barnum's show pulled in more than one million dollars—$600,000 above what the show made the year before. Once again, his courage paid off.

Are You Curious?

Building curiosity also works. In 1886 the letters "W & B" began appearing on posters all over Philadelphia. People would stop and wonder what the initials stood for. Curiosity created attention. Days later, a second poster replaced the first with the words "Wanamaker & Brown." Later still, balloons were released into the air, and anyone who brought one back got a free suit at the new store. As a result, by 1889 W & B became the largest retail dealer in men's clothes in the United States.

This method is still used today because it works. Late in 1996, a client of mine received a postcard with the phrase, "Enjoy the ride" on it. He couldn't find a logo, return address, company name, or any clue to what the card was promoting. Two weeks later, he received another postcard, again with the phrase, "Enjoy the ride" on it, but this time the company name was on the card—Nissan.

A few days after this, my client began noticing billboards and then television commercials saying "Enjoy the ride," further promoting Nissan's new car. Not only did this campaign make my client curious, he ended up going to his local Nissan dealer and buying a new car from them.

Call Yourself Names

Even having the right name can bring attention. Barnum knew few people would pay hard earned money to see a midget named Charles Stratton. But they repeatedly paid to see someone with the distinguished name of General Tom Thumb.

When Barnum hired Lancashire musicians, he renamed them The Swiss Bell Ringers. He knew people would flock to see the more curious group because of the easier, better name.

Many people are still using this method today. Singer John Denver's real name was Henry John Deutschendorf, Jr., and actor John Wayne's real first name was *Marion*.

Mademoiselle Zazel, the world's first human cannonball, was really Rosa M. Richter. She was the first person ever to be shot out of a cannon in a circus. Barnum renamed her to make her sound more colorful (and he billed her as his Human Projectile).

I've used this method, as well. I created the first marketing program based on the ideas in this book and named it Project Phineas. Although the name isn't entirely meaningless (Barnum's first name was Phineas), it is insignificant to most people. However, it also captivates most people. It makes them curious. After the name was decided, it was easy to conjure up the slogan, "Improve your business with Project Phineas."

You Can Count on This

Adding a number can also generate attention. In the 1860s there appeared a patent medicine labeled "S.T. 1860 X." The name was meaningless but unforgettable. It helped make the owners of the medicine millions of dollars.

Also, let's not forget Boeing 727, or Baskin-Robbins 31 flavors, or even Heinz 57. There are more than 57 varieties of Heinz products, but Mr. Heinz loved the ring of "57" and wisely kept it. Heinz has been in business since 1869.

When I wanted to sell a privately printed collection of my sales letters, I came up with the name, "Master Writer 397." The name sounded impressive. It was also meaningless. As a result, I sold out of every edition I printed, and I still do. Again, a unique name for your company, product, or service can also bring attention to your business.

It's no accident that, as a copywriter and speaker, I bill myself as Mr. Fire! People may forget my real name, mispronounce it, or misspell it, but few forget Mr. Fire. What I should probably do next is add a number to it, such as, Mr. Fire 437-X. It would certainly create more curiosity.

Hang from a Helicopter

Beacon Manufacturing Company wanted to promote their blankets in ways that nailed public attention. They turned Ted, their vice-president of sales, into an ad character and named the ads "Adventures of Teddy." The ads showed Ted, aka Teddy, being tossed in the air by a Beacon blanket, dangling from a helicopter by a Beacon blanket, and even keeping sharks away using a Beacon blanket.

Although you might feel sorry for Ted, these calculated risks brought enormous attention to the company because they dramatized their product in order to get attention for it.

Start the Line

Another way to grab attention is to be first to do something noteworthy.

We all remember the first giant elephant that Barnum brought to America, but who remembers what elephant came after Jumbo?

We all know the famous midget Tom Thumb, but how many of us remember Commodore Nutt, who followed Tom Thumb?

Barnum was always scouting for new people, products, or events to show. He hired agents around the world to locate new curiosities for him. He wanted to be the first to display the most interesting people and products in the world because he knew being first would get attention.

You have to be like the Toledo, Ohio man who opened a new franchise called Puppy Hut—the first fast-food restaurant for dogs. He even has a fenced in "Park-N-Bark" area, complete with fire hydrants. Be the first in a new field and you can grab attention, but that's not all you can do.

Become an Audacious Idea Generator

Ask Stanley Arnold. When Piel's desperately needed to sell more beer, they hired the ad agency Young & Rubicam, which hired the professional idea man Stanley Arnold.

The first thing Arnold did was buy an island. Then he buried prizes on it. Then he held a contest. Piel's increased sales dramatically as people lined up to buy their beer, all the customers dreaming of winning a visit to "Treasure Island."

When Gulf Oil was lagging behind in fuel sales, Arnold rented a 40-room chateau in France. He advised Gulf to have a contest in which the grand-prize winner got to live the "Life of Riley" in the castle. Gulf agreed. They were desperate. Did the audacious plan work? Arnold says, "In just four weeks, more than two million three hundred thousand motorists drove into Gulf service stations to make that dream materialize."

Barnum would have loved Arnold's other exploits, as well. When Arnold wanted to present a giant idea to the Continental Baking Company, he hired a real giant to help him. Arnold looked in Ripley's Believe It or Not collection in New York City, found the giant, and hired him.

When Arnold needed to convince The American Tobacco Company that his ideas were confidential and would not be leaked to the competition, he hired a Wells Fargo armored car, complete with armed guards, to drive and accompany him to the business meeting. And when Arnold wanted Macy's as a client, he legally changed his name to Stanley Macy's Arnold.

What is Arnold's secret to success in coming up with these Barnum-like ideas?

He says, "I've built my entire career on putting carts before horses, and feeling before logic."

Ten Easy Ways to Grab Attention

Here are some proven ways to implement this ring of power for you and your business:

1. *Hold a contest.* Barnum invented the baby contest to help promote his museum. When he held his first one, more than 60,000 customers attended—and this was in 1848 when they had to travel by horse. However, any contest will bring attention. Consider fashion contests, poetry contests, cooking contests, sporting events, look-alike contests, even funny guess-the-number-of-M&M's-in-this-jar contests. People love contests and quizzes and involving games. Television shows such as *Wheel of Fortune* are enormously successful for giving people risk-free fun.

2. *Hire a band.* Live music draws crowds. Barnum hired the worst band he could find to play on the balcony outside his famous museum in New York City. He knew the bad music would drive people into his building. I would suggest a good band playing music your target audience would enjoy.

3. *Use costumed characters.* Or even costumed salespeople. Barnum hired real curiosities to draw attention to his enterprises, whether they were midgets or Siamese twins. You can bring a carnival atmosphere to your business by renting costumes and letting your employees role-play their favorite characters. You might even invite customers to join in the fun. Everyone knows Mickey Mouse is an animation, yet millions trek to Florida to see some person in a Mickey Mouse costume. I've considered dressing as P.T. Barnum and giving speeches on his business principles while pretending to be the great showman. Audiences would love it.

4. *Hold psychic readings.* Barnum, like Houdini after him, was a great debunker of spiritualism, seances, and people who claimed to manifest the dead. Yet psychic readings and fortune tellers remain popular. Barnum had them in his museum. You might consider a spoof and hire someone to give comical psychic readings. My friend Connie Schmidt does just that, and even wrote a hilarious book titled *Cosmic Relief.*

5. *Bring in animals.* Barnum loved finding and displaying animals. He cofounded the Bridgeport SPCA and funded many worthy causes for animals. You could invite your local SPCA or Humane Society to bring in animals available for adoption. They will bring attention to your business while helping the community. Customers love it.

6. *Offer collectibles.* As I wrote in one of my earlier books, *CyberWriting: How to Promote Your Product or Service On-line (without being flamed)*, virtually everyone collects something. I collect books by and about Barnum. I also collect magic effects. Barbed wire is worth gold in the West (there are over 1,200 different types of barbed wire); old irons are popular in other areas.

Scout for odd but valuable collectibles and put them on display at your business. This can be as creative as showing the guitar made out of matchsticks that I mentioned earlier or as odd as creating a display of Bic lighters. The local media will probably cover your collection and give you and your business even more attention.

7. *Hold an art show.* I'm no expert here. I once sat down for breakfast with a friend in a small cafe and found a rectangular piece of wood on our table. It had two pieces of sticky putty on one side and the artist's name on the other. My friend held up the wood and said, "This is art." I took the small object and studied the two pieces of putty, trying to find meaning in their shape or size. I couldn't. After a few minutes of bewilderment, we looked up and saw a huge painting on the wall beside our table. The wood I held was supposed to be stuck on the wall under the art: It was the name plate for the artist. Still, art shows grab attention (if not mine).

8. *Sponsor an event.* Fund a walk-a-thon or a fun run. A Schwinn bike dealer in California sponsors bike rodeos for Boy Scouts. Contributing to worthwhile causes, such as environmental improvement, will also help you get attention. Barnum contributed animals to the Smithsonian and to Tufts University. Although he was sincerely helping the world understand nature and history, he also knew his contributions were getting him free publicity.

9. *Hire an entertainer.* This can be as simple as finding a local magician or balloon sculptor to something as complicated (and expensive) as locating a celebrity to appear in your business. Barnum was an amateur magician and often performed magic tricks in his lectures. He knew entertainers helped people feel good and brought attention to his business.

10. *Break a record.* Become the greatest at something. Clearly Barnum became the greatest showman of his time. Think of what you could do to get into the *Guinness Book of World Records*. This may at first seem a bizarre way to increase your business, but when you break a record, the media will refer to you as, "Joe Smith, President of Your Business, today broke a record for. . . ." That simple mention can give you miles worth of publicity.

In short, think audaciously and act courageously. I love the phrase "dreams that stir your blood." Create a way to get attention that stirs your blood, that excites your passions, that makes your eyes light up and your heart beat faster. Answer the question, "What would Barnum do if he were alive today?" and then *do it*.

The World's Oldest Formula

The world's oldest advertising formula—known as AIDA—says you must first get attention before you can urge anyone to take action. It makes sense. If no one looks at your ad, no one will know what you are selling.

AIDA stands for attention, interest, desire, action. Many people in advertising still use this formula (though I updated it in an earlier book of mine, titled *CyberWriting*). AIDA means your ads must first get *attention*, then create *interest* in your product, then develop a *desire* for it, and finally request that the reader take some *action* to buy it. For our purposes, let's just take a peek at the first step: attention.

Although there may be several methods for capturing attention, they all seem to fall into the category that I call contrast.

Barnum used parades, long banners flying in the wind, lighthouse lights on top of a building, and even unusual carriages to get attention. These activities were in contrast to the day-to-day activities of most people in the mid-1800s.

When you go to work every day, you typically see the same things on the road. If one day you see a parade, or a huge man walking down the street on stilts, or a policeman riding a giraffe, you stop and look. The unusual display holds contrast to everyday life, and that contrast grabs your attention.

Barnum had Tom Thumb's picture taken while the little man stood beside a regular sized table, and beside two of London's tallest guards. The resulting images rivet the eyes of everyone who sees it. Even today, the pictures show Tom's size with such contrast that they still capture attention.

Barnum used this same technique to promote his other shows. When he wanted people to see his Fejee mermaid, he displayed signs showing a half woman–half fish. Clearly, this got attention. It was in contrast to any other signs of the time.

When you create advertising or publicity, remember that you have to disrupt the daily preoccupation people have with themselves. Anything you can do to interrupt their automatic flight through life will bring their attention to you. By thinking of the concept of contrast, you can start to brainstorm ways to grab attention for your own business. Imagine something so different, so bizarre, so unusual—something bigger or better than what people see every day—and you will grab attention. The secret is contrast.

This tool is more important today than ever before. With all the competition you have, unless you do something Barnum-like to get noticed, you won't get anyone's attention *or* anyone's business.

Arrest Public Attention

Your task in this chapter is to think of ways to befriend the media and grab public attention. Anything goes. Contests, awards, and surveys work; so does breaking a record, staging a protest, and inventing a quiz. You don't have to be as dramatic as Barnum or Houdini, but you do have to be clever and creative. The idea is to arrest public attention long enough for it to notice your business. After all, the public is a parade walking past you. Unless you get them to turn their heads and look at you, they will simply walk on by. Barnum summed up the need for creative promotion when he wrote:

> I studied ways to arrest public attention; to startle, to make people talk and wonder; in short, to let the world know that I had a Museum.

As Barnum wrote in a letter in 1850, "I need not tell you that even Our Saviour needed John the Baptist as an *avant courier*. . . . The angel Gabriel uses a '*trumpet*,' and *you* know that *we must* do likewise!"

Now is the time to act on these timeless and proven principles. Barnum wrote, "If you hesitate, some bolder hand will stretch out before you and get the prize."

What are *you* going to do to claim the prize?

6

Barnum Knew People Would Spend Their Last Nickel on This One Thing

You must—I repeat it, must—*have always a great and progressive show and also one which is clean, pure, moral, and instructive. Never cater to the baser instincts of humanity, strive as I have always done to elevate the moral tone of amusements, and always remember that the children have ever been our best patrons. I would rather hear the pleased laugh of a child over some feature of my exhibition than receive as I did the flattering compliments of the Prince of Wales.*

—P.T. Barnum, 1891, five days before he died

A friend of mine said his father was able to survive the Great Depression of 1929 and the lean years that followed by simply getting people to spend a nickel on something they didn't need.

"How?" I asked. "My dad said his family nearly starved."

"My father bought a small fold-up merry-go-round," my friend explained. "He would take it to parks and charge people a nickel each to ride on it."

"It worked?"

"People will spend their last nickel to have fun," he said.

Years later, when I was researching material for my book on Bruce Barton, the 1920s advertising genius and bestselling author, I discovered that when radio was invented and swept the country, the same thing happened. Radio became a primary source of entertainment. People became so interested in keeping their radios that when hard times hit and they had to choose between having their refrigerator or their radio repossessed, the fridge went. People would sooner starve then lose their ability to have fun.

P.T. Barnum knew this ring of power long before the rest of the world did. Judging from the number of businesses that are going out of business every day, most business people still don't know this one. Once you have a firm grasp on this fundamental truth, the rest simply requires creativity, audacity, and persistence.

What People Really Want

An unspoken truth in marketing is that the only reason people do anything is for the feelings they expect to get. Without those feelings dangling before them, they will not spend money with you. Although people sometimes spend money to feel frightened (such as when they rent a horror movie), they typically spend money to feel better. In short, make your business more fun and you'll start getting more business.

When Barnum took over the Scudder Museum in 1841, the business had been losing money over the previous three years. Under Barnum's management, all debts on the museum were paid in full within 18 months, and within three years Barnum was making huge profits.

How? Barnum knew he had to attract the public. He went out of his way to draw attention to his establishment with posters and paintings, lights and music. He also knew he had to give people their money's worth. He did. People would arrive when the doors opened at sunrise and spend hours looking at over 850,000 displays (think of it!), some humorous, some bizarre, many living, and many fossilized, but the key word was fun. People enjoyed going to his museum. It was equivalent to visiting Disneyworld today. You felt good there.

Barnum gave people educational entertainment. One visitor in 1864 wrote that he saw Barnum hold up a lump of dry clay and announce to everyone that a live fish would be found inside. Barnum sawed the lump in half and indeed, some sort of creature was there. After exposure to air, and then water, the fish began to swim. Everyone was astonished and delighted. Barnum had just shown them the first example of the African lungfish in America. In the 1800s, this event was historic. People left feeling as if they had seen a miracle.

Safari Adventures

Any business can be injected with fun and made to be exciting. One of my clients teaches seminars on leadership and change. That can be pretty boring stuff, but Rick Butts has a background in rock and roll music, and he speaks with power and passion. I advised him to create a seminar that would actually be an adventure. His book, *The Safari Adventure Company*, can be brought to life on stage. He could even play live music and write songs with important messages.

"Make it a multimedia experience," I urged him. "Use lights and sounds and videos and role-playing to make people actually live the adventure. Help them to have fun."

Butts now delivers Rocky Mountain Safari retreats for business people, and he's currently putting his Safari seminars on CD-ROM so viewers can have a virtual reality experience at their desks.

As Barnum once said, "The noblest art is that of making others happy."

Wilde Terror

I once had breakfast with Stuart Wilde, the roguish businessman who teaches executives how to face their fears by having them jump off high poles, walk on fire, and sit still while pythons crawl across their laps.

"Why in the world would business people pay you good money to be terrorized?" I asked him.

"When I was a child my father told me that the most exciting time of his life was when he was in war and being shot at," Wilde explained. "In those moments, life was thrilling. People are tired of their ho-hum existence. They crave fun and excitement."

The Great New Jersey Buffalo Hunt

Barnum knew how to give people a thrill. In 1843 he bought a herd of skinny buffaloes, hired someone to feed and nurse them back into health, and then announced—anonymously—a "Grand Buffalo Hunt, Free of Charge" to be held in Hoboken, New Jersey.

Thousands of people took the ferry across the river to witness the wild sports of the Western prairies. However, the show didn't go as planned. The buffaloes refused to run, stampede, or even move. The man who was supposed to lasso them didn't know what to do. When the crowd started laughing, the herd became scared, broke through a barrier and ran off into a swamp. No one was hurt and not a single buffalo was lost. Everyone had a good time and the crowd even gave three cheers for the anonymous author of this humbug.

Barnum later admitted that he was the man behind the show, but this news isn't the only way he profited from the event. He had leased the ferry for the day and received one-half of all the receipts. Not only did he give the public more of the excitement they craved, he also received more publicity, and a nice sum of cash, as well.

Create Fun

P.T. Barnum isn't alone in wanting to make businesses more exciting.

- Barnes & Noble bookstores have sofas, music, and coffee to help customers feel relaxed and at home.

- Oshman's sporting stores have full-size basketball courts right in the store so customers can play and even try out shoes.
- Incredible Universe has video games to keep customers feeling great.

You don't need to be in the entertainment business to make your business more entertaining. The idea is to make your place of business fun to visit, a place where your customers can feel good. Whether you are selling wallpaper or accounting services, running a furniture store or managing a company with 300 employees, all it takes is creativity. For example:

- Information-systems employees at Owens Corning in Toldeo, Ohio learn how to juggle at work. They walk down the halls with balls in the air (or on the floor), they practice in the lunchroom, and they encourage each other in meetings. They learn that juggling is like managing: They have many things to keep in the air at one time, but they learn that work also can be fun.
- Price Waterhouse made their training course for entry-level managers exciting by having instructors dress up like clients, wearing funny hats and wild ties. They have found it educational, but more important, they have also found it to be fun.
- Keith Lockhart, conductor for the Boston Pops, found he could increase ticket sales by making entrances in Rollerblades, in a Batman suit, and even on an elephant. He says Barnum is one of his role models.
- Allan Stillman—called "the P.T. Barnum of the restaurant business"—created T.G.I. Fridays as a singles bar and restaurant so he could have some fun. In 1995, all of his restaurants generated over $60 million.
- Harold Ruttenburg pulls customers into his Just For Feet stores with videos, laser beams, basketball courts, and popcorn. He says,

"We think it's important for people to just come in and have a good time."

- Hard Rock Cafe, Harley Davidson Cafe, and Rainforest Cafe all turn eating a meal into an exciting experience.

Again, people do business where they feel good. Help them to feel good and you will get more of their business.

Barnum's Famous Museum

Barnum's museum burned down too many times for there to be any real mementos from the treasures inside. Barnum's illustrated 112-page guide book from 1860 said the museum held over 850,000 items of fascination. A visit to the Barnum Museum in Bridgeport, Connecticut can give you a sense of what the original museum must have contained. On one floor, you will find a mummy as well as a stuffed two-headed calf. You can also view a recreation of the nightmarish looking Fejee mermaid.

Barnum's original museum was much more captivating. It was five stories tall and would take you hours to visit (for only 25 cents). There were phrenologists such as Professor Livingston, who would examine the heads of customers and produce charts for them, in less than 10 minutes, that revealed their personalities. There was a hall of wax figures, thousands of items on display, and numerous animals, including a live whale. (When Barnum learned whales needed salt water to live, he ordered special plumbing to bring the water from New York Harbor right into his museum.)

There were also fortunetellers, including one who would read rocks to reveal the future. There was a rifle and pistol gallery, as well. He even had a bowling alley in the basement. However, when it came to original thinking and creative service, Barnum took the cake. He also had a taxidermist on hand who would take the recently departed bodies of pets, stuff and mount them, and have them ready for customers when they left at the end of their visit to the museum.

Barnum's real gift to his customers was his Lecture Room. Theaters during Barnum's time were dirty, low-class, disreputable areas where prostitutes and hooligans hung out. Respectable people seldom went there. Children were forbidden entrance. Barnum and a handful of others transformed the theater of the 1800s by turning it into family entertainment and education. He called his theater The Lecture Room because he needed a new name that people could feel good about visiting. The Lecture Room was the first home for many stars, including Tom Thumb, and it was the place where Barnum made a very real contribution to American culture by offering such plays as *The Drunkard*, a famous script revealing the evils of drinking alcohol, and even *Uncle Tom's Cabin*. Barnum himself lectured on the stage in The Lecture Room.

How to Give Good Feelings to People

You are an accountant, or a CEO, or a manager of a company with several hundred employees, or the owner of a home-based business. You don't run a sideshow or a circus. How do you give people what they want? How do you help them feel good?

Remember that all people ever buy are good feelings. It doesn't matter what your product or service happens to be. What matters is how people feel as a result of doing business with you. If you make it difficult for them, they won't feel good, and you won't make any money. However, your product or service itself also has inherent feelings attached to it, otherwise no one would buy it.

Someone who wants your accounting service wants to feel safe when it comes to money. Someone who wants your home security system wants to feel good when they leave the house. Someone who wants your nuts and bolts wants to feel that their machinery will hold up as a result of using your product. There are good feelings in every product or service you can name. Finding them and being aware of them will help you understand what your customers are really paying you for, and once you identify those feelings, amplify them in your ads and publicity.

Without exception, people pay money because they expect to feel differently as a result. Barnum intuitively knew this fact. During his day, people loved a good joke or a good story. They didn't have television or radio to entertain them. Barnum provided educational entertainment. He strove to help people feel better, particularly during such high stress times as the Civil War. People gladly paid for this service.

Barnum wasn't the only one to benefit in this way. One of the reasons Mark Twain's humorous stories became popular was because of the Civil War and people's need to feel better during those trying times. Editors published Twain's material and people—desperate to feel happy again—bought it.

Fishing for Good Feelings

I've never been much of a fisherman, but people tell me it's fun. Still, if most people were asked to name the most boring television program, I'm sure fishing shows would be near the top of the list. Although fishing may be fun to do, it isn't necessarily fun to watch. Making it exciting is the challenge Blair Warren faces every day.

Blair is one of the producers of *Alan Warren Outdoors*, a nationally syndicated television program hosted by his brother Alan. They accurately bill their production as "TV's Most Entertaining Outdoor Show." Turn on this program any given week, and there's no telling where Alan and his guests will be fishing. But one thing's for sure: They'll be having a blast doing it. And the viewers—fisherman and non-fisherman alike—will be joining in the fun.

What makes this show so different from its competition?

"Fun," Blair says with a smile. "We work extremely hard to make this show fun—because we have to. We realize that whenever our program is on, we're competing for viewers with dozens of other types of shows, everything from football and basketball, to sitcoms and talk shows. Unless we give viewers a compelling reason to watch, they're gone." So how do you make a fishing show fun? Blair says that aside from the obvious, such as an enthusiastic host and guest, there are a number of different factors that come into play.

> The first thing we look at is the story. The story is almost never watch someone fish. It's a blend of the people, the quest, the challenges involved, and, of course, the natural anticipation and excitement of the sport itself. But these don't automatically come across just by showing a "two shot" of some people trying to catch fish. It takes a lot of time and consideration to pull it off correctly.

Blair also invented a technique to help create more interest for viewers.

> I follow something I call the Twenty Second Rule on every program I produce. That is, I believe that people will watch at most about 20 seconds of any show before changing channels—unless something compels them to keep watching.
>
> That could be anything from changing the angle of a shot, increasing or decreasing the pacing of the edits, or changing a cut of music, cutting away to an interview, or bringing up a title. Anything to constantly give the viewer something new to see, hear, or think about. When a program is fun and exciting, people respond.

Despite Blair's past successes and more than 15 years of experience in the business, not everyone understands his method of operation. He tells a story about producing a promotional tape for a fishing lodge and discovering this firsthand.

> Since they already had established their reputation as a quality fishery, they wanted to specifically target husbands and wives who were looking to take a joint vacation. After reviewing all the footage we had to work with, I saw one shot that stood out.
>
> In it, a man was proudly holding up a nice trophy fish while his wife patted her husband on the belly and then she gave him a big hug and a kiss. The

shot said it all. It was overflowing with good feelings. So I used it to set the tone for the entire piece and chose music, pacing, and voice over accordingly. The final tape was, I felt, one of my best pieces of work. I was very proud of it.

However, Blair was in for a surprise.

When my client reviewed the tape, he not only hated it, he absolutely refused to show it to anyone. He couldn't say enough bad things about it!

Now stop and consider what was happening here. Blair's client was focused on his product, not on his customers. The client wanted to brag about his business; Blair wanted to show the good feelings inherent in the client's business. Big difference.

It turns out he was embarrassed by the fact that I didn't show more "big" fish in my video. After all, that's what he felt set his business apart from the competition. When I told him that the piece was already scheduled to air on our television program and it was too late to change it, he was sick with fury.

What happened when the show was aired?

Their phones lit up. The show was a hit and the phone calls proved it. The owner's wife called in a panic. She didn't know how to handle all the calls! Suddenly they liked the tape. They started using it to close sales and to this day they run it at their booth in trade shows.

Why did Blair's video work? Because he showed people having a good time.

Barnum knew this fact: People will do business where they feel good. Serve them well, provide what they seek, and they'll give you their money.

Barnum would have loved *Alan Warren Outdoors*, because the only hobby the busy showman ever had was occasional fishing.

Barnum or No-Name?

Be aware that everything you offer in business has feelings attached to it, usually created by your own advertising and publicity.

For example, no-name products are often offered in stores, but recognized names always surpass them in sales. Why? Because people have good feelings with a name they trust. A generic product doesn't have any feelings. Some people will buy them simply because they enjoy the feeling of saving money, but most people will opt for the name brand because they enjoy the feeling of safety and reliability. They feel assured they will get what they want.

Barnum plastered his name and image across the world so people would learn to associate him with a good show. This method worked. Barnum's name remains so familiar today that there is a type font named after him, a Broadway play about him, several movies about his life, countless biographies of him, a box of cookies with his name on it, a 1995 *X-Files* television show used him in their plot, and, of course, Ringling Brothers still owns and promotes the circus with his name. The name *Barnum* has brand name recognition, even today.

Not bad long-term publicity for a man who has been dead over one hundred years.

Love Your Customers

Most of us treat our pets better than we do our clients. If you truly loved your customers, what would you do? If you treated them as well as you treat your best friend, what would you do? If you treated them as well as you do your pet, how would you treat them?

I'm referring to how people feel as they interact with your business. Having a product that they can trust helps, but if you don't treat them well and make them feel good, they'll buy that product from someone else. Barnum had competition in his day, yet he stood head and shoulders above the rest. There were two other museums when he opened his. Can you name them? Not likely. They are long forgotten.

From 1840 through 1940 there were hundreds of traveling shows displaying human curiosities. How many can you name? Only Barnum's comes to mind. Barnum became famous due to his flamboyant advertising and publicity and because people felt so good doing business with him that they told the world and kept coming back.

Years ago I went to The Men's Wearhouse, a successful clothing store chain, because a suit jacket I had bought from them developed small moth holes in it. I wanted to see if they could repair the holes. Though I hadn't bought the jacket at this particular Men's Wearhouse store, their service was so extraordinary that they gave me a new jacket on the spot. That was treating me like a loved pet. How did I feel? This happened almost 10 years ago, and I *still* feel good about it. When I wanted new clothes, who did I shop with? And who is getting free publicity, even now, for the service they gave then?

Betty runs a small coffee shop in Houston. She personally talks to every customer, smiling, joking with them, learning what they like and who they are. As a result, people feel they know her and love doing business with her. Even people who stand in line to see her end up talking among themselves and having a good time, catching Betty's good spirits and relaxing. As a result, her business consistently does well.

My late wife, Marian, once visited a Nordstrom's store when she went to Oregon. The clerk at the makeup counter befriended her, found out what she liked, and took down her name and address. When Marian returned home, there was a card from the clerk thanking her for her visit. Three days later, Federal Express delivered a package to us. It was for my wife, from the clerk at Nordstrom. The clerk had taken the time to put together a collection of sample products along the lines of what my wife might like. How did Marian feel? She *beamed* for a week. She never forgot her experience with Nordstrom, and, yes, she ordered more products long distance from the nice clerk. After all, the salesperson felt like a friend and my wife felt good doing business with her.

Barnum treated his customers with respect. He thought about what would fascinate his customers and went out of his way to obtain it. He realized many of his customers came into the city early in the morning to begin their shopping. He opened his museum at dawn and left it open all day. That was unheard of in his day. He thought of his customers, not of himself. As a result, those people made him rich.

However, I'm not just talking about service. Add some spice to your business. Be creative. Think of ways to make your business more entertaining. Although you may not want to become a Disneyland or a Barnum Museum, there's nothing wrong with adding games, curiosities, collections, things to do, pictures, art pieces, or anything else you can imagine. You might take a poll of your existing customers and discover what their common interests happen to be. If they all love baseball, you might start a collection of baseball memorabilia and invite customers to view it or contribute to it.

Let Employees Fight—on Stage!

Encourage your employees to have fun at work. The more they relax and enjoy themselves, the more they will radiate that good will to your customers.

Once, two of Barnum's employees were fighting and threatening to kill each other. Barnum told them to wait and let him promote the battle on stage so all could see the fight to the finish. His employees laughed and lightened up. Keep your employees happy and your customers have a better chance of being happy.

Barnum's View of Customers

"What if you run into a truly abusive customer?" asked Kim, one of my clients.

"They're probably abusive because of lousy service," I replied.

"But some people are just too tough to deal with!" she protested.

"They're probably tough because you didn't satisfy their expectations."

"But some people are unreasonable!"

"There's a story about a man who angrily returned a set of tires to a Nordstrom's store," I said. "The man demanded his money back and the Nordstrom employee gave him a refund."

"So?"

"Nordstrom doesn't sell tires."

Kim sat silently as she realized the importance of what I just told her.

"But what would Barnum do?" she asked.

"At one point Barnum's museum employed over 300 people," I explained. "He taught them to respect their customers. One employee said he wanted to trash a customer for being rude. Barnum pointed out that the customer paid for the right to be rude."

"I don't get it."

"Not only is the customer always right, they are paying us to allow them to be right," I said. "Not only is there a customer born every minute, but you can also lose a customer in a minute. You must always treat them like royalty."

This ring of power can dramatically improve your bottom line. As final evidence that Barnum made people feel so good that they lined up at his door, and didn't mind if he played a gentle trick on them, consider these two facts:

1. In 1865 the total population of the United States was around 35 million people. Yet during Barnum's management of his museum, over 38 million admission tickets were sold. Clearly, many people entered the museum several times. But any way you look at it, Barnum gave people so much that the country came to his door. And this was during a time when people traveled by horse and carriage!

2. At one point the crowds going through the museum packed the hallways so badly that Barnum hung a sign over a door on an upper floor that read, "This way to the Egress." People wondered what odd animal or curiosity stood behind the door, opened it, went down the stairs, and suddenly found themselves in the street. They had unwittingly fallen for a Barnum humbug, as an egress is an exit. Did anyone complain? No. They laughed, felt good, and either went home smiling or reentered the museum—after paying another 25 cents, of course.

How can you make your business more fun, something your customers will feel so good about that they tell all of their friends?

7

P.T. Barnum's Secret for Making Unknowns Famous and Himself Rich

I am indebted to the press of the United States for almost every dollar which I possess and for every success as an amusement manager which I have ever received. The very great popularity which I have attained both at home and abroad I ascribe almost entirely to the liberal and persistent use of the public journals of this country.

—P.T. Barnum, 1891, five days before he died

P.T. Barnum had never heard Jenny Lind sing, but he had heard of her reputation and he was willing to gamble everything he had on that reputation.

The plain-looking 29-year-old Swedish soprano, hair parted in the middle, a nose like a Nordic potato, never known to wear makeup, was the talk of Europe. Critics said her voice sounded like a nightingale. People who watched her sing felt they were in the presence of an angel. Royalty paid homage to her. Queen Victoria loved her. All of Europe treated her like a celestial being. People called her the Swedish Nightingale. Yet few in America had ever heard of her.

Barnum smelled an opportunity, but what he would need to succeed was yet another ring of power.

Barnum Gets Chilling News

Despite everyone telling him he would fail, Barnum went into debt in order to bring Lind to America. He was confident that the reviews he had heard about her would mean money in the bank to him. One day, however, he was hit with news that sent a cold shiver to the very marrow in his bones.

He was having a casual conversation with a doorman when he mentioned he was bringing Lind to America. The doorman asked, "Is she a dancer?"

That's when Barnum knew he had his work cut out for him. He was bringing the greatest operatic soprano in the world to America in only six months and the average American had no idea who she was. Virtually every bank and investor had told him he would fail. After all, his experience was in displaying questionable curiosities and running a museum, not in managing a legitimate entertainer like the great Jenny Lind. Barnum had to educate the public fast.

Lindomania

He did. He hired 26 reporters to feed the media news stories about Lind, her talents, her arrival, her character. He even had Lind give a farewell performance in England so it could be reported to the U.S. papers.

As a result, over 30,000 people met Lind at the docks in New York when her ship arrived. Over 20,000 people followed her to her hotel, waiting to catch a glimpse of her. Within a short time, there were Jenny Lind songs and polkas, gloves, bonnets, riding hats, shawls, robes, and even Jenny Lind cigars, chewing tobacco, and perfume.

Barnum promoted Lind so heavily that he feared the worst. After all, he had never seen or heard her sing. What if the public hated her?

". . . I confess that I feared the anticipations of the public were too high to be realized, and hence that there would be a reaction after the first concert," Barnum wrote in his autobiography, "but I was happily disappointed. The transcendent musical genius of the Swedish Nightingale was superior to all that fancy could paint, and the furor did not attain its highest point until she had been heard."

The press went crazy. A writer for *Holden's Magazine* advised, "Sell your old clothes, dispose of your antiquated boots, hypothecate your jewelry, come on the canal, work your passage, walk, take up a collection to pay expenses, raise money on a mortgage, sell 'Tom' into perpetual slavery, stop smoking for a year, give up tea, coffee and sugar, dispense with bread, meat, garden sass and such luxuries—and then come and hear Jenny Lind."

Barnum had used the ring of power that he often said could make any man rich—publicity.

Barnum Gets Respectable

Barnum's giant gamble became one of his greatest accomplishments. Promoting Lind gave him respectability. He was no longer the shameless showman who exhibited an ugly mermaid. He was now the man who introduced the great Jenny Lind to America, and as a result, both he and Lind became independently wealthy.

Don't think Barnum had it easy, that all he did was offer a diamond to the public and they lined up to touch it.

First, Lind was virtually unknown in America when Barnum signed to bring her here.

Second, under Barnum's management Lind's concerts averaged $7,496 a show, more than *six times* the highest income of the most successful performer of the day. However, when Barnum and Lind split up and she tried managing her own concerts, she failed. Attendance of her concerts grew smaller and smaller. She could not get the crowds to come and see her, yet she was the same person with the same wonderful voice.

Finally, she quit. Within a few months she left America, and very few saw her ship leave dock.

The Value of Publicity

I learned the value of advertising your business when I researched Bruce Barton, cofounder of the BBDO ad agency, for my book, *The Seven Lost Secrets of Success*. Barton said you had to advertise consistently because "You aren't talking to a mass meeting, you're talking to a parade." I discovered all the different ways to advertise a business when I was writing my book for the American Marketing Association, *The AMA Complete Guide to Small Business Advertising*, but it wasn't until I began researching this book that I realized the full power of publicity.

I learned that advertising wasn't enough. I learned that you had to have an integrated marketing plan to achieve success. Barnum was a master at it. He knew that with strategic publicity you could get people to line up at your door to see anything you wanted to show them. He used publicity to get people to see a little boy he renamed General Tom Thumb. He did it again with an elderly black woman he claimed was the nurse for the father of our country. And he did it with Jenny Lind.

How did he use this particular ring of power? And how can you implement these methods today, to bring business to your own door?

Elssler's Secret

Although Barnum was an acknowledged genius at generating publicity for his businesses, he didn't create every technique he used. He was wise enough to learn from others. While still a young man, years before he tasted success running the museum, he found a mentor and witnessed the creation of the world's first superstar.

Jenny Lind was not the world's first celebrity. That distinction went to Fanny Elssler, a ballerina. Now, stop and consider how you might promote a *ballerina* in the 1800s in America. That century was a time of farming, growth, stress, sickness, poverty, poor cultural appreciation, ugly wars on our own land, and slavery. Who really cared about some foreign dancer hopping across a stage?

But publicity can work wonders. Elssler was managed by Chevalier Henry Wikoff, who used puff pieces of publicity to urge the media to write about his client. He also networked relentlessly, arranging for Elssler to perform before the social elite, and then seeing that each performance was covered by the press.

This creative manager didn't stop there. He also held the first auction for the tickets to Elssler's opening public performance. By the time Wikoff had orchestrated public enthusiasm for his dancer, there was Elsslermania across the land. People were eager to spend money to see this now-famous ballerina.

Barnum watched all of this with great fascination. He "... gave her manager the credit for doing what I had considered impossible, in working up public enthusiasm to fever heat." In later years, Barnum used the same publicity techniques to promote Jenny Lind. He learned from watching a master.

Toilet Paper Ends World War I

If you want to learn how to get publicity for your business, get a mentor. Barnum learned from watching Wikoff. You can learn in the same fashion. Find a legend and study his (or her) methods. One of my own heroes in the publicity business was a man who helped stop World War I by giving away toilet paper.

"Harry Reichenbach was the greatest single force in American advertising and publicity since P.T. Barnum," wrote David Freedman, Reichenbach's co-author, in *Phantom Fame: The Anatomy of Ballyhoo.*

Reichenbach worked as a circus press agent at the turn of the century, as a promoter for silent films, and as a propagandist for the first World War. His publicity stunts were jaw-dropping in cleverness as well as effectiveness.

When Reichenbach wanted to get an unknown actor hired at a high salary, he filled his pockets with two thousand pennies. He and the actor then began a long walk to the producer's office, dropping pennies along the way. At first only children picked up the coins, but then adults started following and gathering pennies as well. Of course, this was in the early 1900s, when pennies were worth picking up.

By the time Reichenbach and his client reached the producer's office, a mass of people stood behind them. When the producer looked out his window and saw the parade of smiling people behind the unknown actor, he couldn't help but feel he was about to hire a popular entertainer. Little did he know that no one in the crowd had ever heard of the actor before.

To promote an early *Tarzan* movie, Reichenbach had someone check into a hotel under the name of "T. R. Zann." He then had a lion delivered to his hotel room. Yes, a living, breathing, terrifying lion. The resulting chaos achieved wide press coverage. In every article, the name T. R. Zann was mentioned during the same week that the movie *The Return of Tarzan* hit theaters.

During World War I, Reichenbach created a diploma that the Allies dropped by plane over German lines. The diploma gave any German soldier, upon surrender, status as a prisoner with officer rank. The back of the diploma listed the benefits: bread and meat to eat every day, cigarettes to smoke, a delicing comb, and 24 sheets of toilet paper a day.

About 45 million diplomas were dropped over enemy lines during World War I. Thousands of Germans grabbed the offer and put down their weapons. The German army became so concerned that they passed a law making it a capital offense to pick up any paper on the battlefield. In short, bend over and get shot. This brilliant scheme worked because what the German soldiers wanted, more than anything else, was toilet paper.

"Publicity is the nervous system of the world," Reichenbach said in 1930, shortly before he died. "Through the network of press, radio, film and lights, a thought can be flashed around the world the instant it is conceived. And through the same highly sensitive, swift and efficient mechanism it is possible for fifty people in a metropolis like New York to dictate the customs, trends, thoughts, fads and opinions of an entire nation. . . .

"From Prohibition to hair-dressing and from a national peace policy to a girl's pout, the mass is always a magnified reflection of some individual."

Barnum was such an individual in the 1800s. Reichenbach filled his shoes at the turn of the century. Until 1995, Edward L. Bernays helped push the buttons of publicity to make the public do what he wanted.

The Terrifying Bernays

Edward L. Bernays was the founder of public relations, a nephew of Freud, and the man Hitler tried to hire to promote his cause.

A friend of mine described reading the books by Bernays as "terrifying." He added, "It's as though Bernays was from another planet and knew how to pull our strings."

Bernays once wrote, ". . . While most people respond to the world instinctively—without thought—there have been an 'intelligent few' who have been charged with the responsibility of contemplating and influencing human history."

You can count Bernays as one of those early and few gladiators of publicity. He promoted World War I, made the fashion world learn to love the color green so Lucky Strike cigarettes, which had green on their packaging, would be acceptable, and changed the entire country's attitude toward women smoking with a now famous publicity stunt.

In the 1920s he hired beautiful fashion models to march in New York's Easter parade, each lady waving a lit cigarette and wearing a banner that said it was a "torch of liberty." Overnight, women began to smoke, and Bernays's client, the American Tobacco Company, got rich.

In the 1970s, when Bernays learned that smoking caused lung cancer, he used his talents to create an antismoking movement and fought to have tobacco ads removed from radio and television.

Bernays lived to be 102, and he has been considered one of the 100 most important Americans of the twentieth century. In 1928, Bernays wrote in *Propaganda*, "The business man and advertising man is realizing that he must not discard entirely the methods of Barnum in reaching the public."

One of the people who met Bernays was another publicity wizard: Aaron Cushman. He promoted Dean Martin, Jerry Lewis, The Three

Stooges, and business and political giants. Aaron once told me that his favorite Bernays quote was, "Don't send out news releases, send out news *stories*."

Whether you choose Barnum, Bernays, Reichenbach, Cushman, Wikoff, or some other publicity giant as your role model, find a publicity master to learn from. Read their books. Study their methods. Imagine what they might do if they were running your company, and implement what you feel will work in your own business.

Before we move on, let's meet yet another Barnum-like publicist.

The World's Greatest Hoaxer

One of my favorite media mavericks is Alan Abel. He's been called the World's Greatest Hoaxer. As a jazz drummer turned master spoofer, Abel appeared in a great number of publications and television shows. He is best known for his satirical spoof SINA, the Society for Indecency to Naked Animals, a tongue-in-cheek crusade for the purpose of clothing all pets for the sake of decency. It ran for five years, upsetting some people and delighting others.

Why did this man turn to such ridiculous ideas?

Truth is, Abel was a struggling comedian in the 1950s. To make himself stand out in the crowd, he began to do wild things and create wild events. I love his inventive mind. He once organized a campaign to elect Yetta Bronstein, said to be a Bronx housewife (actually Abel's wife), U.S. president. He also got the media interested when he announced the first International Sex Bowl in 1969.

According to Alex Boesce, in *The Museum of Hoaxes*, Abel hired himself out in the 1970s as a professional hoaxer who would give strange speaking engagements to advertising executives. In Abel's hilarious autobiography, *The Confessions of a Hoaxer*, he states those talks were titled "The Fallacy of Creative Thinking."

In 1979 Abel staged his own death from a heart attack near the Sundance Ski Lodge. He hired a fake funeral director to collect his belongings and his widow notified the *New York Times*. The *Times* published a long obituary (a rare example of a premature obituary). Three days later Abel held a news conference to announce the "reports of my demise have been grossly exaggerated." The *Times* published a retraction the next day, for the first time in its history.

In 1997 Abel invented a special but odd gift: a wrapped pint of urine allegedly from celebrity Jenny McCarthy. The product was supposedly offered in the name of CGS productions, with a contact named Stoidi Puekaw ("Wake up idiots" spelled backwards). The star's copyright lawyer threatened to sue. Abel's pun was based on an appearance by McCarthy in a shoe commercial where she was seen sitting on a toilet.

Abel also ran for Congress on a platform that included paying congressmen based on commission, selling ambassadorships to the highest bidder, installing a lie detector in the White House and truth serum in the Senate drinking fountain, requiring all doctors to publish their medical school grade-point averages in the telephone book after their names, and removing Wednesday to establish a four-day work week.

At the 2000 Republican Convention in Philadelphia, Abel introduced a volatile campaign to ban all breastfeeding because "it is an incestuous relationship between mother and baby that manifests an oral addiction leading youngsters to smoke, drink and even becoming a homosexual." After 200 interviews over two years, Abel confessed the hoax in *U.S. News and World Report*.

Abel knew that getting the media's attention got him attention. He went from unknown comedian to fame. Today there is a documentary about him, called *Abel Raises Cain*.

Barnum would have loved him.

How to Get Free Publicity

In *The Humbugs of the World*, Barnum explains how Pease's Hoarhound Candy became a hot seller in a very unusual way:

"In the year 1842, a new style of advertising appeared in the newspapers and handbills which arrested public attention at once on account of its novelty," Barnum wrote. "The thing advertised was an article called 'Pease's Hoarhound Candy'; a very good specific for coughs and colds."

Pease would read the newspapers to learn what was happening in the country, and then write news commentaries that ended up cleverly and il- logically slipping in a sales pitch for his candy. Barnum explains:

> Mr. Pease's plan was to seize upon the most prominent topic of interest and general conversation, and discourse eloquently upon that topic in fifty to a hundred lines of a newspaper-column, then glide off gradually into a pane- gyric of "Pease's Hoarhound Candy." The consequence was, every reader was misled by the caption and commencement of his article, and thousands of persons had "Pease's Hoarhound Candy" in their mouths long before they had seen it!

If I were practicing Pease's method in this book, I would suddenly in- ject a line such as "Read Joe Vitale's other books, too" whenever I felt like it, not caring if the line fit with the rest of the chapter.

Pease made a fortune, according to Barnum. Although no business person would dare such a sly maneuver today, Pease was on the right track.

In order to get publicity for your business, you can tie your business to current news. Pease did this, but in a deceiving way. Today you can find de- scendants of Pease's method wherever you see an advertisement designed to look like a newspaper editorial. This works because people tend to trust news sources—radio, television, newspapers, magazines, and their re- porters—over ads. You have to advertise (one of the other rings of power) to be able to fully state your message, but you also need to be associated with news to legitimize your business.

How Barnum Made News

Basically you must have news, invent news, or associate your story to news in order to grab the busy media. They don't care about your business until you give them a reason to care, and a news-oriented reason at that.

In the middle 1800s, when the country was obsessed with Darwin's theories and people wondered about evolution, Barnum displayed a black dwarf and billed him as "What Is It?" His copy asked, "Is it a higher order of monkey? None can tell!"

Although most of us today would recoil at such a racist display, people in the 1800s eagerly bought tickets to see if they could tell if this curiosity was the missing link in evolution. Most people didn't realize that "What is it?" was really William Henry Johnson, a lifelong friend of Barnum's. Why did people line up to see Johnson? Because Barnum tied the show to then current news.

Barnum also received publicity when he showed Maximo and Bartola, "The Aztec Children," said to represent a lost race. Barnum had a 40-page booklet printed, complete with endorsements from scientists, to offer the public and the media. Again, this was tying his business to current news interests, because people were very interested in evolution and lost races.

When the country was talking about John Fremont, an explorer who was lost, Barnum displayed an unusual horse that he claimed the explorer had found. Because Barnum tied his display to current news, the people paid attention to his Woolly Horse.

When Barnum was showing Joice Heth, he clearly pointed out that she had been nurse to George Washington, tying his offering to news every patriotic American would be interested in.

When the Civil War was in full swing, Barnum hired men, women, and children who had tasted battle. He showed Robert Hendershot, the 11-year-old Drummer Boy; he displayed Major Pauline Cushman, the actress turned spy; and he hired Samuel Downing, a 102-year-old veteran of the American Revolution. Barnum also showed what he called patriotic dramas twice a day in his Lecture Room. And when Lincoln's wife and son visited the museum, Barnum, of course, let the press know.

When Barnum found and renamed Charlie Stratton, he invented news. The media loved Tom Thumb. He was the news. When Tom was getting married to the tiny Lavinia, Barnum paid for their wedding. He could afford to. He told the public and the press they better see Tom Thumb and his wife-to-be "Now or Never." Museum ticket sales shot to an average of $3,000 a day. Barnum offered $15,000 to the tiny couple if they would postpone their wedding. They declined. When the public tried to buy admission into the little ones' wedding, Barnum declined. He had promised a quiet wedding, and he kept his word. (See Figure 7.1.) Still, all of these events were news, and Barnum saw to it that the press heard of them.

In the 1860s Barnum again created news by importing zebras, polar bears, camels, sea lions, kangaroos, hippos, and white whales. The world had never seen such a display of nature's bounty. Because all of this was new and, therefore, news, the public and the media devoured it.

When Barnum wanted to promote the city of Bridgeport, he tested the city's air with chemically treated paper and then announced that Bridgeport possessed "a higher average rate of ozone than has ever before been found on the face of the earth!" He felt the news would attract health conscious individuals to the city. He was so convinced of his strategy that he made plans to build an Ozone Hotel. This, again, was creating news.

FIGURE 7.1   Tom Thumb's marriage. (Used by permission, The Barnum Museum, Bridgeport, Connecticut.)

Forget Yourself

Most people in business want to promote their business, and only their business. Although it seems logical, it isn't wise. Again, you will get far better results if you tie your business to news—even if you have to produce that news.

For example, how would you promote a new play? You might send out a news release. Will that help you sell more tickets?

In 1914 Edward L. Bernays originated news to promote the play, *Daddy-Long-Legs*, about an orphan and her rescuer. Bernays created a program to encourage private families without children to adopt orphans. It was a brilliant idea. It would help husbands and wives, and it would help homeless kids. Bernays organized Daddy-Long-Legs Groups to help implement the program. The press broadcasted this exciting news nationwide. Every time a story was printed or mentioned, the play was also mentioned. As a result, *Daddy-Long-Legs* ran for three years, an outstanding success.

P.T. Barnum could have focused his news on the singing talents of Jenny Lind when he promoted her concerts, but he didn't. Instead, he played on Lind's very real generosity. He let the press know that Lind donated thousands of dollars to charity, and often gave her entire income from a performance to a worthy cause. This was news, and this news helped promote Lind's appearances.

Note that *Daddy-Long-Legs* was just another play until Bernays created some news around it, and note that Jenny Lind was virtually unknown in America until Barnum told the press about her generous soul.

Don't focus on your business; focus on current news and tie your business to it.

Proactive Success

Phil Morabito learned how to deal with the press while he was a Madison Avenue whiz kid in New York City in the 1980s.

Morabito now runs Pierpont Communications, Inc., a full-service public relations firm. He and his staff handle accounts for individuals as well as Fortune 500 companies. He advises all businesses to run a proactive media campaign.

"Proactive media relations is when you actively send out ideas to media contacts in the hope they'll run something that plugs you or your business," Morabito explains.

"You should *always* be pitching, or presenting, ideas. Send out news releases, feature stories, press kits, letters—everything you can to suggest favorable story ideas. *Never* stop doing this."

Another way to be proactive is by letting the media know you are an expert available for interviews.

Although being an author remains one of the best ways to establish yourself as an authority in your field, you can also write to editors and tell them you are an expert. Morabito suggests a letter such as this:

"Dear Editor: I'm John Smith of XYZ Corporation. I'm an expert in (your field). I'd be happy to act as a source on this subject. My promise to you is that I'll always be available to you, and I will quickly and accurately answer all your questions."

And what do you do once you're on the phone with the press?

"Give them whatever they want—and more," Morabito advises.

"Answer their questions. Offer other ideas, sources, leads, or materials. And follow up to see if they got what they wanted. The people who help the press the most often get featured in the story."

Barnum would agree. He would go out of his way to befriend newspaper editors and feed them stories. He knew he was helping his business when he helped the media.

How Ink Can Make You Rich

Barnum wrote numerous articles and stories for the press throughout the decades to promote his various curiosities. He knew this ring of power could make him wealthy. He said, "Printer's ink can make any man rich."

He knew having and creating news was one thing, informing the press was quite another. He often spent entire mornings writing to press contacts. He kept a secret address book with their names and addresses. He even highlighted the names of those who were most open to news from him.

Barnum also wrote numerous letters to editors, some under his own name, many under fictional names, to draw attention to his business enterprises. The 1800s were a time of invention, and people were curious. When a newly invented machine that could talk was getting attention in the news, Barnum wrote an anonymous letter saying Joice Heth wasn't a person at all but an automaton, a machine. The media swallowed it and printed it. The public again lined up to see Heth, to try and detect if she was indeed a machine. Again, Barnum tied his story to current news by writing a relevant letter to get publicity. The double whammy worked. Crowds increased in size to see Joice Heth.

Barnum was not bashful about visiting editors of newspapers or even royalty. When he wanted to introduce Tom Thumb to the press, he went right to the homes of editors, knocked on their doors, and placed Tom on their dinner tables beside their food.

In 1872 Barnum hired three full-time press agents to travel with his circus and place stories in the local newspapers. Later he hired seven agents and created a huge, colorful railroad car advertising coach that would visit each city one week before the show was to arrive. The agents would paper the city with flyers and flood the newspaper editors with stories. The result was massive publicity and sold-out events.

Don't think this is unusual. The media so badly want news that they will often pay for it. The legendary Charles Lindbergh, before flying to France in his *Spirit of St. Louis*, made a deal with the *New York Times* that he would get paid to give them his exclusive story. So, in 1927, the famous newspaper paid Lindbergh for the exclusive rights to run his story. When the pilot landed, he called a *Times* reporter and gave them the news. It was a win-win for all, and in this case Lindbergh even got paid. The *Times* ran several pages on his flight. When he returned home, he was not only famous, he was a phenomenon.

If you want an even more recent example of how the media loves a good story, consider the case of celebrity magician David Blaine. According to the book *It!* by Paula Froelich, public relations agent Dan Klores saw Blaine perform, was impressed, and brought him right into the editorial offices of *New York* magazine. Blaine performed card tricks for the group. Everyone was impressed. *New York* magazine ran the first feature on the then-unknown magician. That was followed by articles in the *New York Post* and *Daily News*. Blaine then picked up the pace on his own by Barnumizing himself with wild stunts, such as spending two days packed in ice in Times Square.

Barnum would have loved it.

Britney Spears Helps Me

In 2004 I began an international marketing campaign to sell my new home-study course, *Hypnotic Selling Secrets*. The strategy was to hold a teleseminar training where people could listen to me teach them how to use hypnosis in their marketing. At the end of the call, I would promote the course. Obviously, it was imperative that I get a crowd on that call.

I was wondering how I would do it when I saw a commercial on television. It was pop star Britney Spears promoting the perfume Curious. A light bulb went on over my head. I ran upstairs, and wrote the headline to a news release: "Britney Spears Accused of Using Hypnotic Methods in New TV Commercial."

I then wrote the rest of the release, quoting myself (because I'm a hypnotherapist and a marketing expert), and saying that if anyone wanted to learn more about hypnotic selling, they should attend my call and visit my site at www.HypnoticMarketingStrategy.com.

I sent out the news release and was astonished at the results. I knew having the sex kitten's name in the headline would grab attention; I knew talking about a commercial that was airing was current news; and I knew the headline was, well, curious. However, I didn't know over 35,000 people would sign up for the teleseminar. I made a half million dollars virtually overnight from the sales of my course.

All it took was thinking like P.T. Barnum.

News Releases Lead to Fame

When the first edition of this very book, the one you are reading, was published, I sent out a news release asking, "Are P.T. Barnum's Methods to Success Valid Today?" I got a few invitations to do radio shows, and a newspaper wrote a story on me and the book, but nothing much seemed to happen.

Until the bomb exploded.

One night a few months later I started receiving calls, e-mails, and faxes, all congratulating me. On what? I had no idea. The next morning I found out that A&E, the national television network, aired a new biography on Barnum. At the end of it the host held up one book and only one book, saying, "Are P.T. Barnum's methods to success valid today? According to Joe Vitale, author of the book, *There's a Customer Born Every Minute*, they are."

My one-page news release had turned into an ad on national television. As a result, the first edition of this book sold out literally overnight. Book stores couldn't keep the book in stock, and the publisher was stunned.

You never know when a news release will bring fruit, but when it does, fame and fortune can be the happy result.

Three Steps to Publicity

"But who decides what becomes the news of the day?" one of my clients asked me one day. He runs an enterprise creating videos for businesses.

"What do you mean?"

"At work yesterday a co-worker asked me if I had heard that they were releasing George Lucas's *Star Wars* trilogy on the big screen. I told him I hadn't heard anything about it. Later, I went to my car, turned on the radio, and some announcer was talking about the *Star Wars* movies coming out. Then, I went to a store and there was a big sign about the *Star Wars* movies. Who made all of that happen? Who orchestrated that? Who made it the news of the day?"

"The publicity and advertising people working for George Lucas," I answered. "And then editors in the media decided if it was news."

"But how can people like me do the same thing in business?," he asked. "We aren't all like George Lucas or P.T. Barnum."

"There are three steps to getting publicity," I began.

"First, you have to have news. One of the easiest ways to do this is to simply read the headlines in the newspaper and then connect your business to something happening in the news. Retail stores will often have a President's Day sale right when the President's Day holiday is coming around. The holiday is news. The sale is associating your business with that news. However, with a little imagination, you can tie your business to anything happening in the news."

"Give me an example."

"If cold weather freezes pipes and you are a plumber, you might issue a news release advising people how to protect their pipes in the winter."

"But I'm not a plumber."

"I know you're not," I replied. "You have to think like a reporter and you have to think of the public, not yourself. So if you're in a state that wants to pass a new law about increasing property taxes, and you're a tax attorney, you might issue a news release that stems from the news surrounding the new law."

"I still don't get it."

"Go get a newspaper," I said.

He got up, looked around, and found a newspaper. He handed it to me.

"No, you look at it," I said. "What are the headlines?"

"There's one here about the Internet and how senior citizens are going online."

"Okay. Your job would be to think of a way to tie your business to that news."

"You mean maybe writing a news release about how people will soon see television programs and video documentaries on their computer? Or maybe about how senior citizens are putting home movies on computer disks?"

"That's the idea!" I said. "Tie what you do to current news in an interesting way."

"What's the second step, then?"

"Second, you have to saturate the media. Mail, fax, and e-mail news releases about your news. Barnum personally visited the media in his day. Today you can sit in front of your computer and send out news releases over the Internet, but nothing beats personal contacts. Good publicity people get results because they have networked—another ring of power, you remember—and already know who to contact.

"Third, you have to hope that your news connects with the public's readiness to hear it."

"What does that mean?" he asked.

"The world was ready to meet a Tom Thumb in the 1840s," I answered. "I'm not so sure a Tom Thumb would interest anyone today. The public has different interests. If the public isn't ready to hear about something, nothing you do will succeed. Barnum tried to promote a fire extinguisher in the middle 1800s and everyone thought it was a joke. The invention worked, but people weren't ready for it. Barnum's publicity for it failed."

"It did?"

"Yes. And in the 1830s when Cyrus Hall McCormick demonstrated his new machine—a reaper that was destined to transform farming—skeptical farmers thought it was a humbug. The reaper could do the work of six men, and do it in less time, but the public simply wasn't ready to accept it until around 1860."

"So there are no guarantees?"

"No," I answered. "But if you follow all three steps, you increase your likelihood of success. And if what you are doing connects, your success could be on the level of a George Lucas or P.T. Barnum."

How Barnum Turned Blackmail into Gold

One day a woman walked into Barnum's museum office and handed him an article she had written. Barnum thumbed through it and saw that she had written some frightful things about him. Being a man not easily bull-dozed by anyone, he handed it back to her.

The woman said he didn't understand, that she planned to publish and distribute the booklet, and wanted Barnum to buy the copyright to the booklet to prevent her plan from going into action. Barnum nodded, reached into his pocket, and handed her some loose change.

The woman, now shocked by Barnum's cool manner, insisted that Barnum buy her writing or else. Barnum fairly roared with laughter and then said:

> My dear madam, you may say what you please about me or about my Museum; you may print a hundred thousand copies of a pamphlet stating that I stole the communion service, after the Tom Thumb wedding, from the Grace Church altar, or anything else you choose to write. Only have the kindness to say something about me, and then come to me and I will properly estimate the money value of your services to me as an advertising agent.

As far as Barnum was concerned, any publicity would help promote his business.

How President Bush Was Nearly Captured and Eaten

In January of 1997 my friend Dan Poynter, author of *Parachuting: The Sky-diver's Handbook*, volunteered to run the International Parachute Symposium for the Parachuting Industry Association, to be held in Houston the next month. More than 800 people from 30 countries were expected to attend. Dan called me for help in promoting the event. Because I was busy finishing the book you now hold in your hands, I told him to contact a publicist I had been teaching, Linda Credeur, and I said I would help her with anything she needed. What Dan didn't know is that I had already tutored Linda in Project Phineas, my new sales training program based on Barnum's rings of powers.

Dan was about to get Barnumized.

Dan and Linda talked about ways to promote the event, from sending out news releases to calling the media by phone. Linda—remember that she had already studied Barnum's rings of power—knew they needed something bigger. They needed to think like P.T. Barnum and come up with a truly colossal idea. They needed a Jumbo of some sort to draw media attention to the event.

Sometimes the answer sits right in front of our noses. One night Dan told the riveting story of how former U.S. President George Bush had been nearly killed when he had to jump out of his crippled torpedo bomber in 1944, during World War II. Bush had to trust his parachute to save his life and to save him from falling into the hands of a sadistic Japanese commander known for torturing captured allied servicemen, cutting them up, and feeding them to his troops. Despite the odds, and thanks to Bush's parachute, he survived.

Linda recognized a media opportunity. She suggested they create an award for Bush being the only U.S. president to ever parachute and present it to him at the parachuting convention. It was a very Barnum-like idea, but Dan, like most people in business, is a conservative guy. He wanted to send out news releases and play it safe. That's how most publicists would promote any event. However, if you intend to create an empire, you have to go for the gusto. You have to take risks. Linda was willing. Dan was hesitant. Linda called me to discuss the idea.

"Dan thinks George Bush might want a lot of money to appear," Linda said. "After all, Bush gets $50,000 to give a speech."

"But you aren't asking Bush to give a speech," I explained. "You're asking him to show up and accept an award. If he's at all interested, he'll do *that* for free."

Linda understood that when you appeal to anyone's vanity, they will listen and reasonably do what you suggest. She agreed that Bush would probably attend the ceremonies. She started asking around and quickly found the name of Bush's former White House publicist. Linda sent a message to Bush, through the publicist, explaining the award and their offer to present it to him at the opening of the parachuting symposium. What no one knew was that Bush had a presidential library stocked with valuables—including a Navy torpedo bomber—and wanted a

1944 parachute to complete his collection. Bush said he would attend the event if someone could locate a parachute like the one he used during World War II.

Dan's an expert on parachuting. He found the rare parachute and Bush agreed to the awards ceremony. On the morning of February 10, 1997, a gracious and humorous George Bush appeared before the media to accept his award, the 1944 parachute, and to inadvertently publicize the 1997 International Symposium. Five news crews covered the event. CNN gave it national exposure. The local papers saturated the city with the news.

"You took an ordinary industry gathering," Dan later wrote Linda, "and turned it into a major media event."

In short, getting a former president of the United States to attend the convention put the entire event on the map. The media ate it up. The public liked it. The convention attendees, who had never seen anything like this before and for a few seconds couldn't believe their eyes, experienced an exciting kick-off to their convention, and none of it cost a dime.

What it took was thinking like P.T. Barnum.

"I really owe you one," Dan Poynter told me by phone three days after the event.

"You don't owe me," I replied. "You owe Linda Credeur and P.T. Barnum."

Offer the media news about your business because they want—even desperately need—to hear from you.

"Academicians who study media now estimate that about 40 percent of all 'news' flows virtually unedited from the public relations offices," writes journalist Mark Dowie in the introduction to *Toxic Sludge Is Good for You!*

My own study reveals that up to 80 percent of what you read in the papers was planted by people who sent out news releases seeking publicity. Bob Bly, in his excellent *Targeted Public Relations*, cites a *Columbia Journalism Review* survey of the *Wall Street Journal* where they found that more than one hundred stories on the paper's inside pages were taken directly from press releases.

Consider that there are 150,000 well-paid public relations profession-als in America versus 130,000 underpaid reporters and you get a sense of how reporters rely on news releases to get their information. Aaron Cush-man, famous publicity master, says there is no way a major city can find all the news because they simply don't have enough reporters. Help the press and they will help you.

What can you do right now to give the media news while promoting your business?

8

The Shakespeare of Advertising's Rules for Jumbo Success

But it is of no advantage to advertise unless you intend to honestly fulfill the promises made in this manner.

—P.T. Barnum, 1891, five days before he died

How would you like to have your prospects learning about you, discovering you, and even doing business with you while you are at home sleeping?

P.T. Barnum admitted that advertising was a key factor in his success. It was one of his favorite rings of power. People called him the Shakespeare of advertising because of his skill at creating ads. It helped make him and the people close to him millionaires. In the 1800s, that took some doing! In his autobiography and his other writings Barnum repeatedly stressed that persistent advertising was one of the secrets to getting on in the world. In his book, *Humbugs of the World*, he wrote:

Advertising is to a genuine article what manure is to land—it largely increases the product. Thousands of persons may be reading your advertisement while you are eating, or sleeping, or attending to your business; hence public attention is attracted, new customers come to you, and, if you render them a satisfactory equivalent for their money, they continue to patronize you and recommend you to their friends.

Barnum did not write down his method for writing ads, though he left many hints throughout his career. The following are my ideas on how Barnum handled his advertising. For more insights on his ideas, read the talk by him at the end of this book.

1. *Touch a live shark!* Although Barnum didn't know what the term *USP* stood for, because it wasn't invented until the 1950s by Rosser Reeves, he somehow had an intuitive sense of its meaning. A USP is a Unique Selling Proposition, a one-line statement (proposition) that explains (sells) how your product or service differs (unique) from the competition. What does Federal Express say? Dove soap? Their slogans are their USPs.

Barnum scoured the entire planet in search of unique products, whether people, items, or animals, to offer to the public. He knew such items would make his museum unique. He was the first in America to show a live hippopotamus. He was first to display living giraffes, and whales, and an aquarium, and the largest elephant in captivity. His ads focused on the uniqueness of everything he touched.

Sometimes you can create your uniqueness by knowing what people want and focusing on it. A friend of mine saw an ad for an aquarium that began with a boring headline such as, "Come see our fish swim," but buried within their flyer was the line, "Touch a live shark." That was the unique item they had to offer and that should have been their headline. Which would you sooner do, watch fish swim or "TOUCH A LIVE SHARK!"?

2. *Use layout that supports copy.* Graphics, fonts, and layouts don't sell, but they can help bring attention to your sales message. (See Figure 8.1.) You must know the form your sales message will take before you begin to draft your actual message. Knowing you are about to write a classified ad

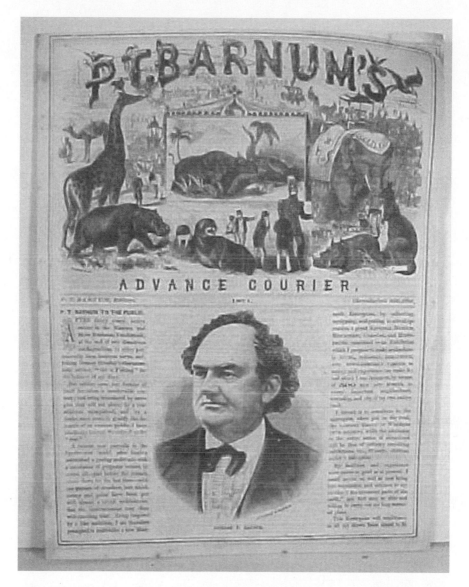

FIGURE 8.1   Here is a vintage newspaper from Barnum. Note how he branded his name and face by placing it prominently on the front page. (From author's private collection.)

will lead you to write differently than if you were about to write a sales letter or a display ad. Barnum's ads were rich in detail. His layout pioneered the way for direct response ads today: He would have a large—no, a *colossal*—headline to capture attention, at least one huge illustration, and many paragraphs of copy under both. This method still works today. Graphic artists who get fancy with typefaces and design can actually confuse potential customers. Barnum's ads were clear and direct.

3. *Barnum's secret cattle call!* Create a bold, riveting, and relevant headline. Barnum's headlines were designed to nail the attention of his readers. He would round up his prospects with a headline that made them sit up and take notice. When he advertised Joice Heth, the woman who was said to be over 160 years old and once wet nurse for George Washington, Barnum's headline screamed "The Greatest Natural & National Curiosity in the World."

A headline calls out to your readers. As later studies by John Caples and others have revealed, a change in headline can bring 19 times more response. In one full-page ad from 1873, a monstrous illustration contained a headline within it that read, "P.T. BARNUM's." By then Barnum's name was known around the world. It alone was a powerful headline. But he didn't stop there. The bold subhead under the illustration read, "GREAT TRAVELING WORLD'S FAIR FOR THE CAMPAIGN OF 1873." And under that read, "P.T. Barnum to the public." It was virtually impossible to not see the ad, and then to not read it. The headlines kept grabbing and pulling readers.

4. *"Go on home."* Write simply, directly, and in the conversational style of your prospects. Who are you trying to reach? Housewives, business executives, children? You must know the type of person you are writing to. Write to one person from that group and you will speak to all people in that group. Forget trying to impress people, win writing awards, or please a past English teacher. Good copy often violates the rules of English but still makes the sale.

In Barnum's time, more than 90 percent of the white population could read. (It's a staggering thought, when half of America cannot read today.) Newspapers were sprouting up and becoming as common then as television today. When Barnum wrote ad copy, he wrote in a style that respected the education of his readers. He did not use words they could not understand. He created rapport with his readers by using the same common language they used in their own writing and speaking.

After one of his shows Barnum said, "The festivities have come to a conclusion." Nobody moved. He repeated, "The festivities have come to a conclusion." Still nobody moved. Finally he said, "It's all over. Go on home." Everyone understood those simple statements. They left. Barnum learned that you can persuade people when you speak in ways they can easily understand.

5. *People want results, not things.* Write of the benefits, not the features. A feature generally describes a product; a benefit generally explains what the product does for you. Don't tell people how great you make your products; tell them how great your products will make them.

A good way to write about benefits would be to keep saying "you get this . . . and the product does this . . . so that you get. . . ." Look at Kodak. People don't buy film for the pictures they create. They are buying memories. Look at their advertising and you'll barely see film anywhere. What you will see are family reunions, graduations, weddings, etc. You get film that helps you take pictures so that you get memories.

Keep asking "So that____?" to dig up benefits. For example, "This computer is a Pentium Pro . . . so that . . . you get a computer that is twice the speed of other computers . . . so that . . . you can get twice the work done in the same amount of time . . . so that . . . you are free to have longer lunches, make more calls, or focus on something else."

Barnum always wrote ads that suggested you would get much more than entertainment. He wanted to educate as well as entertain. When he wrote of Joice Heth, he was sure to mention that she sang religious songs, which connected with the moral values of nineteenth-century people. He also mentioned her relationship to George Washington, thereby touching on the country's admiration for anything American. The feature was Joice Heth; the benefit was cultural and patriotic appreciation.

6. *Use Captain Cook's war club.* People buy for emotional reasons and justify their purchases with logic. Use words that have emotion. In Barnum's hands an Indian war club became "The club that killed Captain Cook." (There were many of them in the 1800s.) A roof on Barnum's museum became "an Aerial Garden." His hippo was called "The Great Behemoth of the Scriptures." All these emotionally charged labels made Barnum's show much more appealing. When Barnum advertised his Fejee mermaid, his copy wove a spell of emotional magic:

> . . . positively asserted by its owner to have been taken alive in the Fejee Islands, and implicitly believed by many scientific persons, while it is pronounced by other scientific persons to be an *artificial* production, and its natural existence claimed by them to be an utter impossibility. The manager can only say that it possesses as *much appearance of reality* as any fish lying on the stalls of our fish markets—but who is to decide when *doctors* disagree? At all events, whether this production is the work of *nature or art*, it is *decidedly* the most stupendous curiosity ever submitted to the public for inspection. If it is artificial, the sense of sight and touch are useless, for art has rendered them totally ineffectual. If it is natural, then all concur in declaring it THE GREATEST CURIOSITY IN THE WORLD!

7. *Plug electricity into your writing.* Activate your writing. Whenever you write the words *is was are*, or *to be*, train yourself to stop and change them to something more active. "The meeting is tonight" sounds dead; "The meeting *starts* at 7 P.M. sharp tonight" feels clear, direct, and alive. "Clair Sullivan is the finest promoter in the country" doesn't convey the excitement that "Clair Sullivan *creates* corporate events better than anyone else on the planet" does.

In one ad Barnum's copy said, "The great street procession, three miles long, takes place every morning at half-past eight o'clock." Notice the clarity and directness of the sentence? Although most business writing permits passive writing, ad copy should virtually always be dynamic. Active writing makes people keep reading; passive reading puts them to sleep. Barnum never gave his prospects a chance to nod off.

8. *Tell them something they don't know.* Fascinate your readers. The more you tell, the more you sell. Long copy usually works better than short copy, as long as the copy holds interest. After all, people read whole books. They will read your copy *if* it interests them. Barnum was a master at this. He was deeply interested in science and natural history. He paid enormous sums of money to find rare animals, mechanical devices, people, or museum pieces. He knew if he could offer people something they didn't know or hadn't seen before, they would pay him to see it for themselves, but he didn't stop there. He also used his ads to educate people.

9. *"What is it?"* Seduce the reader into continued reading. Keep your reader reading any way you can. Questions, unfinished sentences, involving statements, sub-heads, bulleted points, quizzes—all these things work. These techniques also handle the skimmers who just glance at your copy, as well as the word-for-word readers. Barnum's ads were rich with copy, illustrations, and numerous sub-headlines. One of his headlines began, "What is it?" seducing people into reading the rest of his ad to learn what he was referring to.

He often used bold type and unusual capitalization to highlight particular sentences and words. One line in an ad read, "Among the Rare Living Animals are **MONSTER SEA LIONS**, transported in great water-tanks; the largest **RHINOCEROS** ever captured alive, and 500 Wild Beasts and Rare Birds, Elephants, Elands, Gnus, Lions, Tigers, Polar Bears, Ostriches, and every description of Wild Animal hitherto exhibited, besides many never before seen on this Continent."

10. *Say "Jumbo."* Be specific. Whenever you write something vague, such as "they say," or "later on," or "many," train yourself to stop and rewrite those phrases into something more concrete, such as: "Mark Weisser said . . . ," or "Saturday at noon" or "Seven people agreed." Don't say "dog" when you can say "collie." Don't say "elephant" when you can say "Jumbo." Don't say you have "a midget" on display when you have "General Tom Thumb."

Specifics make your copy believable and your ads come alive. Note the details in this 1876 ad by Barnum: "My great Traveling Centennial Academy of Object Teaching cost a million and a half of dollars, employs 1,100 persons, 600 horses and ponies, and will be transported East to Maine and West to Missouri on 100 solid steel railroad cars."

11. *Get Mark Twain's endorsement.* Overwhelm with testimonials. Get as many testimonials as you can. The more specific, the more convincing. In short, deliver proof that your claim is for real. Barnum didn't really care if you believed his claims. He invited doubt. But he also invited scientists, newspaper experts, and other leading authorities to examine his offerings, and he put those invitations right in his ads. In a subtle way, these invitations acted as testimonials. Barnum wrote to presidents and queens, authors and poets, usually soliciting testimonials. He wrote to his friend Mark Twain several times, asking for an endorsement he could reprint. When Barnum went to England with Tom Thumb, he wanted to see the Queen because he knew that once he had, the rest of the country would follow, and they did.

12. *Remove the risk!* Give a guarantee. Less than 2 percent of your customers will ever ask for their money back, so offering a guarantee is a safe risk. Here's the guarantee from my book, *The Seven Lost Secrets of Success*: "Use these seven principles for six months. If you're out of work, you'll find a job. If you're employed, you'll get a raise. If you're in business, you'll see a whopping 25 percent jump in revenues—or return this book and your receipt for a full cash refund!"

Even though I could not find any record of *written* guarantees by Barnum, he apparently stood behind his ads and claims. He offered so much that he was sure no one would ever complain. On the one or two rare occurrences when a display of his backfired, he refunded everyone's money. He wanted no complaints. His guarantee was unexpressed but real.

13. *Use these free magic words.* I was impressed to see one of Barnum's ads from the mid-1800s begin with the words "At last!" Those two words are part of a list proven to help gain attention. When Barnum held his infamous buffalo hunt in New Jersey, his headline contained the magic word "free" and read: "Grand Buffalo Hunt, Free of charge."

If you just string the following magic words together, they sound like fluff. But weave them into your sentences, along with your facts, and they become powerful: *Announcing, astonishing, at last, exciting, exclusive, fantastic, fascinating, first, free, guaranteed, incredible, initial, improved, love, limited offer, powerful, phenomenal, revealing, revolutionary, special, successful, super, time-sensitive, unique, urgent, wonderful, you, breakthrough, introducing, new,* and *how-to.*

And consider the connotations of the words you use: *workshop* sounds like hard work whereas *seminar* sounds easier. *Read* sounds hard whereas *look over* sounds easy. *Write* sounds difficult whereas *jot down* sounds easy. Be aware of the psychological implications of the words and phrases you use. *Sea Lions* sounds interesting but lame; *Monster Sea Lions* sounds like something you must see.

Don't be afraid to use adjectives. One of Barnum's most famous press agents was Richard Tody Hamilton. Hamilton said his secret to success in writing sales copy was knowing how to weave a spell with adjectives. He explained:

> To state a fact in ordinary language is to permit a doubt concerning the statement. Suppose a grocer should advertise fine, fresh codfish and his rival across the street advertised the largest, sweetest, absolutely the best codfish ever caught, with scales as large as quarters and meat whiter than snow—the finest yielded by the Atlantic Ocean. Which grocer do you think will sell the most codfish?

14. *Remember the tattooed man!* A business associate of Barnum's said that when Barnum found a new concept, "He fairly reeked with his idea." Show your excitement for your product. If you aren't pumped up about it, why not? Enthusiasm sells. Barnum always believed in what he was offering. Even when an autopsy (which Barnum sold tickets to attend) revealed Joice Heth had not been a day over eighty, Barnum confessed he had really believed she was over 160 as he had been told. You can sense a certain pride in most of the ads Barnum wrote. His sincere belief that he was offering the public something of genuine value came through. And people lined up. Note how he describes the world's first completely tattooed man:

> Captain John Constantinos, a noble Greek Albanian, tattooed from head to foot in Chinese Tartary as punishment for engaging in rebellion against the

King. Every inch of his body is covered with three hundred and eighty-eight beautifully delineated figures, in indigo and cinnabar, of beasts, birds, fishes, reptiles, and hieroglyphics. The prolonged and horrible agony of this combination of barbaric art and vengeance necessitated over seven million blood-producing punctures.

15. *"Final Week!"* State a believable deadline. Most people won't take any immediate action unless there exists a sound reason to do so. Give them an excuse to act now. Deadlines help, as long as your deadline sounds credible. Barnum would let people know that they could see Jenny Lind, for example, but only if they came to one of her limited performances. When Tom Thumb was about to be married, Barnum saturated New York City with ads saying "Final Week!" to see the midget couple. He knew the deadline would get people to his door. When he advertised the Fejee mermaid, his ad began, "Engaged for a short time. . . ."

16. *Show roaring hippos.* Use dramatic illustrations. Your illustration helps stop people so that they look at your ad. Barnum used stirring illustrations. When he was the first to show a live hippopotamus, he had the artist create a large drawing of a hippo, mouth open, roaring. He didn't show a hippo standing in the water doing nothing. His hippo was dramatic, and unforgettable, and attention getting. The human eye seeks action. Show it in your illustrations.

17. *Be King of the Jungle.* Dominate the media where you advertise. If you don't, the other animals in the marketplace will drown out your roar. Barnum's ads were large and visible. He often placed newspaper ads on the entire top one-third of a page. He wanted his ads noticed by their position on the page. He knew size alone could help make him king of the jungle. In 1879 he ordered "the biggest and best show bill in the world." It took his printers three months and cost Barnum $3,000 to create, but he ended up with a gargantuan poster, big enough to cover the entire side of a building. Talk about an attention getter!

Your potential buyers are preoccupied with the concerns of their lives. And rightly so. You haven't yet earned the right to speak to them. First, you have to get their attention. One of Barnum's first demands of his printer was to create a head of Barnum four times the size of any picture ever made in history. The result was 24 by 36 inches, and it helped people stop, recognize, and remember Barnum throughout his life. The giant picture of Barnum interrupted people. It disrupted their preoccupation. As a result, people know and remember Barnum's name and face on sight even today, a century after his death.

When Barnum took over the poorly managed Scudder Museum, he devoted most of his profits to the ring of power called advertising. Although it hurt him and his family to scrimp on food and lodgings, the result was that he nearly tripled sales within the year, paid off his loan to buy the museum within two years, and quickly made the museum one of the most popular enterprises in America. As Barnum would later say, "A little advertising is a dangerous thing." In short, once you start advertising, never stop. Barnum told a group of New York businessmen:

> You do not any of you advertise enough. You ought to use the printer's ink every day. You are asleep and want your business to run itself. Standing advertisements in a paper command confidence. The man who for a year resides in one community and leads a respectable life, even though he be of moderate ability, will grow in the confidence and esteem of his fellows. On the same principle, a newspaper advertisement becomes familiar in the eye of the reader. It may seldom be read, still it makes the name and business of the man familiar, and its presence in the columns of the paper inspires confidence in the stability of the enterprise.

Where can you advertise your business to reach the largest possible customer base, and what ads can you create to get their attention?

9

How an Unknown P.T. Barnum Met Queen Victoria— and Got Rich

If I was not a remarkably modest man, I should probably brag a little, and say that I had done what no American ever before accomplished; but being "remarkably modest," I shall say nothing, but wait for an American to appear who has visited the queen at her palace twice within eight days.

— P.T. Barnum, *Atlas* newspaper article, 1844

P.T. Barnum had a treasure on his hands and he knew it.

He was already showing his little talented friend, General Tom Thumb, to the American public and getting rich in the process. Everyone loved the doll-sized charmer. They were eagerly lining up to watch Thumb perform, sing, joke, and kiss every lady in sight. Barnum loved it but wanted more. He set his sights on bigger game: Europe.

Barnum, Thumb, and family set sail for England in 1844. So many people bid Barnum farewell that tears came to his eyes. However, Barnum's arrival overseas was disappointing. No one met his ship. The English did not line up to see Tom Thumb. Most of them felt they could see a "dwarf," as midgets were called then, any time, and for very little money. For a short time, Barnum was discouraged. But he had an ace up his sleeve.

What Barnum held up his sleeve was a new ring of power.

Introduced to Royalty

Barnum carried a letter of introduction from his American newspaper friend, Horace Greeley. The letter was for Edward Everett, the American ambassador in England. Barnum knew that if he could get the leading citizens of London to see and talk about General Tom Thumb, the rest of the country would follow.

Barnum began his plan by renting a mansion and holding private performances for upper-class citizens. He wrote, "I sent letters of invitation to the editors and several of the nobility, to visit the General. Most of them called, and were highly gratified. The word of approval was indeed so passed around in high circles that uninvited parties drove to my door in crested carriages, and were not admitted."

Barnum refused uninvited guests because he knew people would more eagerly want what they could not easily have. It was a stroke of genius, a courageous move, and caused royalty to wonder what rare prize lurked behind the mansion walls. Of course, Barnum always found out who the uninvited guests were and sent them engraved invitations a day or so later.

Next, Barnum gave Greeley's letter to Everett, and then introduced Tom Thumb to Everett. Although the famous ambassador previously felt Barnum was a hustler, he had to admit that he was charmed by Barnum's sidekick. As a result, Everett arranged for a meeting with Her Majesty, Queen Victoria.

The result was instant success. Thumb captivated the Queen and everyone else at the royal court. Within weeks Barnum and Thumb were invited back three more times for private performances. (See Figure 9.1.)

This fit right into Barnum's plan. He wisely assumed that if the Queen enjoyed Thumb, the rest of Europe would hear the news and want to see

FIGURE 9.1   P.T. Barnum and the famous General Tom Thumb. When Barnum found little Charlie Stratton, no one saw the superstar that Barnum saw. (Used by permission, The Barnum Museum, Bridgeport, Connecticut.)

the little man, as well. He was right. Word quickly passed through the country. Tom Thumb became an instant celebrity, and Barnum grew so wealthy that he contemplated sending $15,000 back to America for private investment.

As Dr. Arthur Saxon writes in his biography, *P.T. Barnum: The Legend and the Man*, "By enlisting the Queen of England at the outset of his carefully orchestrated campaign in the Old World, by shrewdly playing upon the innate snobbery of his British hosts, Barnum had managed to snare them all, from prince to lowliest commoner."

You Can Meet Anyone

Although Barnum showed boldness in his dealings overseas, he also heavily relied on something that he didn't have a word to describe in the 1800s: networking.

Networking can be described as friends helping friends to achieve a specific result. When Barnum went to Paris in 1844 to attend the Great Exposition, a type of early World's Fair or global trade show where new products were displayed, he picked up 87 business cards from people he wanted to befriend and know more about. That's networking. He was creating a larger circle of friends who could help him meet other friends. The expanding network could become infinite with possibilities.

When Barnum wanted to meet the queen, he got his friend Greeley to introduce him to Everett, who knew and might be able to help Barnum meet the queen. That's networking. When you ask someone you know to help you meet someone else that you don't know, you are networking.

"You are only two or three people from anyone you want to meet," declares Donna Fisher, networking expert and author of *People Power*. She writes:

> Networking is as simple as friendship and as complex as matchmaking. It is gathering, collecting, and distributing information, being a resource for others, and learning how to call on the resources in your network.

When Barnum asked Greeley for a letter of introduction, he was calling on someone in his personal network to help him meet the queen. Greeley wrote the letter to someone in his own personal network of contacts. In essence, Barnum was only two people away from the queen at any time: Greeley, then Everett, were his steps to her.

And it's the same for you. Who do you want to meet? Who do you want as a new client? Or friend? Or business partner? You are probably only two or three people away from anyone you can name.

Who Do You Know Who Knows____?

One day a client of mine said he wanted to get endorsements for his new book but didn't know who to ask. I decided to teach him this ring of power.

"Who do you want to endorse it?" I asked.

"I'd like a celebrity but I know I can't get one," he said.

"Why not?"

"I don't know any."

"You don't have to know any," I explained.

I then urged him to make a wish list of everyone he would love to have endorse his book.

"Just write down everyone who comes to mind," I advised. "Don't edit yourself. As long as the person is alive, write down their name."

He did. I then told him to call the library and ask for the addresses of everyone on his list. I knew that if they were at all famous, they would be listed in *Who's Who* or in some other reference publication. The library would give him the contact information and he could then write each person a letter stating his request.

"Now there's one more thing I want you to do," I began. "I want you to ask your friends and family a question."

"A question?"

"A question. A magical question. I want you to ask them, 'Who do you know that knows ____?' and fill in the blank with someone you really want to meet on your list."

"You mean if I want to meet Dear Abby, I should ask my wife, 'Who do you know that knows Dear Abby?' "

"That's the idea," I explained. "But don't just ask your wife. Ask your friends. Your neighbors. Your clients. Ask the people in your business clubs. Ask people in the elevator. Ask everyone in your own network."

He did, and within 24 hours he discovered a client who was a friend of Dear Abby. My client then called Abby's friend and from there he met the famous columnist herself. He got an endorsement from her for his book, too. And he put it right on the cover.

Join the Cary Salon

Joining professional societies, breakfast, lunch, and dinner groups, or trade associations can extend your network of contacts and increase your chances of doing business with anyone you want.

Barnum often attended the Cary Salon, where he met John Greenleaf Whittier, Horace Greeley, Susan B. Anthony, and many other famous intellectuals, writers, editors, celebrities, clergymen and literary figures of his day. Alice and Phoebe Cary, American poet sisters, wrote popular poetry and attracted famous people. Barnum's choice to be part of the group's Sunday-evening informal meetings helped him when it came time for networking. As a result, he had a larger circle of friends to call on when he needed help.

Lest we forget, Barnum's circle of friends also had *him* to call on when *they* needed help. True networking involves people helping people. It works both ways. After Everett introduced Barnum to the queen, Barnum wrote the minister a letter expressing a thousand thanks and saying he was in the ambassador's debt. He wrote:

I have now attained my *highest* desires and hasten to thank you to whom I am entirely indebted for this great gratification. Rest assured that your goodness will never be forgotten.

Again, networking can achieve surprising results.

Dan's Bake Sale

Take Dan's Bake Sale of May 1993, for example.

When a fan of Rush Limbaugh called and asked the radio show legend for a free copy of his newsletter, Rush declined but instead suggested the caller hold a bake sale to raise the money for the newsletter. Limbaugh got the idea after hearing how third-grade children were selling baked goods and sending the money to Washington to help reduce the national debt. Limbaugh's suggestion was more a satirical comment than sincere advice, but the result was pure Barnum. The caller accepted the challenge.

Limbaugh announced Dan's Bake Sale on his radio show and the networking began. One company donated 15 outdoor billboards. A baker gave 200 pounds of cookies. People started telling other people. Limbaugh said he would attend the sale and give a speech. The word spread.

Did people listen? According to the talk show king, over 65,000 people flocked to the event. And, yes, Dan raised the money he needed for his newsletter subscription, and Mr. Limbaugh also benefited from the free advertising. Again, a little Barnum and a little networking can produce outstanding results.

Network Online with Only E-mail

P.T. Barnum loved technology. He was one of the first people to have a burglar alarm system in his mansion. He was also one of the first to use a telephone, and to profit from using the telegraph. He would no doubt be online today, making rich use of computers, software, and the well hyped Internet. (In fact, Barnum can be found online right now. Visit any search engine online, such as Google, and type in the words "P.T. Barnum.")

If you aren't online with your business, get online today. The Internet can be another leg in your marketing strategy. Don't think you need a giant web site and numerous bells and whistles to profit from cyberspace. You can effectively promote your business and collect new clients with a simple e-mail account.

Skeptical? You won't be much longer. I once couldn't convince a client of the value of being online until I told him the following:

"You attend a networking meeting every Wednesday morning, don't you?"

I knew he did. He had been attending for more than 10 years.

"How many people go to those meetings?" I asked.

"About 30."

"Stop going," I said. "Go online and join a few electronic mailing lists and participate in them. When you do, you will be promoting yourself in the easiest way possible to the widest number of people possible. It's the new way to network."

Right now I'm participating in one book publishers' discussion group that has more than 400 members. When I post something of value to these readers, it's like standing up in a networking meeting. Everyone notices me. Because of this global visibility, I have had business with people from around the world, people I have never met, talked to, or even faxed. They e-mail their orders for press releases and sales letters, and I collect their money in my snail mail box.

The trick, I told my friend, was in participating in appropriate electronic discussion groups or e-mailing lists:

1. Find the e-lists that your prospects are reading. If you are selling fishing lures, find the lists where people discuss fishing. Search Google, using their Groups feature.

2. Join the groups that seem most relevant to you. They are free, and you can join and participate entirely by e-mail. Again, subscribe to the ones your prospects are reading. You may want to join a marketing e-list to keep up with marketing dialogues, but your prospects probably aren't reading it.

3. Monitor the group for two weeks. Most of the lists will have daily postings. That means people are reading and responding to the list by the second. It's like getting your newspaper delivered to your door every few minutes, which you can read online, immediately reply to, and then see your comments published seconds later.

4. Offer practical information relevant to the readers. Ask yourself, "Will the readers be glad I posted this e-message?" If so, mail it. If not, delete it. Blatant ads will get you burned, or *flamed*, online.

5. Use your sig file to promote yourself. A sig file is a signature file, a short biography of who you are. Your sig should be no more than four lines. Ask your online provider how to create a sig file (it's easy). Then write one that gives your contact information and a one-line statement about what you do or offer. When people get interested in what you say, the sig file tells them how to reach you.

Networking online works the same way networking offline does: You meet people, let them get to know and respect you, and then you transact business. Barnum would be online today, networking, promoting his enterprises, being seen, continuing to let the world know about his business. You can do the same.

Balloon Flights and the Free Museum

In 1865 Barnum planned to create the largest free museum in the world. His strategy was to open his own paying museum next to it. The only reason he was able to continue with the grand idea was because he networked with the people who could make it happen. He even got an endorsement from President Andrew Jackson. After Barnum's second museum burned down in 1868, he lost interest in this project. Later, in 1882, he helped build and stock the Barnum Museum of Natural History at Tufts College.

In 1873 Barnum wanted to finance the world's first manned balloon flight across the Atlantic. He obtained a letter of introduction from Joseph Henry, a famous physicist, stating Barnum's genuine interest in the "promotion of aerial navigation." Barnum then went to Europe to network with experts in orchestrating the flight. Barnum's idea was to finance the transatlantic voyage out of his own pocket, and then display the balloon afterwards for pay. The only thing that stopped this from happening was the sudden death of Barnum's wife of 44 years. Later, Barnum was talked out of the idea by experts. He settled on short, highly publicized flights over his shows.

How do you know who, among your friends, family, clients, and peers, might be the ones to help you network your way to success?

"You don't know," Donna Fisher once told me. "So love everybody."

Ask yourself, "Who do I know who can help me achieve my dreams?

10

How Barnum Purchased the Business of His Dreams with No Money

You know I had rather be laughed at than not to be noticed at all. . . .

—P.T. Barnum, 1876, to Samuel L. Clemens/Mark Twain

In 1841 the contents of Scudder's Museum in New York City went up for sale and Barnum knew he wanted it. There was only one catch: He had no money.

He was then making four dollars a week writing ads for the Bowery Amphitheater and struggling to keep his family fed. When a friend asked Barnum how in the world he would ever buy the contents of the museum, which was selling for $15,000, Barnum replied, "With brass, for silver and gold I have none."

I've always been amazed at the true brass Barnum showed in making his offer to buy the collection inside the museum. Maybe Barnum knew that his first name, *Phineas*, means "mouth of brass" in Hebrew.

Whatever the case, somehow Barnum knew the museum would be his claim to fame and fortune. All he had to do was buy it.

But how?

Barnum was about to discover another ring of power.

"Bind Me in Any Way"

Barnum wrote and hand delivered a letter to the owner of the museum outlining his offer. It was one of the most creative proposals I've ever heard of in any business anywhere in history.

In short, Barnum asked the museum owner, a retired merchant named Mr. Francis Olmstead, to buy the museum's collection in his own name and then lease it and the building to Barnum. Barnum added:

> Allow me twelve dollars and a half a week to support my family—and if at any time I failed to meet the installment due, I would vacate the premises and forfeit all that might have been paid to that date.

Barnum didn't stop there. He continued:

> In fact, Mr. Olmstead, you may bind me in any way, and as tightly as you please—only give me a chance to dig out, or scratch out, and I will either do so or forfeit all the labor and trouble which I may have incurred.

Olmstead checked Barnum's references and asked for some security (backed into a corner, Barnum offered Ivy Island as collateral). The deal was complete. Barnum was able to accomplish the seemingly impossible: He bought the museum and its contents with nothing but his wits, an honest desire to succeed, and brass.

However, that's not all that made this offer work (and it's not the end of the story). Barnum was respecting the other person involved in the transaction, something unusual in business then and now. Barnum wanted the museum, but he wanted it in a way that satisfied the other person involved. He wanted a win-win negotiation for all concerned.

He got it—for the moment.

How Barnum Made Tom Thumb Rich

When Barnum began managing Tom Thumb, he offered Thumb $3 a week. Soon after he raised the wages to $7 a week, then to $25, and then to $50 a week. Later Barnum made Tom a full partner and they split all ticket sales 50–50, making Tom and Barnum very rich men. Around 1870, after Tom had traveled the world with his new wife and gave over 1,471 performances, Barnum gave up all profit concerning Tom Thumb.

Barnum did not have to do this. The raises were voluntary. He knew it was a smart thing to do because if he kept his employees happy, they would stay with him and continue to do good service. They did. Tom and most of Barnum's other partners and employees stayed with him for decades, loved him, and always spoke of him with respect.

When Barnum surrendered all rights to profits from Tom Thumb's performances, he sincerely felt he had earned all he was entitled to. He permitted Tom to continue his success, but without having to pay anything to Barnum ever again.

Why Barnum Gave Lind More Money

When Barnum wanted to bring Jenny Lind to America, he mortgaged and borrowed everything he could to make the enterprise work. Bankers and friends said Barnum would fail, but he believed in Lind's reputation and he believed in his idea. He negotiated with her, gave her what she wanted—a colossal $187,500 *in advance*—and brought her here.

Very soon after their first shows, he voluntarily raised her fee. He offered to pay Lind her original fee of $1,000 a performance plus—after $5,500 a show for expenses—half of all the profits, as well.

Why? Again, he knew if he kept his employees happy, they would remain loyal to him and continue to perform their duties exceptionally well. Lind was so shocked that she threw her arms around Barnum and hugged him.

Barnum had discovered another ring of power: Negotiating with respect.

The Swedish Bikini Team

Most people don't realize that negotiation plays a role in every aspect of business. Take publicity, for example.

Barnum was a master at wheeling and dealing with editors to get newspaper coverage for his shows. He would often place an ad but also inform the editor that he expected full newspaper coverage by a reporter in exchange for the ad. In the 1800s this type of negotiating was common. The editorial and advertising departments were often the same person or in the same office. However, negotiating with the media is not so uncommon today. For example: R.J. Garis works as a publicist in California. Several years ago a major beer company approached him about increasing their sales. Garis invented a publicity stunt, of the sort which, he says, are now called magnet events, that people are still talking about.

Garis and his staff combed the beaches of California looking at beautiful women. They also went to bikini contests. They had a tough job. They selected a handful of attractive women, renamed them, bought them blonde wigs, taught them how to speak with an accent, and called the group The Swedish Bikini Team.

Then they told the media.

The press immediately jumped and wanted to cover the story. However, Garis wouldn't agree to any stories without some bartering.

"Everything is negotiable," he says.

Although most people would be elated to have the media exposure, Garis said that wasn't enough. "You also want the media to mention your product," he explains. "That's negotiable. You can ask for that."

And he did. The Swedish Bikini Team traveled for two years, appearing as walk-ons for television shows, showing up at conventions, doing modeling, selling posters of themselves, and much more. It was a very Barnum event. The girls got wealthy in the process. Garis made some money, and his client, Strohs beer, received over a billion dollars in free publicity.

Not bad.

"It's All Negotiation"

Garis offers a staggering thought: He says that when you get on one good television show, you can reach more people in one moment than Barnum did in his entire lifetime.

"But getting on the shows is negotiable," he reminds. "We often pitch a strong story to five different shows and let them make offers to us."

Those offers can be everything from money to plane tickets. An amateur will accept free tickets to and from the show while a professional will negotiate for something bigger—like the right to plug his product or service on the air.

"The media needs news," Garis explains. "There are over 4,000 radio programs producing five-day-a-week shows and the print space that needs to be filled every day is unimaginable. The media needs news and will negotiate for it. It's fun to be famous, but you also need to take that publicity to the bank."

New Jersey Man Sells Brooklyn Bridge

Barnum, like Garis, knew that negotiating wisely can bring you whatever you want in terms of business success or publicity. When dealing with the press, you are dealing with people who want something. Help them get what they want and they will help you get what you want. No one knows this better than my friend Paul Hartunian, a publicity specialist who once made news history by selling the Brooklyn Bridge—one piece at a time—for $14.95.

Hartunian collects Barnum's letters, books, and mementos. He's learned from the showman's examples. Years ago, Hartunian saw a television news story about how the pedestrian walkway of the famous Brooklyn Bridge was being replaced. Construction workers were tearing up the rotting and unsafe old wood and replacing it with new material. The ghost of Barnum must have been sitting in the room at the time, because Hartunian had a sudden brainstorm that would lead him to megapublicity.

First, Hartunian went to the construction workers and asked if he could buy the old wood. Because they considered it junk and were going to throw it away, they agreed to sell the truckload for $500. They thought Hartunian was nuts.

Second, Hartunian called a carpenter to pick up the wood and cut it into small square pieces, each about one inch thick.

Third, he went to his typewriter (he didn't have a computer at the time) and wrote a headline that he knew would get attention: "New Jersey Man Sells Brooklyn Bridge . . . for $14.95!"

Finally, Hartunian mailed his press releases to the media.

What happened as a result?

Nothing for the first two or three days. But then everything went wild.

Hartunian's phone rang incessantly. Reporters came right to his door. Newspapers, magazines, radio shows, and television shows contacted him, all wanting to interview him. CNN sent one of their vans to his house. Their news coverage was aired on CNN every 30 minutes for the next three days.

Things died down for a while. That gave Hartunian time to fulfill all the orders he had received from all the free publicity he had generated.

However, a few months later, Johnny Carson spent 10 minutes on his television show spoofing the man who sold the Brooklyn Bridge, and the media again ran to Hartunian's front door.

How does all of this pertain to negotiating with the media? As Paul Hartunian puts it, "I tell them they have to give out my phone number or I won't do the interview."

Hartunian had something the media desperately wanted: a hot story. The media had something Hartunian wanted: the ability to broadcast his product to millions. So they negotiated a deal that was fair to both.

As a result, checks and moneyorders poured in from around the world—all for $14.95 each—all from people wanting to buy a small but authentic piece of the Brooklyn Bridge.

Talk about a modern day humbug!

Getting Schools to Sell Products

You can negotiate with anyone. In the 1920s, when soap sales needed a rise and research unveiled that kids didn't like soap because it burned their eyes, Edward L. Bernays created a soap-sculpting contest. He then negotiated with schools to get their support. The schools saw that they could get children involved in art, and the soap manufacturer saw they could get free publicity by helping to promote the event. It was a win-win negotiation.

Within a year, 22 million children were using soap. Soap sales boomed. Bernays wrote in his autobiography, *Biography of an Idea*, ". . . as a result millions of school children carved Ivory soap for the next quarter century."

Besides illustrating that you can negotiate with anyone, this story further proves that publicity can alter what people think and feel. As a side benefit of this innovative strategy, kids quit complaining that soap burned their eyes. Children, the enemies of soap, became conditioned to enjoy soap.

Trump

If anyone can be called a modern day P.T. Barnum, it's Donald Trump. This colorful billionaire knows the power of wheeling and dealing, whether to negotiate for a hotel or to capture media attention. He's had everything from his own hit television show to numerous bestselling books. In his early bestseller, *The Art of the Deal*, he writes:

> You can have the most wonderful product in the world, but if people don't know about it, it's not going to be worth much. There are singers in the world with voices as good as Frank Sinatra's, but they're singing in their garages because no one has ever heard of them.

In 1985 Trump bought one hundred acres and announced he was going to build the tallest building in the world on it. That's news. It's also pure Barnum. The press leaped to cover the story. The *New York*

Times put it on their front page. Dan Rather announced it on television. And every architect stated their opinion. Trump explains:

> If I take a full-page ad in the *New York Times* to publicize a project, it might cost $40,000, and in any case, people tend to be skeptical about advertising. But if the *New York Times* writes even a moderately positive one-column story about one of my deals, it doesn't cost me anything, and it's worth a lot more than $40,000.

Trump knows how to negotiate with the press to get the kind of media coverage he describes. If he has news, such as creating the world's tallest building, the press comes to him. He then answers their questions honestly. However, if a reporter asks a negative question, Trump skillfully redirects or renegotiates the outcome. He writes:

> For example, if someone asks me what negative effects the world's tallest building might have on the West Side, I turn the tables and talk about how New Yorkers deserve the world's tallest building, and what a boost it will give the city to have that honor again.

Even when negotiating with the media, you can hold the cards and deal yourself a winning hand. Remember that you have news and want something in exchange for it: free press. It worked for Barnum. It works for Trump. And this ring of power can work for you.

Malice in Dallas

Sometimes you can turn a negotiation into a media event.

When Herb Kelleher of Southwest Airlines and Kurt Herwalkd of Stevens Aviation argued over the rights to an advertising slogan, they wisely left the courtroom and went into a wrestling arena. There they arm wrestled to decide who would win. Their Malice in Dallas spectacle gave immeasurable free publicity to both companies. Even though Kelleher lost, Southwest Airlines continues to fly ahead of other airlines, partly because they know how to have fun, no matter what challenges they face.

Even President George Bush commented on the inventive negotiation tactic with a note that began, "Just *Plane* Terrific!"

Donkey Marketing

My first taste of the power of marketing combined with negotiation probably happened around 1970.

I was a teenager in Ohio. I was assistant sports editor for the school newspaper. I had heard on the radio that the disc jockeys in Youngstown, Ohio were available to play basketball games as fund-raisers. The twist was they would ride donkeys on the court.

Yes, donkeys.

P.T. Barnum would have loved it. It was show business. It was outrageous. It was attention getting. It was *different*.

I don't remember how I got elected to be the one to set this game up. That was over 30 years ago. However, I do recall calling the radio station and telling them I wanted to arrange a donkey basketball game between the popular DJs and my high-school faculty.

It was as easy as making a phone call. The station manager agreed. I then went to the school principal and asked him if he would approve. He seemed confused. Donkeys? Basketball? Say what? Once he realized it wouldn't cost the school anything, he gave his nod and the game was on.

The next call was to the newspaper. That was easy, too. Teachers playing basketball against popular DJs while riding donkeys? They saw the news value and covered the story.

I have vague memories of the actual game. My parents, brothers, and sister were there. So were all my friends. So was most of the small city of Niles, Ohio. I remember asking an overweight policeman standing at a door for an estimate of how many people were there. He didn't know but agreed that it was standing room only.

The game itself was a delight. Teachers and DJs fell off donkeys. Some donkeys wouldn't move at all, but the game went on and someone won. Who, I don't recall.

I'm pretty sure I didn't even know what the word *marketing* meant at that point in my young life. All I was doing was creating a fun experience for people, something they would want to attend, something that would be a win–win for all. The negotiations were easy because the benefits were clear: The DJs got more attention for their station, the faculty got a little fame, the media got a fun story, and the school made a little money.

There's the essence of good Barnum-like marketing. Focus on fun, win–win, and making a little money. And if you can get donkeys involved, all the better.

After all, isn't life a circus?

"Friend Barnum, What Is Up?"

When Barnum began promoting the auction for the tickets to Jenny Lind's opening concert in America, he secretly went to see one other man besides John Genin the Hatter.

Barnum had already advised Genin to buy the first ticket, no matter what the cost, saying, ". . . the higher the price, the greater renown it will give you all over the country within twenty-four hours after purchase!"

However, Barnum feared that the others at the auction might be too conservative or slow to join in the high bidding. He wanted a buying frenzy—the bigger, the better. A few days before the auction, he went to see Dr. Brandreth, a successful patent medicine producer and heavy advertiser in the 1800s.

The doctor greeted Barnum warmly, led him to an easy chair, locked the office door, turned and asked, "Friend Barnum, what is up?"

"A mighty big thing for you," Barnum replied. "If you will keep it a profound secret for three days."

Now, stop right here and notice how Barnum focuses on how the other person will benefit in this negotiation. Barnum didn't say he needed help in promoting the auction. Instead, he said he has something "mighty big" for Brandreth.

The doctor's eyes sparkled with interest. He promised to keep whatever Barnum had up his sleeve a secret. Barnum continued:

"Buy the first Jenny Lind ticket at auction, even if you have to pay high for it, and let every newspaper in America and Europe announce that Dr. Brandreth, Jr., the maker of the celebrated Brandreth Pills, secured the first Jenny Lind ticket at fifty or one hundred dollars, as the case may be."

At first Brandreth suspected Barnum was just trying to run up the price of concert tickets for his own profit.

"Doctor Brandreth, I have long admired your ingenious methods of advertising Brandreth Pills," Barnum said. "But if you can't see the value to your business of my suggestion, I beg to say you will surely regret it when that first Jenny Lind ticket falls into other hands."

The doctor agreed to bid at the auction, but said he would play it safe. He did, too, by sending his cashier to the event with instructions to bid as high as two hundred dollars, but no more. Genin, on the other hand, sent his agent to the auction with instructions to bid as high as one thousand dollars. Genin, of course, bought the first ticket for two hundred and twenty-five dollars, became internationally famous, and then rich.

Brandreth regretted his loss and later said, "I had better have paid $5,000 than to have missed securing the first Jenny Lind ticket. Such a splendid chance for notoriety will never offer itself again."

The point here is that Barnum knew his auction would promote his Lind concert and generate reams of free publicity across the land. What he focused on in his negotiations with people was what *they* would get out of the arrangement.

Barnum Books an Unknown Juggler

In 1836 Barnum met a juggler named Signor Antonio. Barnum saw potential in the performer and offered to manage him on two conditions:

1. Signor "submit to be thoroughly washed."
2. Signor Antonio change his name to the more foreign sounding "Signor Vivalla."

Signor Antonio/Vivalla agreed. Barnum began promoting him by sending articles to the local papers. He then called on William Dinneford, manager of the Franklin Theatre in New York. However, Dinneford wasn't interested in booking the juggler, saying he had seen many performers of that kind before.

Here's where Barnum employed his negotiating ring of power. He did not give up. He did not admit defeat. Instead, he made an offer that was hard to refuse.

"You shall have him one night for nothing," Barnum said. "If you like him after one trial, you shall have him the remainder of the week for fifty dollars—but, understand me, this is only that the public may be able to see what he is. After that, my terms are fifty dollars per night."

Dinneford accepted. Why not? He had nothing to lose. Barnum had made the negotiation easy.

To guarantee success, Barnum immediately began promoting his performer. He explained:

> I invoked the powers of "printer's ink" and wood-cuts for three days and nights previous to the first appearance of the "renowned and extraordinary Italian artist, Signor Vivalla," and they were potent for my purpose. The house was crammed.

Barnum took a risk in giving the manager a night's performance for free, but it paid off. Barnum said, "Manager Dinneford was delighted, and before we left the stage he engaged Vivalla for the week."

Barnum Gets Thunderstruck

Barnum's incredible offer to buy the Scudder Museum with nothing but brass isn't the real brass he ended up showing in this negotiation.

Although he had made a grand offer to buy the museum and fully expected to honor it, he was in for a surprise. When he went to see John Heath, Olmstead's administrator, he was told that their deal was off.

"I was thunderstruck," wrote Barnum later. "I appealed to his honor. He replied that he had signed no writing with me, was not therefore legally bound. . . ."

Barnum then went and pleaded with Olmstead, but Olmstead said nothing could be done.

"Mr. Olmstead said he felt sorry for me, but could not help me," Barnum wrote.

The directors of the Peale Museum, a longtime rival of Scudder's American Museum, had offered more money than Barnum and had already paid $1,000 down in cash. As far as Olmstead was concerned, Barnum was out of luck.

Barnum did not give up. He did some investigating and discovered that the potential new owners of the museum were planning to swindle the public by selling stock in the museum and then abandoning the business.

Armed with these facts, Barnum visited the editors of the New York newspapers. He asked that they give him columns to expose the potential stock swindle. No doubt, the editors knew this hot news would help sell more papers. They eagerly agreed.

Barnum immediately began to write articles designed to "blow the speculation sky-high." Barnum later said, ". . . I wrote a large number of squibs, cautioning the public against buying the Museum stock."

Barnum's plan worked. The Peale administrators issued their stock, and almost no one bought it. People had heard too much bad press about it.

"The stock was as dead as a herring!" Barnum wrote.

However, the story doesn't end here, either.

Barnum Renogiates to Win

Barnum went back to Heath and asked when the Peale directors were required to pay the rest of the money for the museum. The answer: in seven weeks, on December 26, 1841. Barnum then negotiated a new deal.

He said that if the Peale group did not make their payment on the appointed day, he wanted their contract to be considered void and his own offer to buy the museum to be accepted. Heath agreed. And this time—at Barnum's request—signed a letter stating so.

Barnum continued to write his columns exposing Peale's attempt to sell stock and then dump the business. Before long, the Peale administrators invited Barnum to a meeting with them. There they offered him $3,000 a year—to manage the museum when they bought it. Barnum agreed to take the job, saying he would start work on January 1, 1842. As he was leaving, the president of the group said, "Of course, Mr. Barnum, we shall have no more of your squibs through the newspapers."

Barnum smiled and said, "I ever try to serve the interests of my employers."

The Peale group relaxed. From what they could see, they just shut up the man causing them the most damage. They also assumed that that same man could not afford to buy the museum they had signed to buy. When December 26 arrived, the Peale group did not make their payment. They didn't feel any rush to do so. Consequently, they let their deadline pass. Barnum wrote, "In fact, so unconcerned were they upon this point, that they did not even call on the administrator on the 26th, nor send him the slightest apology for not doing so!"

And on December 27, Barnum, with an attorney at his side, met with Heath and Olmstead to finalize their negotiations.

The Scudder Museum and its contents now belonged to P.T. Barnum.

Smart negotiation—and a lot of brass—gave him the business that would change his life forever.

Barnum's Friends Try to Rescue Him

As further proof that Barnum treated his employees as friends and negotiated deals that satisfied everyone, look at what happened when he went bankrupt in 1856: His business associates ran to help him. On May 12, 1856, General Tom Thumb wrote:

> My Dear Mr. Barnum, — I understand your friends (and that means "all creation") intend to get up some benefits for your family. Now, my dear sir, just

be good enough to remember that I belong to that mighty crowd, and I must have a finger (or at least a "thumb") in that pie. . . .

Barnum refused all handouts, preferring to pay off his debts using the ring of power you'll read about in Chapter 14. Although it's true that much of the jealous public showed glee at seeing the famous Barnum fall to his knees financially, Barnum's own partners, employees, and friends— the people who knew him best—offered their time, energy, and money to help him recover from his losses.

Gerard Nierenberg, author of *The Art of Negotiating*, generally considered the father of negotiation, told me that the word *negotiating* wasn't in use when Barnum was alive. "But he knew the value of win-win partnerships and the lasting value of relationships," Nierenberg explained.

When you want better employees, better deals with suppliers, or even more press coverage for your business, remember this ring of power: Think of the other people involved, and focus on what they will get from the partnership. As the famous salesman Zig Ziglar has said, "You can get whatever you want if you help enough people get what they want."

How can you make better deals with your employees, vendors, or customers; how can you make arrangements that respect them while helping you?

11 | P.T. Barnum's Secret for Surviving Disasters and Tragedies

But why dwell on this unpleasant theme? I have been and still am overwhelmed with financial embarrassments.

—P.T. Barnum, private letter, 1860

Anyone who thinks we live in an alarming period now has forgotten their history.

Pick up any newspaper from the mid-1800s and you'll think we live in heaven today. Although we live in an age of high stress, constant crime, and a shark-eat-shark business environment, Barnum lived through the Civil War, Indian wars, economic panics, terrible crime, robber barons, disease, famine, poverty, slavery, and extreme political and religious chaos. He also experienced appalling personal tragedies. In spite of all that, he seemed to smile and roll with the ebb and flow of life—and prospered no matter what happened.

I was rereading the first edition of his autobiography one night when I realized he finished it in 1854 while sitting in luxury in his Iranistan mansion. He was rich, famous, and in his 40s, but hell was just around the corner.

He would have to move out of his palace when money troubles hit him. The mansion itself would later burn to the ground. His famous museum in New York City would burn once again. He was to lose his wife and two daughters. He would go bankrupt. He was still some time away from any involvement with the circus, which would lead to his discovery, and then loss of, Jumbo the elephant.

Barnum did not know what was in store for him as he sat in his manor and finished his book in 1854, yet those disasters came to be and did not stop him. He weathered the storms with a calmness that most people would envy. Throughout it all Barnum maintained this optimistic attitude toward life in general. He somehow knew all would be well.

Why? How? Where did he get this fortitude? I wanted to know. I knew it could help me as well as others in business today.

I knew another ring of power was waiting to be found.

Barely Batting an Eye

When Barnum's museum burned down the first time, he was in the Connecticut state capital giving a speech. He was handed a telegram with the news. He read the message, folded the paper, and went on with his speech. He did not bat an eye. When he was finished with his delivery, he headed back to the city and began to rebuild his museum. Because he was always dramatically underinsured, he basically had to rebuild his museum from scratch.

When his museum burned down the second time in 1868, Barnum read about it in the newspaper while eating breakfast. He simply put down his fork, sent off some telegrams ordering his coworkers to restock their inventory and rebuild the museum, and then he finished breakfast. Again he was underinsured, he lost all his income while the new museum was being created, he had to restock treasures he had traveled the planet to find, and yet he did not get upset.

How many of us have that tenacity and faith today? Most people would have been crushed and even suicidal from any one of the disasters Barnum endured. When he went bankrupt because of his involvement with the Jerome Clock Company, he was only 46, a millionaire, living in a mansion, and set for life. This tragic event may have destroyed any other man.

Why did it barely faze Barnum?

Barnum Gets Stunned

The only times Barnum seemed to momentarily lose his inner strength were when his wife died in 1873 while he was in Hamburg, and when Jumbo the elephant was killed by a train in 1885. Even his unexpected bankruptcy didn't seem to affect him as much as these two deaths.

When Barnum's wife passed on, he was so depressed he locked himself in a hotel room for several days. He quickly recovered, returned to America, and went on with his life, even marrying once again.

When Jumbo was killed, Barnum momentarily gasped. The death stunned the world, as well as the showman. Within minutes he was giving orders to have the hide stuffed and the bones erected into a standing skeleton. He then arranged to display both hide and bones—two Jumbos for the price of one—until the day when he donated Jumbo's skin to Tufts College and his bones to the Smithsonian.

Once again, Barnum's faith carried him through, and faith became another of his rings of power.

Barnum's Secret

I remember reading about Mark Twain, and how the personal and professional tragedies of his life made him an angry man. Barnum suffered bankruptcy. So did Twain. Barnum lost his wife. So did Twain. Barnum invested in businesses that failed. So did Twain. Yet Twain became bitter and broke and Barnum continued to feel happy and prosper. What was the difference?

I wanted to know. I needed to know. I thought there may be a clue in his faith, because Barnum was a very religious man. He was a devout Universalist since a young man and wrote a short article titled, "Why I Am a

Universalist." I wanted to find that article. When I went to Bridgeport and visited Dr. Arthur Saxon, the author of the definitive biography of Barnum, I asked him about the article.

"That won't help you understand Barnum as a businessman," he said.

"I'm not so sure," I replied. "Barnum survived monstrous losses and yet kept going. I want to know why. How did he survive all those fires? How did he survive family loss and bankruptcy?"

"He was a better man than most of us," Dr. Saxon said.

"But what made him that way? I can't help but feel his religion gave him a fortitude to stomach the worst of all possible events. In short, he had faith. And I want to know where he got it."

"He got that from his religion," agreed Dr. Saxon.

I finally found the article by Barnum. Although I don't want to make this chapter a call for each of us to choose a religion and get back into a church, I want to point out that having faith in a power greater than yourself brings an ability to survive and prosper in any situation. Let me explain by telling you a possibly very bizarre, but true, story about visiting Barnum's grave.

A Discovery at Barnum's Grave

Imagine a cemetery so big you need a guide or a roadmap to find anything in it. That's Mountain Grove in Bridgeport, Connecticut. Tom Thumb and P.T. Barnum are buried there.

I went there with a friend on a gorgeous day in August 1996 to pay my respects to the great entertainers. My friend drove while we both scanned the cemetery, trying to find the statute of Tom Thumb on top of his plot or any sign or monument to indicate Barnum's site. We drove for several minutes, fascinated by the graves with cannon balls on top of them, feeling sad to see the crowd of small markers in one area from around 1919, after the First World War, and reflecting on the turbulent times these people had lived through.

However, we couldn't find Tom or Barnum. We went over a few hills, turned left, turned right, tried to flag down a man driving a riding lawnmower (he zipped by us, waving as he apparently went on his way to lunch), but we couldn't find our heroes. Finally I took a deep breath and decided to tune in to the spirit of P.T. Barnum himself.

"Okay, Barnum," I began, trusting that my friend driving wouldn't think I had lost my mind, "lead me to you."

We drove a few more minutes. I put out my hands, acting as if I were a magnet for energy, trying to pretend I was a dowsing rod, tuning in to any signal I might pick up from the great showman. It only took a moment before I felt something.

Off in the distance I saw a monument that seemed to glow.

"Drive that way," I said.

We headed the car in the direction of the monument I pointed at. The marker wasn't bigger, or smaller, or stranger than any other, but something about it called me. As we got closer to it, and I could read the name carved on it, I was shocked. The inscription said one word: "Seeley."

I couldn't believe it. I couldn't believe I had been wrong. My intuition had felt so right. We continued to drive, and as we got on the road that went toward the marker I had pointed at, my friend noticed something on her left that made us both stop and look.

"There's Tom Thumb," she said.

We parked the car, got out, and walked over to Tom's graveside. It was a tall monument with a life-size replica of Tom Thumb on top of it. Tom had a sculptor create it when he was in his 20s and wondering if the world would remember him after his death. It's an eye-opener to look at. Thumb was a perfectly proportioned miniature man, three feet tall. He must have truly been a person who commanded attention wherever he went in the 1800s, particularly when he used to travel in a tiny carriage made just for him.

After we walked around Tom Thumb's gravesite, we turned back to the car. That's when I noticed that the monument I had been drawn to earlier, the one that said "Seeley" on it, was only a few yards away. I could now see the front of it, but what amazed me was that the face of the monument had a different word on it, and that word was "Barnum."

I shot over to the monument. It was a marker for the Barnum family, covering his daughters and the people they married, including the family named Seeley. I looked around a little longer and finally found a tiny, unadorned headstone with the words on top of it, carved out of stone, "P.T. Barnum." (See Figure 11.1.) And on the front of it, still legible after over 100 years, was the phrase Barnum loved: "Not my will, but thine, be done."

I knelt on the grave, the home of the body of Barnum, the world's most famous marketing genius, and I placed my hands on his tombstone. I suddenly felt an electric current drift into my body, a soft and subtle energy that entered my being as I knelt and held onto Barnum's marker.

It was a moment I will never forget.

Call it my imagination. Call it madness. I prefer to call it a bonding of souls, for in those cherished moments on that sunny day in Bridgeport, I felt like I was inhaling the essence of the man I was about to write about. I

FIGURE 11.1 Barnum's simple grave site in Bridgeport, Connecticut. (Photo from author's private collection.)

soaked in his spirit, his entrepreneurial mind, his business ingenuity, his marketing bravado, and when I felt full and complete, I dropped my hands and stood over the grave.

"We can go now," I told my friend. "I have a book to write."

Understanding Barnum's Message

It was several weeks later before the full impact of the graveyard experience hit home.

I was having breakfast with Carol Marashi, a dear friend in Austin, and I was telling her about all the stresses of my life in Houston, which was where I was living at the time. After an hour of pouring out my heart, I told her the story I just told to you. Her brown eyes lit up as she asked me the million dollar question, "How did Barnum handle the stresses of his life?"

"He had faith that it would all be well," I instantly replied, "that there was a benevolent divine plan that put the personal tragedies in perspective."

"And what do you think the message is for you?"

I thought for a moment before answering.

"Have faith," I replied.

That was the answer. Barnum found his faith in a Universalist church, but people find faith everywhere. The point here is to find the inner security that allows you to weather the storms. Barnum had an optimistic view of life because he believed in a creator that was benevolent. He knew that blessings often looked like dark nights of the soul at first glance. Faith made getting on, as Barnum would call it, possible.

I can't tell you what to believe, but I know few in business can feel happy and stay healthy without faith in a higher order, a higher spirit, and a benevolent universe. When Tom Thumb died of a stroke at the age of 46, Barnum sent a warm note to Tom's widow, saying, "Yourself and family have my warmest sympathies. Death is as much a part of The Divine Plan as birth. The Heavenly Father finally overcomes evil with good. His will be done."

Find your faith and you will find an invincible supply of power that will carry you through as you pursue your dreams. You will have a ring of power no one can destroy. When I was researching material for my book on Bruce Barton, the advertising legend who founded the BBDO ad agency, I stumbled across this inspiring line in Barton's 1927 book, *What Can A Man Believe?*:

> Faith in business, faith in the country, faith in one's self, faith in other people—this is the power that moves the world. And why is it unreasonable to believe that this power, which is so much stronger than any other, is merely a fragment of the Great Power which operates the universe.

Barnum's Secret for Living at No-Stress Level

In a real way, Barnum's faith allowed him to live at a no-stress level. This may be hard to grasp, as many people today think you need stress in order to have energy. However, energy comes to us naturally as we eat and breathe, and gets stronger as we have dreams that fuel us with passion.

Barnum pursued numerous projects and seemed to have endless energy. When he was an elderly man visiting London, the reporter who followed him around that day was exhausted from the day's activities while Barnum seemed ready to keep moving. Barnum was experiencing this level of no stress.

Jonathan Jacobs, a therapist friend of mine in Seattle, who I write about in my book, *The Attractor Factor*, works with people's energy and belief systems. He once told me that the goal for each of us is to live without stress.

"When you are in stress, you are experiencing a negative thought or an unfinished experience," he explained to me. "When you are at no stress, you are free to make clear choices about what you want in each moment."

"But what about appropriate anger?" I asked.

"Anger is something unfinished in you. It's a sore spot that gets rubbed when you encounter something that reminds you of the past. Clear the past and you won't have the anger."

This was very chewy food for thought. However, I noticed that when Jonathan and I went out, he always seemed cheerful. One day we were having dinner at a fine restaurant and I spotted a hair on his plate. I pointed it out and Jonathan stopped eating, put his fork down, and called our waiter over. He was not upset. He was not angry. He simply informed the waiter of the hair and was neutral about what happened next. The waiter gave him his meal free. He also gave me my meal free, as well. But anger was never involved.

The Power of Belief

Barry Neil Kaufman, another dear friend, the author of the book, *Happiness Is A Choice*, once told me that people use unhappiness, stress, anger, guilt, and most of the other negative emotions, as tools to manipulate themselves and others. However, when you are clear of those beliefs, you are free to see clearly each situation as well as to see clearly how to respond to each. In short, you don't need to be unhappy in order to achieve what you want in business (or anywhere else).

Self-help author Mandy Evans says certain beliefs can lead to a very bad day. Beliefs cause stress, not your business situations.

"There's what happened to you in your life and then there's what you decided it meant," says Evans, author of *Travelling Free: How to Recover from the Past by Changing Your Beliefs*.

"Change your conclusions, or your beliefs about the events in your past," explains Evans, "and you can change the way you live your life today. Certain beliefs can really trip us up."

Beliefs shape the way we feel, think, and act, says Evans, an expert in personal belief systems, but you can't change them until you know what they are. Evans offers a list of "The Top 20 Self-Defeating Beliefs" in *Travelling Free*, her second book, as a way to begin exploring them.

"As you look at each belief, ask yourself if you believe it," suggests Evans. "If you do, then ask yourself why you believe it. Gently explore your own reasons for buying into any self-limiting belief."

Here are 10 of her Top 20 limiting beliefs:

1. I'm not good enough to be loved.
2. No matter what I do, I should be doing something else.
3. If it hasn't happened yet, it never will.
4. If you knew what I'm really like, you wouldn't want me.
5. I don't know what I want.
6. I upset people.
7. Sex is dirty and nasty; save it for the one you love.
8. Better stop wanting; if you get your hopes up, you'll get hurt.
9. If I fail, I should feel bad for a long time and be really scared to try again.
10. I should have worked this out by now.

Just look at belief number nine. Clearly Barnum did not buy into it. When he suffered tragedy and setback, he almost immediately took action to recreate what he lost. He did not sit around and feel bad. That's hard evidence that when you are free of limiting beliefs, when you are living at a no-stress level, you are capable of creating what you want in life, including great wealth in your own business. None of your energy gets tied up in the past or in negativity. You have full power to create the business you want.

Barnum lived a predominately happy life. Major Pond booked him as a speaker and said Barnum had "a smile all over his face." Others said his eyes danced with charm and he was amiable to everyone. He had to be to befriend presidents and kings. Barnum's faith helped him to be clear of the beliefs and limitations most people in business today are programmed and limited by.

For example, when Barnum learned that his circus winter camp burned to the ground and most of his treasures were lost in the fire, he simply began sending out telegrams requesting new treasures. He was at no stress and used that as his power base to create a new empire.

The King's Magic Ring

I once heard a story about a king who wanted to know how to handle every unpleasant situation that came his way.

The king called his court-appointed royal wizard and told him the problem. "I want something that will solve every crisis I encounter," said the king. "Make a talisman or potion or spell for me."

The wizard went off, created something, and returned with it. He handed the little package to the king and said, "My king, this will help you weather any storm."

The king opened the tiny box and saw that it was a simple but elegant looking ring. At first he was angry, thinking his wizard had created something worthless, but as he rolled the ring around in his hand, he noticed an inscription on it. He squinted a bit to read it, and then saw the words, "This, too, will pass."

The king looked at the wizard, awaiting an explanation.

"My dear King, no matter what occurs in your day-to-day business, simply look at the ring. Let it remind you that the situation, no matter what it may be, is momentary. It, too, will pass. The skies will clear. The crops will grow. The sun will rise again."

Barnum's Daily Strength

Knowing that you can live with an attitude of optimism will help you in your day-to-day business challenges. Knowing that "This, too, will pass" can give you the inner strength needed to handle whatever life brings your way. Just *knowing* this can make your life easier because you are no longer restricted to a negative or limited view of the world.

It will also help you to find tools to remind yourself that all is well. It may be a magic ring. It might also be a book. Barnum had a book of inspiration that he looked at whenever he felt the urge. He wrote:

> I own a small dollar book which I would not sell for a thousand dollars if I could not replace it. It is an admirable selection of fine thoughts, finely expressed by ancient and modern writers. It teaches in a marked degree the whole philosophy of living happily and living long. Its title is "Daily Strength for Daily Needs."

Barnum isn't the only person to receive inspiration from that small dollar book he mentioned. When *Daily Strength for Daily Needs* was first published in 1884, it immediately sold out. The publisher reprinted the book 68 times and sold 208,459 copies in 1884 alone. Most books rarely go into second or third printings. *Daily Strength for Daily Needs* has been reprinted hundreds of times over the last century. It remains in print today.

Mary Wilder Tileston created the book by selecting inspiring biblical passages, poetry, and spiritual writings, one of each for every day of the year. It's easy to see how Barnum gained inner strength from these passages. For July 5th, Barnum's birthday, part of the reading for the day says: "We never have more than we can bear. The present hour we are always able to endure." And the biblical passage for the same day reads, "A bruised reed shall He not break." No wonder Barnum was able to tolerate the challenges of his life. He used the wisdom he found in Tileston's book to help him stay focused on the tasks at hand. He used the book to think positively.

I keep books of inspiration within reach, and use an inspiring planning calendar called *The Science of Deliberate Creation*, by Jerry and Esther Hicks, to help me plan each day's events with a positive outlook. Barnum kept a small memo book with him to write his to-do lists, and, of course, relied on his *Daily Strength for Daily Needs* book of quotes for inner nourishment. He also attended his church regularly, and often spoke about his beliefs. These extra tools helped him maintain his faith.

Modeling this aspect of Barnum's personality can give you the strength needed to weather any storm. It will give you an indestructible ring of power. Find your own inner faith, your own tools for inspiration and comfort, and you, too, will be able to create empires without letting obstacles stop you.

Barnum wrote, ". . . If one does right his mind should never be disturbed by anything which he cannot prevent. He should be thoroughly convinced that if he does his duty Providence will take care of the rest, and never send accident, poverty, disease, or any other apparent evil except for an ultimate good purpose."

Where is *your* faith?

12

How P.T. Barnum Wrote His Own Ticket to Success

I shall send you a small package of queer letters this week.
—P.T. Barnum, 1876, to Samuel L. Clemens/Mark Twain

P.T. Barnum discovered the power of the written word in 1832 when he was a 22-year-old man in Connecticut—in jail.

During that period of American history, people were beginning to mix politics with religion, a no-no according to the Bill of Rights. Barnum objected by writing articles for the local paper, but the editors refused to print them. Never daunted, Barnum began his own newspaper.

The Herald of Freedom was a success right from the start. People loved reading Barnum's spirited, well-thought-out arguments against intertwining church and state business. However, Barnum was often reprimanded by the law for speaking a little too loudly against prominent people. At one point, he accused a clergyman of usury, and Barnum was arrested for libel. He was sentenced to jail for 60 days. Instead of hurting his career, it made him more famous.

His jail cell was lined with carpet, the door was left open for his many visitors, and he continued to write his newspaper while in confinement. When he was released, there was a party thrown in his honor. There were songs, orations, toasts, a cannon was fired, and a wagon drawn by six horses led a parade for him. Barnum became a hero throughout Connecticut.

Barnum never forgot the power of the pen. It became one of his most potent rings of power. He used it to promote Tom Thumb, Jenny Lind, his museum, his circus, and himself. He wrote biographies of Lind, Tom, and even Jumbo the elephant. He created an illustrated newspaper to promote his circus, called it *P.T. Barnum's Advance Courier*, printed 500,000 copies, and had it distributed free one week before his show's arrival in each city.

Barnum's own autobiography helped secure his place in American history. It became so famous during his lifetime that Barnum decided to add to it every year, making his life story a serialized national thriller. In 1884 he turned the copyright to his book over to the public, letting anyone print their own version of his autobiography. Barnum knew the resulting publicity would be worth gold, and letting others print the books meant he didn't have any printing bills to pay.

Writing shouldn't be considered a new technique for anyone in business. Name any prominent person and there will probably be a book out by or about him or her. Being an author is so powerful that many businessmen hire ghostwriters to have the work done without lifting a pen themselves. They aren't doing this because of their ego; it's good business to be seen in print.

The Greatest Marketing Tool on Earth

"Write a book? *Me?* Are you kidding?"

No, I'm not. Besides being the most powerful marketing tool around, here are three reasons why *you* ought to consider writing a book: fame, fortune, and immortality.

1. *Fame:* The world bows to experts. Write a book and you're considered the *author*-ity on that subject. Being an author brings a lot of attention to your business. Look at Harvey MacKay, author of *Swim with the Sharks Without Being Eaten Alive.* Who ever heard of him or his envelope company before he wrote his blockbuster? The same can be said for such household names as Tom Peters, Anthony Robbins, and Stephen Covey. They were all virtually unknown before they wrote books.

2. *Fortune:* James Fixx, author of *The Complete Book of Running,* the bestseller that sent people in shorts to sweat through the streets, made over $500,000 from book sales. He made *yet another* $500,000 from all the speaking engagements he did as a result of being a rich and famous author. Not bad. And not too unusual. Peters's books set him up as the expert to call for insights on service excellence. Last I heard, he now gets paid somewhere around $10,000 per talk. His business is booming. And let's not forget Benjamin Franklin, who made his fortune from his book, *Poor Richard's Almanac,* which is still in print.

3. *Immortality:* You've probably read a book that dramatically altered your life, or the way you do business. Did you tell the author? Probably not. Books touch people in ways authors may never imagine. It's your opportunity to make a difference in the world. One of the reasons we even know of people like P.T. Barnum is the books written by and about him. Books can keep your customers remembering you for a long, long time.

And there's more. Your book also becomes a networking tool that is far more powerful than any business card. Iacocca's autobiography sold more than 6.5 million copies. That means a huge audience became aware of him and his business. He couldn't shake hands with that many people in a year.

Not a writer? J. Paul Getty hired a ghostwriter. Trump and Iacocca hired co-authors. You don't have to write the book yourself. Just don't hire a budding novelist. Hire a professional writer. A seasoned author can help you package your story, and even help you identify the uniqueness of your business, so it becomes a salable product in the marketplace. That's what other smart business people have done, including Wal-Mart's Sam Walton and Wendy's Dave Thomas. Barnum wrote all of his own books, but a few of his later articles may have been ghostwritten. It doesn't matter. The effect is the same. Being an author makes you an *author*-ity.

Being a businessperson with a book may be the most powerful marketing tool on the face of the Earth. The public loves you and the press writes about you. If you don't believe us, ask the business tycoons who already have books available—*if* you can get them on the phone!

The Barnum–Twain Queer Letters

Few people know that P.T. Barnum almost co-authored a book with Mark Twain.

Twain became a genuine fan of the showman's career after reading Barnum's famous autobiography, probably the 1869 edition. They later became friends. Sometime around 1874, Barnum showed Twain some of the letters he received from people with wild ideas for making money or wild requests for borrowing money. Barnum called them his queer letters.

Twain loved the letters from people trying to sell Barnum three-legged chickens with two rectums, or those from people wanting to borrow $50 to flee a Benedictine monastery. Twain saw that these letters could make a profitable book. He asked Barnum to forward the letters to Twain at his home in Nook Farm. Barnum was delighted. He felt the letters would reveal "almost a new page in the volume of human nature." He also knew a book by Mark Twain, written with material from P.T. Barnum, would bring enormous free publicity.

Barnum kept his word to Twain but Twain did not keep his to Barnum. When a Reverend Powers visited Barnum in 1876 and saw some of the famous queer letters, he wanted to use them in an article. Barnum declined, saying he had promised the material to Twain. For whatever reasons, Twain never got around to writing the book. Still, both men recognized that having such a book would have helped both of their careers.

What Do Customers Keep Asking You?

"But don't you have to have something to say in order to write a book?" asked David Willis, president of Relationship Marketing, a telemarketing service.

"You already have something to say."

"I do?"

"Your customers are paying you for information, aren't they? They are calling you and asking questions, aren't they?"

"They call on me to teach them how to conduct phone sales, yes, but how can I make a book out of that?"

"Easy," I replied. "Write down the most common questions you get. What do your customers call and ask you over and over again? There's your book."

"You mean, if they keep asking me what they should say on the phone when making cold calls to people, I can turn that into a book?"

"Yes."

"So I write down reoccurring questions. Then what?"

"Then write out your answers," I said. "This is easy. All you have to do is record a few of your phone conversations with clients. When someone calls you and asks for advice, record your answer. Later, type up your answer. You're then on your way to writing a book."

"But won't I be giving away for free what I should be charging to give?"

"It looks that way, I know," I said. "But what often happens is this: People buy your book because they want your information. They read your book, discover they can't or won't do what you say in the book, and then who do you think they hire?"

"The author of the book?"

"You got it," I said. "I've written several books. One tells people how to create their own ads. Well, some people read the book and write their own ads, but most people read the book and still can't or won't write their own ads. However, they now know who to call and hire—the author of the book they just read."

Willis went on to write a small book titled, *In Search of Gold: A Guide for Using Stress-Free Prospecting to Find and Mine Customers.* Having the book gives him further credibility as a telemarketing expert, selling the book gives him another income stream, and everyone who buys the book becomes a potential prospect for his services.

When Barnum began writing *The Humbugs of the World*, his rollicking exposé of spiritualism and other humbugs of his day, he paid attention to what people asked him about and turned their questions and interests into his next book.

You can do the same thing in your business. Think of what clients keep asking you, write out your answers, and add life to your pages with examples and quotes. You may also want to hire an editor (Willis did) to be sure you are expressing yourself with clarity. The result will be a marketing tool that can bring fame, fortune, and immortality.

You can't ask for much more than that, can you?

Barnum's Bestseller

P.T. Barnum wrote, edited, and polished his famous autobiography in less than four months. When it was first published in 1854, it immediately sold more than 160,000 copies. It became a controversial bestseller in England and America. Barnum loved it. It added to his fame, and increased attention to his projects.

In later years Barnum bought back the rights to publish his book and came out with his own edition. He revised and expanded the book several times. He changed the title of it from *The Life of P.T. Barnum* to *Struggles and Triumphs*. He sold it for $1.50 when it cost him nine cents a copy to print. He made money from selling the book as well as from the notoriety the book gave him.

Even when Barnum released the copyright to his work in 1884, he continued to profit. Numerous editions of his book came out under different titles, from *Dollars and Sense* to *How I Made Millions*. Although each title had a different publisher, and none of the royalties went to the showman, the person who benefited the most was always one man— P.T. Barnum. The free advertising he received was worth millions of dollars.

How can you begin writing your own ticket to success? You don't need to write your autobiography (yet) but you do need to begin somewhere.

You might write articles for the local newspaper, or for trade publication. Later, they can be compiled into a book.

You might write a brief work answering common questions from clients or customers. Or maybe you can draft a how-to manual that you sell.

If you're online (and you should be), consider writing a weekly tip or memo as a way to stay in touch with people and build and maintain relationships. For an example, register at www.mrfire.com for my complimentary newsletter by e-mail.

The point is, you can write your ticket to fame and fortune by writing. It worked for P.T. Barnum, and it can work for you, too.

13 | Bonus

My Exclusive Interview with P.T. Barnum

I created the following interview by thinking of questions to ask Barnum and then finding the answers in his writings. If it were not for the words he left behind over one hundred years ago, we would not know what the man thought about what he did.

Pull up a chair. Imagine you are facing a robust, sanguine, portly man with curly hair, a large nose, twinkling eyes, and a sunny, contagious, peculiar mirthful smile.

Author: *I've discovered your 10 rings of power for building an empire in business, but how much of your wealth has been due to luck?*

Barnum: Luck is in no sense the foundation of my fortune; from the beginning of my career, I planned and worked for my success.

Then let's start at the beginning. When were you born?

My first appearance upon this stage was on the 5th day of July, Anno Domini 1810. Independence Day had gone by, the cannons had ceased to thunder forth their remembrances of our National Anniversary, the smoke had all cleared away, the drums had finished their rattle, and when peace and quiet were restored, I made my debut.

What did you do to make money growing up?

Among the various ways which I had for making money on my own account, from the age of twelve to fifteen years, was that of lotteries. . . . Lotteries in those days were patronized by both Church and State. As a writer has said, "People would gamble in lotteries for the benefit of a church in which to preach *against* gambling."

You did very well, I understand.

I sold from five hundred to two thousand dollars' worth of tickets per day.

That's incredible! But then lotteries were declared illegal and you moved to New York?

By this time it was clear to my mind that my proper position in this busy world was not yet reached. I had displayed the faculty of getting money, as well as getting rid of it; but the business for which I was destined, and, I believe, made, had not yet come to me; or rather, I had not found that I was to cater for that insatiate want of human nature—the love of amusement.

Your first exhibition was Joice Heth in 1834, the alleged nurse of George Washington, when you were 24 years old?

I had long fancied that I could succeed if I could only get hold of a public exhibition.

Did you really believe she was 161 years old and could sing and recite psalms?

The question naturally arises, if Joice Heth was an impostor, *who* taught her these things? And how happened it that she was so familiar, not only with ancient psalmody, but also with the minute details of the Washington family? To all this, I unhesitatingly answer, *I do not know.* I taught her none of these things.

But didn't an autopsy prove she was not a day over eighty?

I assert, then, that when Joice Heth was living, I never met with six persons out of the many thousands who visited her, who seemed to doubt the claim of her age and history. Hundreds of medical men assured me that they thought the statement of her age was correct.

How do you feel about having exhibited Heth?

The least deserving of all my efforts in the show line was the one which introduced me to the business; a scheme in no sense of my own devising; one which had been some time before the public and which had so many vouchers for its genuiness that at the time of taking possession of it I honestly believed it to be genuine—such was the "Joice Heth" exhibition which first brought me forward as a showman.

How did you come to buy Scudder's Museum with no money, when you were barely making four dollars a week writing ads for the Bowery Amphitheater?

I repeatedly visited that Museum as a thoughtful looker-on. I saw, or believed I saw, that only energy, tact, and liberality were needed, to give it life and to put it on a profitable footing; and although it might have appeared presumptuous, on my part, to dream of buying so valuable a property without having any money to do it with, I seriously determined to make the purchase, if possible.

But what drove you to make the museum into such a success?

No one will doubt that I now put forth all my energy. It was strictly "neck or nothing." I must either pay for the establishment within a stipulated period, or forfeit it, including all that I might have paid on account.

How did you transform the enterprise so quickly?

Valuable as the collection was when I bought it, it was only the beginning of the American Museum as I made it. In my long proprietorship I considerably more than doubled the permanent attractions and curiosities of the establishment. In 1842, I bought and added to my collection the entire contents of Peale's Museum; in 1850, I purchased the large Peale collection in Philadelphia; and year after year, I bought genuine curiosities, regardless of cost, wherever I could find them, in Europe or America.

That was a great love of yours, wasn't it?

From the first, it was my study to give my patrons a superfluity of novelties, and for this I make no special claim to generosity, for it was strictly a business transaction. To send away my visitors more than doubly satisfied, was to induce them to come again and to bring their friends. I meant to make people talk about my Museum. . . . It was the best advertisement I could possibly have, and one for which I could afford to pay.

Why did you create such outrageous advertising?

It was the world's way then, as it is now, to excite the community with flaming posters, promising almost everything for next to nothing. I confess that I took no pains to set my enterprising fellow-citizens a better example. I fell in with the world's way; and if my "puffing" was more persistent, my advertising more audacious, my posters more glaring, my pictures more exaggerated, my flags more patriotic and my transparencies more brilliant than they would have been under the management of my neighbors, it was not because I had less scruple than they, but more energy, far more ingenuity, and a better foundation for such promises. . . . I have yet to learn of a single instance where a visitor went away from the Museum complaining that he had been defrauded of his money.

How did you come up with your ideas?

I often seized upon an opportunity by instinct, even before I had a very definite conception as to how it should be used, and it seemed, somehow, to mature itself and serve my purpose.

Can you give me an example?

I had not the remotest idea, when I bought this horse, what I should do with him; but when the news came that Colonel John C. Fremont (who was supposed to have been lost in the snows of the Rocky Mountains) was in safety, the "Whoolly Horse" was exhibited in New York, and was widely advertised as a most remarkable animal that had been captured by the great explorer's party in the passes of the Rocky Mountains. . . . When it was generally known that the proprietor of the American Museum was also the owner of the famous "Whoolly Horse," it caused yet more talk about me and my establishment. . . .

How did you master the art of publicity?

I studied ways to arrest public attention; to startle, to make people talk and wonder; in short, to let the world know that I had a Museum.

But why in the world stoop to showing something like the fabricated half monkey–half fish called the Fejee mermaid?

The receipts for the American Museum for the four weeks immediately preceding the exhibition of the mermaid, amounted to $1,272. During the first four weeks of the mermaid's exhibition, the receipts amounted to $3,341.93.

But wasn't the thing manufactured?

Assuming, what is no doubt true, that the mermaid was manufactured, it was a most remarkable specimen of ingenuity and untiring patience. For my own part I really had scarcely cared at the time to form an opinion of this creature.

Not everyone will agree with your actions, you know.

We cannot all see alike, but *we can all do good.*

But some people may say you misled them.

I don't believe in "duping the public," but I believe in first *attracting* and then pleasing them. While I do not attempt to justify all I have done, I know that I have generally given the people the *worth of their money twice told.*

Why did you hold so many baby shows at the Museum?

These shows were as popular as they were unique, and while they paid in a financial point of view, my chief object in getting them up was to set the newspapers to talking about me, thus giving another blast on the trumpet which I always tried to keep blowing for the Museum.

You also held poultry shows, didn't you?

Eight thousand chickens in the Museum. Gods! What a crowing!

But these were all advertisements, weren't they?

Flower shows, dog shows, poultry shows, and bird shows, were held at intervals in my establishment and in each instance the same end was attained as by the baby shows.

Speaking of babies, meeting the child who became Tom Thumb changed your life—as well as his—didn't it?

Much as I hoped for success, in my most sanguine moods, I could not anticipate the half of what was in store for me; I did not foresee nor dream that I was shortly to be brought in close contact with kings, queens, lords, and illustrious commoners, and that such association, by means of my exhibition, would afterwards introduce me to the great public and the public's money, which was to fill my coffers.

Describe Charles Stratton to me, the way he looked when you first saw him in 1842, before you tutored him and changed his name to General Tom Thumb.

He was not two feet high; he weighed less than sixteen pounds, and was the smallest child I ever saw that could walk alone; but he was a perfectly formed, bright-eyed little fellow, with light hair and ruddy cheeks, and he enjoyed the best of health. He was exceedingly bashful, but after some coaching he was induced to talk to me. . . . I at once determined to secure his services from his parents and exhibit him in public.

After you returned from three years of traveling with Tom Thumb in Europe, what did the neighbors back in Connecticut say about him?

"We never thought Charlie much of a phenomenon when he lived among us," said one of the first citizens of the place, "but now that he has become 'Barnumized,' he is a rare curiosity."

And what about Jenny Lind?

It was in October, 1849, that I conceived the idea of bringing Jenny Lind to this country. I had never heard her sing, inasmuch as she arrived in London a few weeks after I left that city with General Tom Thumb. Her reputation, however, was sufficient to me.

How did you promote her?

I then began to prepare the public mind, through the newspapers, for the reception of the great songstress. How effectually this was done, is still within the remembrance of the American public.

Why did you voluntarily increase Lind's salary?

Let it not be supposed that the increase of her compensation was wholly an act of generosity on my part.

What do you mean?

I had become convinced that there was money enough in the enterprise for all of us, and I also felt that although she should have been satisfied by my complying with the terms of the agreement, yet envious persons would doubtless endeavor to create discontent in her mind, and it would be a stroke of policy to prevent the possibility of such an occurrence.

Tell me about your dealings with the Jerome Clock Company.

What a dupe I had been! Here was a great company pretending to be worth $587,000, asking temporary assistance to the amount of $110,000, coming down with a crash, so soon as my helping hand was removed, and sweeping me down with it. It failed; and even after absorbing my fortune, it paid but from twelve to fifteen percent of its obligations, while, to cap the climax, it never removed to East Bridgeport at all, notwithstanding this was the only condition which ever prompted me to advance one dollar to the rotten concern!

They caused you to go bankrupt, but you didn't give up.

I was in the depths, but I did not despond. I was confident that with energetic purpose and divine assistance I should, if health and life were spared, get on my feet again; and events have fully justified and verified the expectation and the effort.

How have you been able to tolerate such losses as fires and bankruptcy?

Time rolls on, troubles come and go, we have darkness at one hour and sunlight at another—but away up, *high* up above all, is calmness and everlasting quietude. . . . We cannot control fate or destiny, but out of all our chaos and troubles, our excitements and disappointments, we gather lessons of experience and wisdom.

Then what have you learned from losing Iranistan and from the Jerome Clark troubles?

I have learned to be patient and submissive, and that was a great and most important lesson for me to acquire. It was just the lesson which I needed—in fact, my whole troubles have been and are just what I most stood in need of.

What do you mean?

. . . I humbly hope and believe that I am being taught humility and reliance upon Providence, which will yet afford a thousand times more peace and true happiness than can be acquired in the din, strife and turmoil, excitements and struggles of this money-worshipping age.

You are strongly against alcohol. Why?

I have been both sides of the fence in this liquor-drinking custom, and I know whereof I speak. From 1840 to 1848 I was a pretty free drinker and prouder of my 'wine cellar' than any of my other possessions. . . . I became a total abstainer. Had I not done so, I should doubtless have been in my grave long since. . . .

Do you really believe that?

If men would fill their pockets with cold boiled potatoes every morning, and whenever they met a friend would draw out a potato, take a bite, and say, "Here is your good health, my boy," it might appear ludicrous, but it would be a thousand times more sensible than drinking one's "health" in poison, as all intoxicants are.

Is it true that in your developing of East Bridgeport, you created a way for people to buy their own homes, but they had to sign a temperance pledge?

Quite a number of men at once availed themselves of my offer, and eventually succeeded in paying for their homes without much effort. I am sorry to add, that rent is still paid, month after month, by many men who would long ago have owned neat homesteads, free from all incumbrances, if they had accepted my proposals, and had signed and kept the temperance pledge, and given up the use of tobacco. The money they have since expended for whiskey and tobacco, would have given them a house of their own.

You seem to truly want to help people. Are you a philanthropist?

I have certainly made some expensive improvements, which I felt sure could *never* repay me, but I am glad to have it understood that mine is usually a *profitable philanthropy*. I have no desire to be considered much of a philanthropist in any other sense. If by helping those who try to help themselves, I can do it without ultimate loss, the inducement is all the greater to me; and if by improving and beautifying our city, and adding to the pleasure and prosperity of my neighbors, I can do so at a profit, the incentive to "good works" will be twice as strong as if it were otherwise.

Why did you get involved in politics in 1865?

It always seemed to me that a man who "takes no interest in politics" is unfit to live in a land where the government rests in the hands of the people.

You were previously a Democrat but accepted a Republican nomination?

I accepted from the Republican party a nomination to the Connecticut legislature from the town of Fairfield, and I did this because I felt that it would be an honor to be permitted to vote for the then proposed amendment to the Constitution of the United States to abolish slavery forever from the land.

What about Jumbo?

Jumbo, the largest elephant ever seen, either wild or in captivity, had been for many years one of the chief attractions of the Royal Zoological Gardens, London. I had often looked wistfully on Jumbo, but with no hope of ever getting possession of him, as I knew him to be a great favorite of Queen Victoria, whose children and grandchildren are among the tens of thousands of British juveniles whom Jumbo has carried on his back. I did not suppose he would ever be sold.

But you made an offer anyway?

Two days afterwards my agent cabled me that my offer of $10,000 for Jumbo was accepted.

But didn't Europe go into a rage?

All England seemed to run mad about Jumbo; pictures of Jumbo, the life of Jumbo, a pamphlet headed "Jumbo-Barnum," and all sorts of Jumbo stories and poetry, Jumbo Hats, Jumbo Collars, Jumbo Cigars, Jumbo neckties, Jumbo Fans, Jumbo Polkas, etc., were sold by the tens of thousands in the stores and streets of London and other British cities. . . . These facts stirred up the excitement in the United States. . . .

Then you never paid a cent for advertising? When it came time for Jumbo to leave London and he refused to move, what did you do?

My agent, dismayed, cabled me, "Jumbo has laid down in the street and won't get up. What shall we do?" I replied, "Let him lie there a week if he wants to. It is the best advertisement in the world."

Why do you rarely talk about your family?

My private personal affairs I always have kept distinct from *business*. . . . *Business* considerations should never be mixed up with other affairs. . . .

You are almost eighty years old. Do you have any concerns or regrets?

I awaken each morning with surprise and gratitude to find myself so vigorous and free from aches and pains at my time in life. But the closing scene is near, and it is *all right*. Our last hours will be all the more pleasant if, with all our faults, we can feel assured that the world is better and happier for our having lived in it.

Finally, do you have anything you want to tell my readers?

If you would be happy as a child, please one.

Childish wonder is the first step in human wisdom.

To best please a child is the highest triumph of philosophy.

A happy child is the most likely to make an honest man.

To stimulate wholesome curiosity in the mind of the child is to plant golden seed.

I would rather be called the children's friend than the world's king.

Amusement to children is like rain to flowers.

He that makes useful knowledge most attractive to the young is the king of sages.

Childish laughter is the echo of heavenly music.

The noblest art is that of making others happy.

Wholesome recreation conquers evil thoughts.

Innocent amusement transforms tears into rainbows.

The author of harmless mirth is a public benefactor.

I say—as the poet said of his ballads—if I might provide the amusements of a nation, I would not care who made its laws.

14

How P.T. Barnum Got Rich Right after Going Broke

The clock folks have wound me up.

—P.T. Barnum, private letter, 1856

Barnum loved the city of East Bridgeport, Connecticut so much that he invested thousands of dollars and almost half of his life in developing it. But this also led to one of the darkest periods of his life—and to the discovery of a new ring of power for making a fortune.

Barnum wanted to bring the Jerome Clock Company to Bridgeport to help the local economy and give jobs to people. The company agreed on one condition: that Barnum sign notes lending them money to make the move. Barnum agreed.

He began signing promissory bank notes with the understanding that the limit would be $100,000, but the company kept having Barnum sign notes, and Barnum—in his blind desire to see his city prosper—kept signing. Before he knew it, he had signed notes promising nearly half a million dollars. By the time Barnum realized he had been swindled, he was bankrupt.

He was in his 40s and had just suffered a loss that would have crippled most other men. Not Barnum. He remained true to his character and said he would pay off every dime he owed on every note he signed. It took him several years, but he did it, and soon after that, he created an even larger fortune.

Chapter 11 explained how Barnum could weather any storm because of his inner strength. This chapter will reveal the action Barnum took to recover from his losses and regain his empire—and how you can do the same thing today by simply opening your mouth.

Money Getting

Barnum began speaking in the 1850s when he became passionate about the temperance (against drinking alcohol) movement. All the money from those talks was donated to worthy causes. After Barnum's bankruptcy, friends urged him to start giving professional lectures about how to make money. Barnum resisted the idea, saying he knew more about losing money than making it, but his friends insisted that he had to know how to earn it in order to ever have it. As a result, Barnum began giving a talk called "The Art of Money Getting."

He (of course) heavily advertised his talk. The results were staggering. Not only did 2,500 people buy tickets at 50 cents each to his first paid lecture on December 29, 1858, in London, but Barnum gave the talk so many times that within only four years it helped him pay off all his debts. As Barnum himself said, "The talk became a fine example of the art of money getting."

The morning after his first talk, the London *Times* wrote:

We are bound to admit that Mr. Barnum is one of the most entertaining lecturers that ever addressed an audience on a theme universally intelligible. The appearance of Mr. Barnum, it should be added, has nothing of the "charlatan" about it, but is that of the thoroughly respectable man of business; and he has at command a fund of dry humor that convulses everybody with laughter, while he himself remains perfectly serious. A sonorous voice and an admirably clear delivery complete his qualifications as a lecturer, in which capacity he is no "humbug," either in a higher or lower sense of the word.

Barnum spoke on the lecture circuit during the same period as Mark Twain and Charles Dickens. Other popular orators of the day included gorilla expert Paul Du Chaiilu (gorillas were discovered in the mid-1800s), poet Henry Wadsworth Longfellow, minister Henry Ward Beecher, and philosopher Ralph Waldo Emerson. Barnum was just as popular, if not more so, as his contemporaries. One newspaper reported:

> His [Barnum's] account of the meeting of Tom Thumb and the Queen was acted as if the old man had included the stage as one of his many professions. Mr. Barnum told yarns about Irish pilots, Irish waiters, funny deacons, mean men, and all sorts of funny people whom the great showman had met in his travels through life. Mr. Barnum is a born storyteller, and in his hands the stalest chestnut would make you roar with laughter.

Barnum could also display his razor sharp wit at a moment's notice. Once a heckler asked how alcohol affected a person, "Internally or externally?" Barnum shot back, "*E*-ternally."

And when Barnum heard the Bishop of London end his speech with, "I hope I shall see you in heaven," Barnum said, "You will if you are there."

Defending Himself

Barnum's speaking ability served him in many ways, including defending himself before crowds of people and police.

Henry Bergh, founder of the American Society for the Prevention of Cruelty to Animals (ASPCA), won such legal power that he and his crew were permitted to stop and arrest anyone on the spot who they felt was hurting an animal. On several occasions Bergh went after Barnum. What Bergh didn't realize was that Barnum knew more about animals than most people of his time, including Bergh.

At one point Bergh heard that Barnum was displaying a rhinoceros. He immediately demanded that the rhino be given a tank of water to swim in. Barnum had to explain that rhinos did not live in water and, in fact, would die in a tank of it. Another time Bergh was outraged to hear that Barnum fed live toads and lizards to snakes. Again, Barnum had to educate Bergh that snakes require live frogs in order to survive.

However, the real showdown came in 1880 when Bergh heard that Barnum's circus included a horse named Salamander who jumped through a fiery hoop. Bergh sent his troops to close the show. Barnum, not batting an eye and sensing a publicity opportunity, invited Bergh and his followers to the circus ring where he promised to answer Bergh's accusations. As Barnum predicted, crowds packed the tents—including a crowd of policemen, ready to arrest Barnum. The only person who did not appear was Bergh, who sent one of his aides instead.

This is where Barnum's skills as a performer and speaker came into full play. He stood in the center of the ring and addressed the crowd:

> Ladies and Gentlemen: I have been catering to the public for forty-eight years, yet I am here today expecting arrest by this large force of police, and imprisonment and trial by a jury of my countrymen. The patent fact is just this: Mr. Bergh or I must run this show.

Barnum then continued with a recounting of Bergh's attempts to stop Barnum from hurting animals. He added that he had been a protector of animals in this country, and overseas working with the queen, long before Bergh ever began his animal rights crusade. Barnum ended his delivery with a demonstration that brought cheers. Barnum lit the fiery hoops. Then he stepped through them. Then 10 clowns performed ludicrous antics through the hoops. And finally Salamander passed through "without showing any signs of fear and without singeing a hair," but Barnum didn't stop with this dramatic moment. He then had Bergh's representative walk through the blaze. When the aide was finished, he announced to Barnum and the crowd that his superior, Mr. Bergh, had apparently made a mistake.

"I love animals too well to torture them," Barnum explained.

Bergh and Barnum later became friends, but it was Barnum's speaking abilities that saved him in 1880.

How I Gave the Talk of My Life

In the summer of 1996 I spoke at the Publishers Marketing University in Chicago. It was my first time to address the hundreds who attend the yearly conference. I was nervous. I also knew that several of my mentors spoke to the same group, and had been doing so for many years. That didn't help me relax. I felt intimidated.

I wanted to give one of the best talks of my life, so I prepared. I thought about Barnum and how he used stories to entertain people. I thought about Twain and how he carefully rehearsed everything he wanted to do before giving a speech. I read books. I listened to tapes. I outlined my presentation. And then I stumbled across one of the most powerful secrets of all time.

There's an old Greek word called *synaesthesia*, which means "a merging of the senses," that saved the day for me. What you do is imagine your talk as something other than a speech. In other words, if your presentation was a piece of music, what type of music would you want it to be? If your talk was a color, what color would it be? You cross and merge senses in an attempt to make your actual talk richer and more alive.

I used synaesthesia to prepare for my Chicago talk. I would lie down, close my eyes, breathe deeply and evenly, and see myself giving my talk. I would then ask myself, "If your talk was a color, what would it be?" I imagined a fiery red color with white streaks in it. That symbolized to me high energy, enthusiasm, and inspiration, all qualities I wanted to project.

I then asked myself, "If your talk was a piece of music, how would it sound?" I immediately conjured up an image of Melissa Etheridge, the passionate rock star who stirs her crowds with music that pulsates and a voice that soars. I chose Melissa as a role model because I had seen her performance on MTV's famous "Unplugged" show and was stunned. That little woman, singing and playing her acoustic guitar alone before the packed house, made people feel her magic. I later discovered that she used to perform before small groups of people where she learned that if she didn't captivate them and hold their attention, the people would leave and she would lose her job. Consequently, Melissa rocks when she plays and everyone feels her presence. I felt that if my talk could express some of her passion and punch, I would knock my Chicago crowd on their rears.

I mentally rehearsed my talk in this fashion for several weeks. I would pretend that my speech was a piece of music being sung by Melissa. Although I never saw myself actually singing, I infused my imagery with high energy. I allowed my subconscious to integrate the dynamic elements of a Melissa Etheridge concert into my talk. I remembered what Melissa had said in an America Online interview when someone asked her for advice on performing. Melissa replied, "Be strong . . . do not be afraid of your power . . . *rock*." I wondered what would happen if I let my inner power as a speaker "rock" through my words and gestures when I spoke. I wasn't sure how my mind would make this happen, but I trusted that it would. I knew that I was programming my mind for success.

When the day of the event arrived, I was ready. I felt strong, clear, articulate, enthusiastic. I gave my speech, sat down, and listened as the crowd applauded. The fellow who was speaking after me got up and said, "I have to catch my breath after Joe's talk."

He never did catch his breath, and the crowd seemed sleepy as he spoke. When the audience was polled several weeks later, and asked which of the 24 classes had been the best, my talk got rated the highest with a score of 9.84 out of a possible 10. When you consider that I was the newcomer and over 20 presentations had been given by more experienced speakers, you have to take note.

I'm not relating this story to brag about myself as a speaker. My point is that anyone—even you—can learn to become a powerful speaker. When you do, you begin to implement one of Barnum's most important rings of power. I acquired several new clients as a result of my Chicago talk. When you stand up in front of a crowd of prospects, they see you as an authority. When you entertain and educate them, they remember you. When they need your services, they'll hire you.

Although Barnum probably did not know about mental imaging and synaesthesia, he knew preparation was a key to success. Because most of us aren't Barnum or Twain, we can use all the help we can get. Twain, for example, rehearsed his talks as if they were theatrical performances and his words were the script. Barnum apparently used notes for his talks and was very animated in his delivery.

What can you do today to speak and grow rich?

Barnum's Incredible Speaking Tips

Use these tips to create your own winning talk:

1. *Know your audience.* Think about what people are interested in, not in what you want them to be interested in. When Barnum began speaking for money, he knew the vast majority of his audience would want to know how to increase their wealth. So Barnum told them how in his talk, "The Art of Money Getting." Although he could have created interesting talks about life in the circus, or even continued to give his talks on temperance, he knew that what people would pay to hear were his ideas on success. Give your audience what they want.

2. *Know your message.* If you don't have a key principle or point to convey, your talk will drift aimlessly and your speech will come across as empty. Barnum knew that his temperance lectures were about the evils of alcohol. He knew that his lectures on money were about the wisdom of following certain principles for success. Know your own essential points before you try to give a speech. Barnum used an outline of his talk to help him recall his points and stories.

3. *Have stories to illustrate your points.* Stories entertain as well as educate. Barnum stuffed his talks with delightful and humorous stories that happened to illustrate his key points. Delivering your principles or message without stories will make you sound lifeless and boring. Breathe life into your speech with relevant stories. When you read Barnum's lecture in the next chapter, notice how often he tells a joke, offers a quotation, or relates a story that illustrate his main points. Enrich your presentation with stories. Barnum made crowds roar with delight as he related stories of the people he met as he traveled around the world. Audiences loved it. Many said his talk was the lecture event of the year.

4. *Use visual props.* In the 1800s lecturers did not have overhead slide projectors or use easels to stand up illustrations. They also didn't have microphones and rarely used introductions. Yet they knew the value of keeping people interested. Barnum often performed magic tricks at his lectures. You must keep your audience riveted on you. Use overhead projectors with stimulating illustrations that reinforce your message. Although you and your words will account for a small percentage of the impact you make on people, your visual aids will help you make an unforgettable impression. One of the reasons my talk in Chicago was so successful was that I used slides of old ads to illustrate my points whereas the speaker who followed me used nothing.

5. *End with a bang.* Psychologists say people will remember the opening and the ending of your talk more than any other part of your speech. If you want people to remember you, end your presentation on a memorable note. I like to tell stories that inspire people. Barnum wrapped up his talks with an overview of his message and a wonderful quote. As you'll see shortly, his use of a quote by Shakespeare makes his talk all the more unforgettable. Save your biggest bang—your best story, quote, or illustration, for example—as the final item you deliver before stepping off stage.

In the late 1880s Barnum used his anecdotal talks as a way to test and rehearse material for his next book, *Funny Stories Told by Phineas T. Barnum.* He was so convinced of the power of public presentations that, while mayor of Bridgeport, he established a scholarship to be given to a high school student who excelled in public speaking. The award continues to be given today.

By his own count, Barnum gave his lectures more than 700 times to about 1,300,000 people. His speaking skills helped him as a businessman, showman, publicist, politician, and as crusader against alcohol, but by far, his speaking talents helped save him financially.

When Barnum stood on the stage of his museum on March 24, 1860, and announced he was back on his feet again after four long years of struggle to get out of debt, the jammed house gave him such loud cries of support and such thunderous applause that the showman had to fight from breaking down into tears.

How can you begin speaking about your product or service?

15 | Bonus

The Art of Money Getting
by P.T. Barnum

The speech you are about to read comes from the 1869 edition of Barnum's autobiography, *Struggles and Triumphs*. Although Barnum gave other speeches, this was the one he became most famous for delivering and the one that audiences considered the most helpful to those in business.

It certainly helped Barnum. Giving it helped him crawl out of debt. The famous newspaper editor Horace Greeley said this speech was worth "a hundred dollar greenback" to a beginner in business. Many people said Barnum's advice helped them become wealthy.

I'm including the entire lecture here because of its historic importance, and because the principles—even though now well over 100 years old—have stood the test of time. Some of the fundamentals will sound familiar to you because Barnum used material from his earlier article, "Barnum's Rules for Success in Business," in preparing his talk. (See Figure 15.1.) So you have the complete speech, I am not editing it at all.

Imagine you are in a theater in the late 1800s when P.T. Barnum, one of the most colorful and successful men in American history, strolls out, his

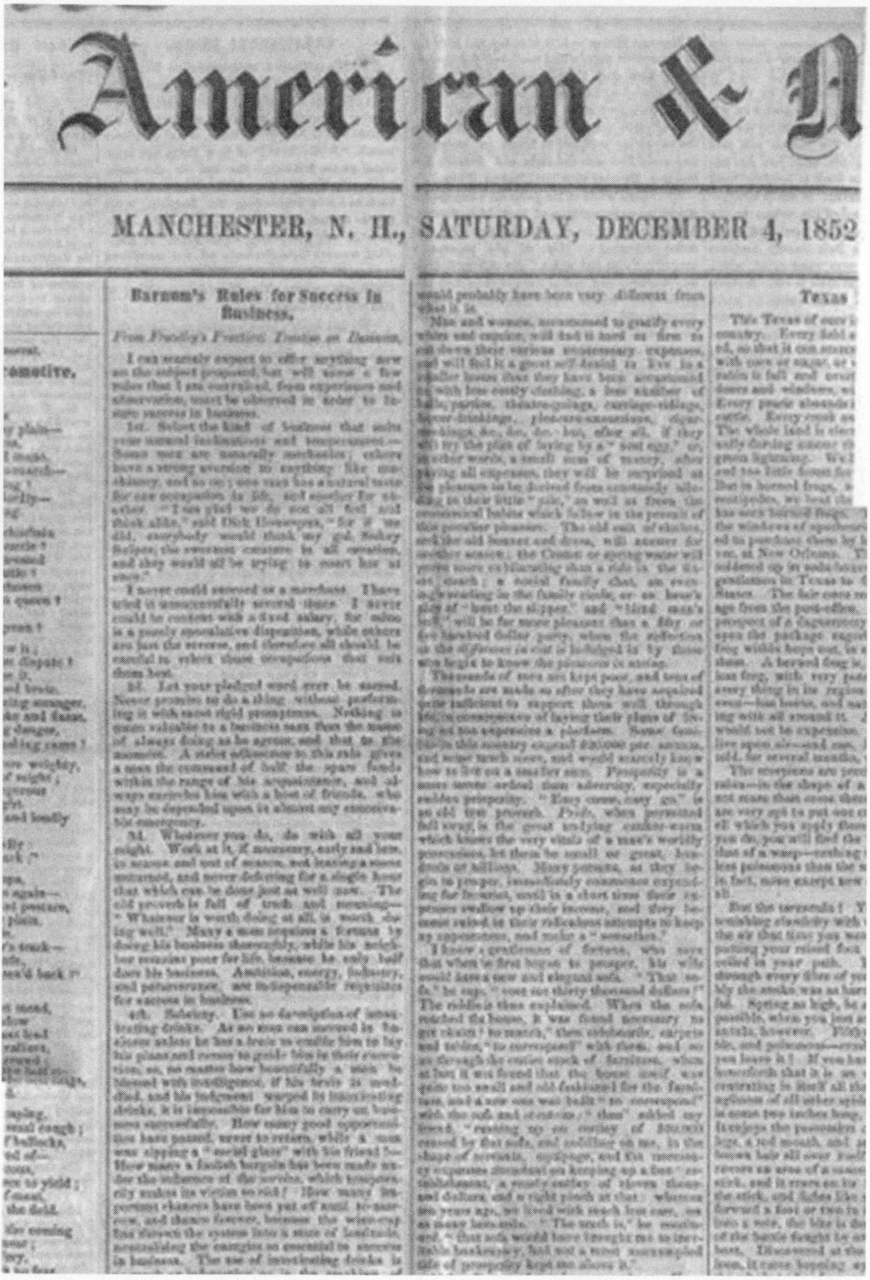

American & M

MANCHESTER, N. H., SATURDAY, DECEMBER 4, 1852

Barnum's Rules for Success in Business.

From Freedley's Practical Treatise on Business.

FIGURE 15.1 Barnum's "Rules for Success" were so popular they were printed in the newspaper. (From author's private collection.)

eyes bright, his smile lighting up the stage. You and the rest of the packed house have eagerly waited to hear what the greatest showman of all time has to say about becoming a success in life. And now . . .

In the United States, where we have more land than people, it is not at all difficult for persons in good health to make money. In this comparatively new field there are so many avenues of success open, so many vocations which are not crowded, that any person of either sex who is willing, at least for the time being, to engage in any respectable occupation that offers, may find lucrative employment.

Those who really desire to attain an independence, have only to set their minds upon it, and adopt the proper means, as they do in regard to any other object which they wish to accomplish, and the thing is easily done. But however easy it may be found to make money, I have no doubt many of my hearers will agree it is the most difficult thing in the world to keep it. The road to wealth is, as Dr. Franklin truly says, "as plain as the road to mill." It consists in expending less than we earn; that seems to be a very simple problem. Mr. Micawber, one of those happy creations of the genial (Charles) Dickens, puts the case in a strong light when he says that to have an income of twenty pounds, per annum, and spend twenty pounds and sixpence, is to be the most miserable of men; whereas, to have an income of only twenty pounds, and spend but nineteen pounds and sixpence, is to be the happiest of mortals. Many of my hearers may say, "We understand this; this is economy, and we know economy is wealth; we know we can't eat our cake and keep it also." Yet I beg to say that perhaps more cases of failure arise from mistakes on this point than almost any other. The fact is, many people think they understand economy when they really do not.

True economy is misapprehended, and people go through life without properly comprehending what that principle is. Some say, "I have an income of so much, and here is my neighbor who has the same; yet every year he gets something ahead and I fall short. Why is it? I know all about economy." He thinks he does, but he does not. There are many who think that economy consists in saving cheese-parings and candle ends, in cutting off two pence from the laundress' bill and doing all sorts of little, mean, dirty things. Economy is not meanness. The misfortune is also that this class of persons let their economy apply in only one direction. They fancy they are so wonderfully economic in saving a half-penny where they ought to spend two pence, that they think they can afford to squander in other directions. A few years ago, before kerosene oil was discovered or thought of, one might stop over night at almost any farmer's house in the agricultural districts and get a very good supper, but after supper he might attempt to read in the sitting room, and would find it impossible with the inefficient light of one candle. The hostess, seeing his dilemma, would say: "It is rather difficult to read here evenings; the proverb says 'You must have a ship at sea in order to be able to burn two candles at once'; we never have an extra candle except on extra occasions." These extra occasions occur, perhaps, twice a year. In this way the good woman saves five, six, or ten dollars in that time; but the information which might be derived from having the extra light would, of course, far outweigh a ton of candles.

But the trouble does not end here. Feeling that she is so economical in tallow candles, she thinks she can afford to go frequently to the village and spend twenty or thirty dollars for ribbons and furbelows, many of which are not necessary. This false economy may frequently be seen in men of business, and in those instances it often runs to writing paper. You find good business men who save all the old envelopes and scraps, and would not tear a new sheet of paper, if they could avoid it, for the world. This is all very well; they may in this way save five or ten dollars a year, but being so economical (only in note paper), they think they can afford to waste time; to have expensive parties, and to drive their carriages. This is an illustration of Dr. (Benjamin) Franklin's "saving at the spigot and wasting at the bung-hole"; "penny wise and pound foolish." "Punch" in speaking of this "one-idea" class of people says "they are like the man who bought a penny herring for his family's dinner and then hired a coach and four to take it home." I never knew a man to succeed by practicing this kind of economy

True economy consists in always making the income exceed the out-go. Wear the old clothes a little longer if necessary; dispense with the new pair of gloves; mend the old dress; live on plainer food if need be; so that under all circumstances, unless some unforeseen accident occurs, there will be a margin in favor of the income. A penny here, and a dollar there, placed at interest, goes on accumulating, and in this way the desired result is attained. It requires some training, perhaps, to accomplish this economy, but when once used to it, you will find there is more satisfaction in rational saving, than in irrational spending. Here is a recipe which I recommend; I have found it to work an excellent cure for extravagance and especially for mistaken economy: When you find that you have no surplus at the end of the year, and yet have a good income, I advise you to take a few sheets of paper and form them into a book and mark down every item of expenditure. Post it every day or week in two columns, one headed "necessaries" or even "comforts," and the other headed "luxuries," and you will find that the latter column will be double, treble, and frequently ten times greater than the former. The real comforts of life cost but a small portion of what most of us can earn. Dr. Franklin says, "It is the eyes of others and not our own eyes which ruin us. If all the world were blind except myself I should not care for fine clothes or furniture." It is the fear of what Mrs. Grundy may say that keeps the noses of many worthy families to the grindstone. In America many persons like to repeat "We are all free and equal," but it is a great mistake in more senses than one.

That we are born "free and equal" is a glorious truth in one sense, yet we are not all born equally rich, and we never shall be. One may say, "There is a man who has an income of fifty thousand dollars per annum, while I have but one thousand dollars; I knew that fellow when he was poor like myself; now he is rich and thinks he is better than I am; I will show him that I am as good as he is; I will go and buy a horse and buggy;—no, I cannot do that but I will go and hire one and ride this afternoon on the same road that he does, and thus prove to him that I am as good as he is."

My friend, you need not take that trouble, you can easily prove that you are as good as he is; you have only to behave as well as he does, but you cannot make anybody believe that you are as rich as he is. Besides, if you put on these "airs," and waste your time and spend your money, your poor wife will be obliged to scrub her fingers off at home, and buy her tea two ounces at a time, and everything else in proportion, in order that you may keep up "appearances," and after all, deceive nobody. On the other hand, Mrs. Smith may say that her next-door neighbor married Johnson for his money, and "everybody says so." She has a nice one-thousand-dollar camel's hair shawl, and she will make Smith get her an imitation one and she will sit in a pew right next to her neighbor in church, in order to prove that she is her equal.

My good woman, you will not get ahead in the world, if your vanity and envy thus take the lead. In this country, where we believe the majority ought to rule, we ignore that principle in regard to fashion, and let a handful of people, calling themselves the aristocracy, run up a false standard of perfection, and in endeavoring to rise to that standard, we constantly keep ourselves poor; all the time digging away for the sake of outside appearance. How much wiser to be a "law unto ourselves" and say, "We will regulate our out-go by our income, and lay up something for a rainy day." People ought to be as sensible on the subject of Money Getting as on any other subject. Like causes produce like effects. You cannot accumulate a fortune by taking the road that leads to poverty. It needs no prophet to tell us that those who live fully up to their means, without any thought of a reverse in this life, can never attain a pecuniary independence.

Men and women accustomed to gratify every whim and caprice, will find it hard, at first, to cut down their various unnecessary expenses, and will feel it a great self denial to live in a smaller house than they have been accustomed to, with less expensive furniture, less company, less costly clothing, fewer servants, a less number of balls, parties, theater-goings, carriage-ridings, pleasure excursions, cigar-smokings, liquor-drinkings, and other extravagances; but, after all, if they will try the plan of laying by a "nest-egg," or in other words, a small sum of money, at interest or judiciously invested in land, they will be surprised at the pleasure to be derived from constantly adding to their little "pile," as well as from all the economical habits which are engendered by this course.

The old suit of clothes, and the old bonnet and dress, will answer for another season; the Croton or spring water will taste better than champagne, a cold bath and a brisk walk will prove more exhilarating than a ride in the finest coach; a social chat, an evening's reading in the family circle, or an hour's play of "hunt the slipper" and "blind man's buff," will be far more pleasant than a fifty- or a five-hundred-dollar party, when the reflection on the difference in cost is indulged in by those who begin to know the pleasures of saving. Thousands of men are kept poor, and tens of thousands are made so after they have acquired quite sufficient to support them well through life, in consequence of laying their plans of living on too broad a platform. Some families expend twenty thousand dollars per annum, and some much more, and would scarcely know how to live on less, while others secure more solid enjoyment frequently on a twentieth part of that amount. Prosperity is a more severe ordeal than adversity, especially sudden prosperity. "Easy come, easy go," is an old and true proverb. A spirit of pride and vanity, when permitted to have full sway, is the undying cankerworm which gnaws the very vitals of a man's worldly possessions, let them be small or great, hundreds or millions. Many persons, as they begin to prosper, immediately expand their ideas and commence expending for luxuries, until in a short time their expenses swallow up their income, and they become ruined in their ridiculous attempts to keep up appearances, and make a "sensation."

I know a gentleman of fortune who says, that when he first began to prosper, his wife would have a new and elegant sofa. "That sofa," he says, "cost me thirty thousand dollars!" When the sofa reached the house, it was found necessary to get chairs to match; then sideboards, carpets and tables "to correspond" with them, and so on through the entire stock of furniture; when at last it was found that the house itself was quite too small and old-fashioned for the furniture, and a new one was built to correspond with the new purchases; "thus," added my friend, "summing up an outlay of thirty thousand dollars caused by that single sofa, and saddling on me, in the shape of servants, equipage, and the necessary expenses attendant upon keeping up a fine 'establishment,' a yearly outlay of eleven thousand dollars, and a tight pinch at that; whereas, ten years ago, we lived with much more real comfort, because with much less care, on as many hundreds. The truth is," he continued, "that sofa would have brought me to inevitable bankruptcy, had not a most unexampled tide of prosperity kept me above it, and had I not checked the natural desire to 'cut a dash.' "

The foundation of success in life is good health; that is the substratum of fortune; it is also the basis of happiness. A person cannot accumulate a fortune very well when he is sick. He has no ambition; no incentive; no force. Of course, there are those who have bad health and cannot help it; you cannot expect that such persons can accumulate wealth; but there are a great many in poor health who need not be so.

If, then, sound health is the foundation of success and happiness in life, how important it is that we should study the laws of health, which is but another expression for the laws of nature! The closer we keep to the laws of nature, the nearer we are to good health, and yet how many persons there are who pay no attention to natural laws, but absolutely transgress them, even against their own natural inclination. We ought to know that the "sin of ignorance" is never winked at in regard to the violation of nature's laws; their infraction always brings the penalty. A child may thrust its finger into the flame without knowing it will burn, and so suffers; repentance even will not stop the smart. Many of our ancestors knew very little about the principle of ventilation. They did not know much about oxygen, whatever other "gin" they might have been acquainted with; and consequently, they built their houses with little seven-by-nine-feet bedrooms, and these good old pious Puritans would lock themselves up in one of these cells, say their prayers, and go to bed. In the morning they would devoutly return thanks for the "preservation of their lives" during the night, and nobody had better reason to be thankful. Probably some big crack in the window, or in the door, let in a little fresh air, and thus saved them.

Many persons knowingly violate the laws of nature against their better impulses, for the sake of fashion. For instance, there is one thing that nothing living except a vile worm ever naturally loved, and that is tobacco; yet how many persons there are who deliberately train an unnatural appetite, and overcome this implanted aversion for tobacco, to such a degree that they get to love it. They have got hold of a poisonous, filthy weed, or rather that takes a firm hold of them. Here are married men who run about spitting tobacco juice on the carpet and floors, and sometimes even upon their wives besides. They do not kick their wives out of doors like drunken men, but their wives, I have no doubt, often wish they were outside of the house. Another perilous feature is that this artificial appetite, like jealousy, "grows by what it feeds on"; when you love that which is unnatural, a stronger appetite is created for the hurtful thing than the natural desire for what is harmless. There is an old proverb which says that "habit is second nature," but an artificial habit is stronger than nature. Take for instance an old tobacco-chewer; his love for the "quid" is stronger than his love for any particular kind of food. He can give up roast beef easier than give up the weed.

Young lads regret that they are not men; they would like to go to bed boys and wake up men; and to accomplish this they copy the bad habits of their seniors. Little Tommy and Johnny see their fathers or uncles smoke a pipe and they say, "If I could only do that I would be a man, too; Uncle John has gone out and left his pipe of tobacco, let us try it." They take a match and light it, and puff away. "We will learn to smoke; do you like it, Johnny?" That lad dolefully replies: "Not very much; it tastes bitter"; by and by he grows pale, but he persists, and he soon offers up a sacrifice on the altar of fashion;

but the boys stick to it and persevere until at last they conquer their natural appetites and become the victims of acquired tastes.

I speak "by the book," for I have noticed its effects on myself, having gone so far as to smoke ten or fifteen cigars a day, although I have not used the weed during the last fourteen years, and never shall again. The more a man smokes, the more he craves smoking; the last cigar smoked, simply excites the desire for another, and so on incessantly.

Take the tobacco-chewer. In the morning when he gets up, he puts a quid in his mouth and keeps it there all day, never taking it out except to exchange it for a fresh one, or when he is going to eat; oh! yes, at intervals during the day and evening, many a chewer takes out a quid and holds it in his hand long enough to take a drink, and then pop! it goes back again. This simply proves that the appetite for rum is even stronger than that for tobacco. When the tobacco chewer goes to your country seat and you show him your grapery and fruit house and the beauties of your garden, when you offer him some fresh, ripe fruit, and say, "My friend, I have got here the most delicious apples and pears and peaches and apricots; I have imported them from Spain, France, and Italy, — just see those luscious grapes; there is nothing more delicious nor more healthy than ripe fruit, so help yourself; I want to see you delight yourself with these things," he will roll the dear quid under his tongue and answer, "No, I thank you, I have got tobacco in my mouth." His palate has become narcotized by the noxious weed, and he has lost, in a great measure, the delicate and enviable taste for fruits. This shows what expensive, useless, and injurious habits men will get into. I speak from experience. I have smoked until I trembled like an aspen leaf, the blood rushed to my head, and I had a palpitation of the heart which I thought was heart disease, till I was almost killed with fright. When I consulted my physician, he said, "Break off tobacco using." I was not only injuring my health and spending a great deal of money, but I was setting a bad example. I obeyed his counsel. No young man in the world ever looked so beautiful as he thought he did behind a fifteen-cent cigar or a meerschaum!

These remarks apply with ten-fold force to the use of intoxicating drinks. To make money, requires a clear brain. A man has got to see that two and two make four; he must lay all his plans with reflection and forethought, and closely examine all the details and the ins and outs of business. As no man can succeed in business unless he has a brain to enable him to lay his plans, and reason to guide him in their execution, so, no matter how bountifully a man may be blessed with intelligence, if the brain is muddled, and his judgment warped by intoxicating drinks, it is impossible for him to carry on business successfully. How many good opportunities have passed, never to return, while a man was sipping a "social glass" with his friend! How many foolish bargains have been made under the influence of the "nervine" which temporarily makes its victim think he is rich. How many important chances have been put off until to-morrow, and then forever, because the wine cup has thrown the system into a state of lassitude, neutralizing the energies so essential to success in business. Verily, "wine is a mocker." The use of intoxicating drinks as a beverage is as much an infatuation as is the smoking of opium by the Chinese, and the former is quite as destructive to the success of the business man as the latter. It is an unmitigated evil, utterly indefensible in the light of philosophy, religion, or good sense. It is the parent of nearly every other evil in our country.

DON'T MISTAKE YOUR VOCATION. The safest plan, and the one most sure of success for the young man starting in life, is to select the vocation which is most congenial to his tastes. Parents and guardians are often quite too negligent in regard to this. It is very common for a father to say, for example: "I have five boys. I will make Billy a clergyman; John a lawyer; Tom a doctor, and Dick a farmer." He then goes into town and looks about to see what he will do with Sammy.

He returns home and says, "Sammy, I see watch-making is a nice, genteel business; I think I will make you a goldsmith." He does this regardless of Sam's natural inclinations, or genius.

We are all, no doubt, born for a wise purpose. There is as much diversity in our brains as in our countenances. Some are born natural mechanics, while some have great aversion to machinery. Let a dozen boys of ten years get together and you will soon observe two or three are "whittling" out some ingenious device; working with locks or complicated machinery. When they were but five years old, their father could find no toy to please them like a puzzle. They are natural mechanics; but the other eight or nine boys have different aptitudes. I belong to the latter class; I never had the slightest love for mechanism; on the contrary, I have a sort of abhorrence for complicated machinery. I never had ingenuity enough to whittle a cider tap so it would not leak. I never could make a pen that I could write with, or understand the principle of a steam engine. If a man was to take such a boy as I was and attempt to make a watchmaker of him, the boy might, after an apprenticeship of five or seven years, be able to take apart and put together a watch; but all through life he would be working uphill and seizing every excuse for leaving his work and idling away his time. Watch-making is repulsive to him.

Unless a man enters upon the vocation intended for him by nature, and best suited to his peculiar genius, he cannot succeed. I am glad to believe that the majority of persons do find the right vocation. Yet we see many who have mistaken their calling, from the blacksmith up (or down) to the clergyman. You will see, for instance, that extraordinary linguist the "learned blacksmith," who ought to have been a teacher of languages; and you may have seen lawyers, doctors, and clergymen who were better fitted by nature for the anvil or the lapstone.

SELECT THE RIGHT LOCATION. After securing the right vocation, you must be careful to select the proper location. You may have been cut out for a hotel keeper, and they say it requires a genius to "know how to keep a hotel." You might conduct a hotel like clock-work, and provide satisfactorily for five hundred guests every day; yet, if you should locate your house in a small village where there is no railroad communication or public travel, the location would be your ruin. It is equally important that you do not commence business where there are already enough to meet all demands in the same occupation. I remember a case which illustrates this subject. When I was in London in 1858, I was passing down Holborn with an English friend and came to the "penny shows." They had immense cartoons outside, portraying the wonderful curiosities to be seen "all for a penny." Being a little in the "show line" myself, I said, "Let us go in here." We soon found ourselves in the presence of the illustrious showman, and he proved to be the sharpest man in that line I had ever met. He told us some extraordinary stories in reference to his bearded ladies, his albinos, and his armadillos, which we could hardly believe, but thought it "better to believe it than look after the proof." He finally begged to call our attention to some wax statuary, and showed us a lot of the dirtiest and filthiest wax figures imaginable. They looked as if they had not seen water since the Deluge.

"What is there so wonderful about your statuary?" I asked.

"I beg you not to speak so satirically," he replied. "Sir, these are not Madam Tussaud's wax figures, all covered with gilt and tinsel and imitation diamonds, and copied from engravings and photographs. Mine, sir, were taken from life. Whenever you look upon one of those figures, you may consider that you are looking upon the living individual."

Glancing casually at them, I saw one labeled "Henry VIII" and feeling a little curious upon seeing that it looked like Calvin Edson, the living skeleton, I said:

"Do you call that 'Henry the Eighth'?"

He replied, "Certainly, sir; it was taken from life at Hampton Court by special order of His Majesty, on such a day."

He would have given the hour of the day if I had insisted. I said, "Everybody knows that Henry VIII was a great, stout old king, and that figure is lean and lank. What do you say to that?"

"Why," he replied, "you would be lean and lank yourself, if you sat there as long as he has."

There was no resisting such arguments. I said to my English friend, "Let us go out; do not tell him who I am; I show the white feather; he beats me."

He followed us to the door, and seeing the rabble in the street he called out, "Ladies and gentlemen, I beg to draw your attention to the respectable character of my visitors," pointing to us as we walked away. I called upon him a couple of days afterward; told him who I was, and said:

"My friend, you are an excellent showman, but you have selected a bad location."

He replied, "This is true, sir; I feel that all my talents are thrown away; but what can I do?"

"You can go to America," I replied. "You can give full play to your faculties over there; you will find plenty of elbow room in America; I will engage you for two years; after that you will be able to go on your own account."

He accepted my offer and remained two years in my New York Museum. He then went to New Orleans and carried on a traveling show business during the summer. To-day he is worth sixty thousand dollars, simply because he selected the right vocation and also secured the proper location. The old proverb says, "Three removes are as bad as a fire," but when a man is in the fire, it matters but little how soon or how often he removes.

AVOID DEBT. Young men starting in life should avoid running into debt. There is scarcely anything that drags a person down like debt. It is a slavish position to get in, yet we find many a young man hardly out of his "teens" running in debt. He meets a chum and says, "Look at this; I have got trusted for a new suit of clothes." He seems to look upon the clothes as so much given to him. Well, it frequently is so, but, if he succeeds in paying and then gets trusted again, he is adopting a habit which will keep him in poverty through life. Debt robs a man of his self-respect, and makes him almost despise himself. Grunting and groaning and working for what he has eaten up or worn out, and now when he is called upon to pay up, he has nothing to show for his money: this is properly termed "working for a dead horse." I do not speak of merchants buying and selling on credit, or of those who buy on credit in order to turn the purchase to a profit. The old Quaker said to his farmer son, "John, never get trusted; but if thee gets trusted for anything, let it be for manure, because that will help thee pay it back again."

Mr. Beecher advised young men to get in debt if they could to a small amount in the purchase of land in the country districts. "If a young man," he says, "will only get in debt for some land and then get married, these two things will keep him straight, or nothing will." This may be safe to a limited extent, but getting in debt for what you eat and drink and wear is to be avoided. Some families have a foolish habit of getting credit at the stores, and thus frequently purchase many things which might have been dispensed with.

It is all very well to say, "I have got trusted for sixty days, and if I don't have the money, the creditor will think nothing about it." There is no class of people in the world who have such good memories as creditors. When the sixty days run out, you will have to pay. If you do not pay, you will break your promise and probably resort to a falsehood. You may make some excuse or get in debt elsewhere to pay it, but that only involves you the deeper.

A good-looking, lazy young fellow, was the apprentice boy Horatio. His employer said, "Horatio, did you ever see a snail?" "I—think—I—have," he drawled out. "You must have met him then, for I am sure you never overtook one," said the "boss." Your creditor will meet you or overtake you and say, "Now, my young friend, you agreed to pay me; you have not done it, you must give me your note." You give the note on interest and it commences working against you; it is a "dead horse." The creditor goes to bed at night and wakes up in the morning better off than when he retired to bed because his interest has increased during the night, but you grow poorer while you are sleeping, for the interest is accumulating against you.

Money is in some respects like fire—it is a very excellent servant but a terrible master. When you have it mastering you, when interest is constantly piling up against you, it will keep you down in the worst kind of slavery. But let money work for you, and you have the most devoted servant in the world. It is no "eye-servant." There is nothing animate or inanimate that will work so faithfully as money when placed at interest, well secured. It works night and day, and in wet or dry weather.

I was born in the blue-law State of Connecticut, where the old Puritans had laws so rigid that it was said they fined a man for kissing his wife on Sunday. Yet these rich old Puritans would have thousands of dollars at interest, and on Saturday night would be worth a certain amount; on Sunday they would go to church and perform all the duties of a Christian. On waking up on Monday morning, they would find themselves considerably richer than the Saturday night previous, simply because their money placed at interest had worked faithfully for them all day Sunday, according to law!

Do not let it work against you; if you do, there is no chance for success in life so far as money is concerned. John Randolph, the eccentric Virginian, once exclaimed in Congress, "Mr. Speaker, I have discovered the philosopher's stone: pay as you go." This is indeed nearer to the philosopher's stone than any alchemist has ever yet arrived.

PERSEVERE. When a man is in the right path, he must persevere. I speak of this because there are some persons who are "born tired"; naturally lazy and possessing no self-reliance and no perseverance. But they can cultivate these qualities, as Davy Crockett said:

> "This thing remember, when I am dead,
> Be sure you are right, then go ahead."

It is this goaheaditiveness, this determination not to let the "horrors" or the "blues" take possession of you, so as to make you relax your energies in the struggle for independence, which you must cultivate.

How many have almost reached the goal of their ambition, but losing faith in themselves have relaxed their energies, and the golden prize has been lost forever.

It is, no doubt, often true, as Shakespeare says:

> "There is a tide in the affairs of men,
> Which, taken at the flood, leads on to fortune."

If you hesitate, some bolder hand will stretch out before you and get the prize. Remember the proverb of Solomon: "He becometh poor that dealeth with a slack hand: but the hand of the diligent maketh rich."

Perseverance is sometimes but another word for self-reliance. Many persons naturally look on the dark side of life, and borrow trouble. They are born so. Then they ask for advice, and they will be governed by one wind and blown by another, and cannot rely upon themselves. Until you get so that you can rely upon yourself, you need not expect to succeed. I have known men personally who have met with pecuniary reverses, and absolutely committed suicide, because they thought they could never overcome their misfortune. But I have known others who have met more serious financial difficulties, and have bridged them over by simple perseverance, aided by a firm belief that they were doing justly, and that Providence would "overcome evil with good." You will see this illustrated in any sphere of life.

Take two generals; both understand military tactics, both educated at West Point, if you please, both equally gifted; yet one, having this principle of perseverance, and the other lacking it, the former will succeed in his profession, while the latter will fail. One may hear the cry, "The enemy are coming, and they have got cannon!"

"Got cannon?" says the hesitating general.

"Yes."

"Then halt every man."

He wants time to reflect; his hesitation is his ruin. The enemy passes unmolested, or overwhelms him. The general of pluck, perseverance, and self-reliance goes into battle with a will, and amid the clash of arms, the booming of cannon, and the shrieks of the wounded and dying, you will see this man persevering, going on, cutting and slashing his way through with unwavering determination, and if you are near enough, you will hear him shout, "I will fight it out on this line if it takes all summer."

WHATEVER YOU DO, DO WITH ALL YOUR MIGHT. Work at it, if necessary, early and late, in season and out of season, not leaving a stone unturned, and never deferring for a single hour that which can be done just as well now. The old proverb is full of truth and meaning, "What-ever is worth doing at all, is worth doing well." Many a man acquires a fortune by doing his business thoroughly, while his neighbor remains poor for life because he only half does it. Ambition, energy, industry, perseverance, are indispensable requisites for success in business.

Fortune always favors the brave, and never helps a man who does not help himself. It won't do to spend your time like Mr. Micawber, in waiting for something to "turn up." To such men one of two things usually "turns up": the poor-house or the jail; for idleness breeds bad habits, and clothes a man in rags. The poor spendthrift vagabond said to a rich man:

"I have discovered there is money enough in the world for all of us, if it was equally divided; this must be done, and we shall all be happy together."

"But," was the response, "if everybody was like you, it would be spent in two months, and what would you do then?"

"Oh! divide again; keep dividing, of course!"

I was recently reading in a London paper an account of a like philosophic pauper who was kicked out of a cheap boarding-house because he could not pay his bill, but he had a roll of papers sticking out of his coat pocket, which, upon examination, proved to be his plan for paying off the national debt of England without the aid of a penny. People have got to do as Cromwell said: "not only trust in Providence, but keep the powder dry." Do your part of the work, or you cannot succeed. Mahomet, one night, while encamping in the desert, overheard one of his fatigued followers remark: "I will loose my camel, and trust it to God." "No, no, not so," said the prophet, "tie thy camel, and trust it to God!" Do all you can for yourselves, and then trust in Providence, or luck, or whatever you please to call it, for the rest.

DEPEND UPON YOUR OWN PERSONAL EXERTIONS. The eye of the employer is often worth more than the hands of a dozen employees. In the nature of things, an agent cannot be so faithful to his employer as to himself. Many who are employers will call to mind instances where the best employees have overlooked important points which could not have escaped their own observation as a proprietor. No man has a right to expect to succeed in life unless he understands his business, and nobody can understand his business thoroughly unless he learns it by personal application and experience. A man may be a manufacturer; he has got to learn the many details of his business personally; he will learn something every day, and he will find he will make mistakes nearly every day. And these very mistakes are helps to him in the way of experiences if he but heeds them. He will be like the Yankee tin-peddler, who, having been cheated as to quality in the purchase of his merchandise, said: "All right, there's a little information to be gained every day; I will never be cheated in that way again." Thus a man buys his experience, and it is the best kind if not purchased at too dear a rate.

I hold that every man should, like Cuvier, the French naturalist, thoroughly know his business. So proficient was he in the study of natural history, that you might bring to him the bone or even a section of a bone of an animal which he had never seen described, and reasoning from analogy, he would be able to draw a picture of the object from which the bone had been taken. On one occasion his students attempted to deceive him. They rolled one of their number in a cow skin and put him under the Professor's table as a new specimen. When the philosopher came into the room, some of the students asked him what animal it was. Suddenly the animal said, "I am the devil and I am going to eat you." It was but natural that Cuvier should desire to classify this creature, and examining intently, he said,

"Divided hoof; graminivorous; it cannot be done!"

He knew that an animal with a split hoof must live upon grass and grain, or other kind of vegetation, and would not be inclined to eat flesh, dead or alive, so he considered himself perfectly safe. The possession of a perfect knowledge of your business is an absolute necessity in order to insure success.

Among the maxims of the elder Rothschild was one, an apparent paradox: "Be cautious and bold." This seems to be a contradiction in terms, but it is not, and there is great wisdom in the maxim. It is, in fact, a condensed statement of what I have already said. It is to say, "You must exercise your caution in laying your plans, but be bold in carrying them out." A man who is all caution, will never dare to take hold and be successful; and a man who is all boldness, is merely reckless, and must eventually fail. A man may go on "change" and make fifty or one hundred thousand dollars in speculating in stocks, at a single operation. But if he has simple boldness without caution, it is mere chance, and what he gains to-day he will lose to-morrow. You must have both the caution and the boldness, to insure success.

The Rothschilds have another maxim: "Never have anything to do with an unlucky man or place." That is to say, never have anything to do with a man or place which never succeeds, because, although a man may appear to be honest and intelligent, yet if he tries this or that thing and always fails, it is on account of some fault or infirmity that you may not be able to discover, but nevertheless which must exist.

There is no such thing in the world as luck. There never was a man who could go out in the morning and find a purse of gold in the street to-day, and another to-morrow, and so on, day after day. He may do so once in his life; but so far as mere luck is concerned, he is as liable to lose it as to find it. "Like causes produce like effects." If a man adopts the proper methods to be successful, "luck" will not prevent him. If he does not succeed, there are reasons for it, although perhaps he may not be able to see them.

USE THE BEST TOOLS. Men in engaging employees should be careful to get the best. Understand, you cannot have too good tools to work with, and there is no tool you should be so particular about as living tools. If you get a good one, it is better to keep him, than keep changing. He learns something every day, and you are benefited by the experience he acquires. He is worth more to you this year than last, and he is the last man to part with, provided his habits are good and he continues faithful. If, as he gets more valuable, he demands an exorbitant increase of salary on the supposition that you can't do without him, let him go. Whenever I have such an employee, I always discharge him; first, to convince him that his place may be supplied, and second, because he is good for nothing if he thinks he is invaluable and cannot be spared.

But I would keep him, if possible, in order to profit from the result of his experience. An important element in an employee is the brain. You can see bills up, "Hands Wanted," but "hands" are not worth a great deal without "heads." Mr. Beecher illustrates this, in this wise:

An employee offers his services by saying, "I have a pair of hands and one of my fingers thinks." "That is very good," says the employer. Another man comes along, and says he has two fingers that think. "Ah! that is better." But a third calls in and says that all his fingers and thumbs think. That is better still. Finally another steps in, and says, "I have a brain that thinks; I think all over; I am a thinking as well as a working man!" "You are the man I want," says the delighted employer.

Those men who have brains and experience are therefore the most valuable and not to be readily parted with; it is better for them, as well as yourself, to keep them, at reasonable advances in their salaries from time to time.

DON'T GET ABOVE YOUR BUSINESS. Young men after they get through their business training, or apprenticeship, instead of pursuing their avocation and rising in their business, will often lie about doing nothing. They say, "I have learned my business, but I am not going to be a hireling; what is the object of learning my trade or profession, unless I establish myself?"

"Have you capital to start with?"

"No, but I am going to have it."

"How are you going to get it?"

"I will tell you confidentially; I have a wealthy old aunt, and she will die pretty soon; but if she does not, I expect to find some rich old man who will lend me a few thousands to give me a start. If I only get the money to start with, I will do well."

There is no greater mistake than when a young man believes he will succeed with borrowed money. Why? Because every man's experience coincides with that of Mr. Astor, who said it was more difficult for him to accumulate his first thousand dollars, than all the succeeding millions that made up his colossal fortune. Money is good for nothing unless you know the value of it by experience. Give a boy twenty thousand dollars and put him in business and the chances are that he will lose every dollar of it before he is a year older. Like buying a ticket in the lottery, and drawing a prize, it is "easy come, easy go." He does not know the value of it; nothing is worth anything, unless it costs effort. Without self-denial and economy, patience and perseverance, and commencing with capital which you have not earned, you are not sure to succeed in accumulating. Young men instead of "waiting for dead men's shoes" should be up and doing, for there is no class of persons who are so unaccommodating in regard to dying as these rich old people, and it is fortunate for the expectant heirs that it is so. Nine out of ten of the rich men of our country to-day, started out in life as poor boys, with determined wills, industry, perseverance, economy, and good habits. They went on gradually, made their own money and saved it; and this is the best way to acquire a fortune. Stephen Girard started life as a poor cabin boy, and died worth nine million dollars. A. T. Stewart was a poor Irish boy; now he pays taxes on a million and a half dollars of income per year. John Jacob Astor was a poor farmer boy, and died worth twenty millions. Cornelius Vanderbilt began life rowing a boat from Staten Island to New York; now he presents our government with a steamship worth a million of dollars, and he is worth fifty millions.

"There is no royal road to learning," says the proverb, and I may say it is equally true there is no royal road to wealth. But I think there is a royal road to both. The road to learning is a royal one; the road that enables the student to expand his intellect and add every day to his stock of knowledge, until, in the pleasant process of intellectual growth, he is able to solve the most profound problems, to count the stars, to analyze every atom of the globe, and to measure the firmament—this is a regal highway, and it is the only road worth traveling.

So in regard to wealth. Go on in confidence, study the rules, and above all things, study human nature; for "the proper study of mankind is man," and you will find that while expanding the intellect and the muscles, your enlarged experience will enable you every day to accumulate more and more principal, which will increase itself by interest and otherwise, until you arrive at a state of independence. You will find, as a general thing, that the poor boys get rich and the rich boys get poor. For instance, a rich man at his decease, leaves a large estate to his family. His eldest sons, who have helped him earn his fortune, know by experience the value of money, and they take their inheritance and add to it. The separate portions of the young children are placed at interest, and the little fellows are patted on the head, and told a dozen times a day, "You are rich; you will never have to work, you can always have whatever you wish, for you were born with a golden spoon in your mouth." The young heir soon finds out what that means; he has the finest dresses and playthings; he is crammed with sugar candies and almost "killed with kindness," and he passes from school to school, petted and flattered. He becomes arrogant and self-conceited, abuses his teachers, and carries everything with a high hand. He knows nothing of the real value of money, having never earned any; but he knows all about the "golden spoon" business. At college, he invites his poor fellow-students to his room where he "wines and dines" them. He is cajoled and caressed, and called a glorious good fellow, because he is so lavish of his money. He gives his game suppers, drives his fast horses, invites his chums to fetes and parties, determined to have lots of "good times." He spends the night in frolics and debauchery, and leads off his companions with the familiar song, "We won't go home till morning." He gets them to join him in pulling down signs, taking gates from their hinges and throwing them into back yards and horse-ponds. If the police arrest them, he knocks them down, is taken to the lock-up, and joyfully foots the bills.

"Ah! my boys," he cries, "what is the use of being rich, if you can't enjoy yourself?"

He might more truly say, "if you can't make a fool of yourself"; but he is "fast," hates slow things, and don't "see it." Young men loaded down with other people's money are almost sure to lose all they inherit, and they acquire all sorts of bad habits which, in the majority of cases, ruin them in health, purse, and character. In this country, one generation follows another, and the poor of to-day are rich in the next generation, or the third. Their experience leads them on, and they become rich, and they leave vast riches to their young children. These children, having been reared in luxury, are inexperienced and get poor; and after long experience another generation comes on and gathers up riches again in turn. And thus "history repeats itself," and happy is he who by listening to the experience of others avoids the rocks and shoals on which so many have been wrecked.

LEARN SOMETHING USEFUL. Every man should make his son or daughter learn some trade or profession, so that in these days of changing fortunes—of being rich to-day and poor to-morrow—they may have something tangible to fall back upon. This provision might save many persons from misery, who by some unexpected turn of fortune have lost all their means.

LET HOPE PREDOMINATE, BUT BE NOT TOO VISIONARY. Many persons are always kept poor, because they are too visionary. Every project looks to them like certain success, and therefore they keep changing from one business to another, always in hot water, always "under the harrow." The plan of "counting the chickens before they are hatched" is an error of ancient date, but it does not seem to improve by age.

DO NOT SCATTER YOUR POWERS. Engage in one kind of business only, and stick to it faithfully until you succeed, or until your experience shows that you should abandon it. A constant hammering on one nail will generally drive it home at last, so that it can be clinched. When a man's undivided attention is centered on one object, his mind will constantly be suggesting improvements of value, which would escape him if his brain was occupied by a dozen different subjects at once. Many a fortune has slipped through a man's fingers because he was engaging in too many occupations at a time. There is good sense in the old caution against having too many irons in the fire at once.

BE SYSTEMATIC. Men should be systematic in their business. A person who does business by rule, having a time and place for everything, doing his work promptly, will accomplish twice as much and with half the trouble of him who does it carelessly and slipshod. By introducing system into all your transactions, doing one thing at a time, always meeting appointments with punctuality, you find leisure for pastime and recreation; whereas the man who only half does one thing, and then turns to something else and half does that, will have his business at loose ends, and will never know when his day's work is done, for it never will be done. Of course there is a limit to all these rules. We must try to preserve the happy medium, for there is such a thing as being too systematic. There are men and women, for instance, who put away things so carefully that they can never find them again. It is too much like the "red tape" formality at Washington, and Mr. Dickens' "Circumlocution Office"—all theory and no result.

When the Astor House was first started in New York City, it was undoubtedly the best hotel in the country. The proprietors had learned a good deal in Europe regarding hotels, and the landlords were proud of the rigid system which pervaded every department of their great establishment. When twelve o'clock at night had arrived and there were a number of guests around, one of the proprietors would say, "Touch that bell, John"; and in two minutes sixty servants with a water bucket in each hand, would present themselves in the hall. "This," said the landlord, addressing his guests, "is our fire bell; it will show you we are quite safe here; we do everything systematically." This was before the Croton water was introduced into the city. But they sometimes carried their system too far. On one occasion when the hotel was thronged with guests, one of the waiters was suddenly indisposed, and although there were fifty waiters in the hotel, the landlord thought he must have his full complement, or his "system" would be interfered with. Just before dinner time he rushed down stairs and said, "There must be another waiter, I am one waiter short, what can I do?" He happened to see "Boots" the Irishman. "Pat," said he, "wash your hands and face; take that white apron and come into the dining-room in five minutes." Presently Pat appeared as required, and the proprietor's: "Now, Pat, you must stand behind these two chairs and wait on the gentlemen who will occupy them; did you ever act as a waiter?"

"I know all about it sure, but I never did it."

Like the Irish pilot, on one occasion when the captain, thinking he was considerably out of his course, asked, "Are you certain you understand what you are doing?"

Pat replied, "Sure and I knows every rock in the channel."

That moment "bang" thumped the vessel against a rock.

"Ah! be jabers, and that is one of 'em," continued the pilot. But to return to the dining-room. "Pat," said the landlord, "here we do everything systematically. You must first give the gentlemen each a plate of soup, and when they finish that, ask them what they will have next."

Pat replied, "Ah! an' I understand parfectly the vartues of shystem."

Very soon in came the guests. The plates of soup were placed before them. One of Pat's two gentlemen ate his soup, the other did not care for it. He said, "Waiter, take this plate away and bring me some fish." Pat looked at the untasted plate of soup, and remembering the injunctions of the landlord in regard to "system," replied:

"Not till ye have ate yer supe!"

Of course that was carrying "system" entirely too far.

READ THE NEWSPAPERS. Always take a trustworthy newspaper and thus keep thoroughly posted in regard to the transactions of the world. He who is without a newspaper is cut off from his species. In these days of telegraphs and steam, many important inventions and improvements in every branch of trade are being made, and he who don't consult the newspapers will soon find himself and his business left out in the cold.

BEWARE OF "OUTSIDE OPERATIONS." We sometimes see men who have obtained fortunes, suddenly become poor. In many cases this arises from intemperance, and often from gaming and other bad habits. Frequently it occurs because a man has been engaged in "outside operations" of some sort. When he gets rich in his legitimate business, he is told of a grand speculation where he can make a score of thousands. He is constantly flattered by his friends, who tell him that he is born lucky, that everything he touches turns into gold. Now if he forgets that his economical habits, his rectitude of conduct, and a personal attention to a business which he understood, caused his success in life, he will listen to the syren voices. He says:

"I will put in twenty thousand dollars. I have been lucky, and my good luck will soon bring me back sixty thousand dollars."

A few days elapse and it is discovered he must put in ten thousand dollars more; soon after he is told it is all right, but certain matters not foreseen require an advance of twenty thousand dollars more, which will bring him a rich harvest; but before the time comes around to realize, the bubble bursts, he loses all he is possessed of, and then he learns what he ought to have known at the first, that however successful a man may be in his own business, if he turns from that and engages in a business which he don't understand he is like Samson when shorn of his locks—his strength has departed, and he becomes like other men.

If a man has plenty of money, he ought to invest something in everything that appears to promise success and that will probably benefit mankind; but let the sums thus invested be moderate in amount, and never let a man foolishly jeopardize a fortune that he has earned in a legitimate way, by investing it in things in which he has had no experience.

DON'T INDORSE WITHOUT SECURITY. I hold that no man ought ever to indorse a note or become security for any man, be it his father or brother, to a greater extent than he can afford to lose and care nothing about, without taking good security. Here is a man that is worth twenty thousand dollars; he is doing a thriving manufacturing or mercantile trade; you are retired and living on your money; he comes to you and says:

"You are aware that I am worth twenty thousand dollars, and don't owe a dollar. If I had five thousand dollars in cash, I could purchase a particular lot of goods and double my money in a couple of months. Will you indorse my note for that amount?"

You reflect that he is worth twenty thousand dollars, and you incur no risk by indorsing his note; you like to accommodate him, and you lend your name without taking the precaution of getting security. Shortly after, he shows you the note with your indorsement canceled, and tells you, probably truly, that he made the profit that he expected by the operation. You reflect that you have done a good action, and the thought makes you feel happy. By and by, the same thing occurs again, and you do it again; you have already fixed the impression in your mind that it is perfectly safe to indorse his notes without security.

But the trouble is, this man is getting money too easily. He has only to take your note to the bank, get it discounted and take the cash. He gets money for the time being without effort; without inconvenience to himself. Now mark the result. He sees a chance for speculation outside of his business. A temporary investment of only $10,000 is required. It is sure to come back before a note at the bank would be due. He places a note for that amount before you. You sign it almost mechanically. Being firmly convinced that your friend is responsible and trustworthy, you indorse his notes as "a matter of course."

Unfortunately the speculation does not come to a head quite so soon as was expected, and another $10,000 note must be discounted to take up the last one when due. Before this note matures the speculation proved an utter failure and all the money is lost. Does the loser tell his friend, the indorser, that he has lost half of his fortune? Not at all. He don't even mention that he has speculated at all. But he has got excited; the spirit of speculation has seized him; he sees others making large sums in this way (we seldom hear of the losers), and like other speculators, he "looks for his money where he loses it." He tries again. Indorsing his notes has become chronic with you, and at every loss he gets your signature for whatever amount he wants. Finally you discover your friend has lost all of his property and all of yours. You are overwhelmed with astonishment and grief, and you say, "It is a hard thing, my friend here has ruined me," but, you should add, "I have also ruined him." If you had said in the first place, "I will accommodate you, but I never indorse without taking ample security," he could not have gone beyond the length of his tether and he would never have been tempted away from his legitimate business. It is a very dangerous thing, therefore, at any time to let people get possession of money too easily; it tempts them to hazardous speculations, if nothing more. Solomon truly said: "He that hated suretiship is sure."

So with the young man starting in business; let him understand the value of money by earning it. When he does understand its value, then grease the wheels a little in helping him to start business, but remember men who get money with too great facility cannot usually succeed. You must get the first dollars by hard knocks, and at some sacrifice, in order to appreciate the value of those dollars.

ADVERTISE YOUR BUSINESS. We all depend, more or less, upon the public for our support. We all trade with the public—lawyers, doctors, shoemakers, artists, blacksmiths, showmen, opera singers, railroad presidents, and college professors. Those who deal with the public must be careful that their goods are valuable; that they are genuine, and will give satisfaction. When you get an article which you know is going to please your customers, and that when they have tried it, they will feel they have got their money's worth, then let the fact be known that you have got it. Be careful to advertise it in some shape or other, because it is evident that if a man has ever so good an article for sale, and nobody knows it, it will bring him no return. In a country like this, where nearly everybody reads, and where newspapers are issued and circulated in editions of five thousand to two hundred thousand, it would be very unwise if this channel was not taken advantage of to reach the public in advertising. A newspaper goes into the family and is read by wife and children, as well as the head of the house; hence hundreds and thousands of people may read your advertisement, while you are attending to your routine business. Many, perhaps, read it while you are asleep. The whole philosophy of life is, first "sow," then "reap." That is the way the farmer does; he plants his potatoes and corn, and sows his grain, and then goes about something else, and the time comes when he reaps. But he never reaps first and sows afterwards. This principle applies to all kinds of business, and to nothing more eminently than to advertising. If a man has a genuine article, there is no way in which he can reap more advantageously than by "sowing" to the public in this way. He must, of course, have a really good article, and one which will please his customers; anything spurious will not succeed permanently, because the public is wiser than many imagine. Men and women are selfish, and we all prefer purchasing where we can get the most for our money; and we try to find out where we can most surely do so.

You may advertise a spurious article, and induce many people to call and buy it once, but they will denounce you as an impostor and swindler, and your business will gradually die out, and leave you poor. This is right. Few people can safely depend upon chance custom. You all need to have your customers return and purchase again. A man said to me, "I have tried advertising, and did not succeed; yet I have a good article."

I replied, "My friend, there may be exceptions to a general rule. But how do you advertise?"

"I put it in a weekly newspaper three times, and paid a dollar and a half for it."

I replied: "Sir, advertising is like learning—a little is a dangerous thing."

A French writer says that "The reader of a newspaper does not see the first insertion of an ordinary advertisement; the second insertion he sees, but does not read; the third insertion he reads; the fourth insertion he looks at the price; the fifth insertion he speaks of it to his wife; the sixth insertion he is ready to purchase, and the seventh insertion he purchases." Your object in advertising is to make the public understand what you have got to sell, and if you have not the pluck to keep advertising until you have imparted that information, all the money you have spent is lost. You are like the fellow who told the gentleman if he would give him ten cents it would save him a dollar. "How can I help you so much with so small a sum?" asked the gentleman in surprise. "I started out this morning," hiccuped the fellow, "with the full determination to get drunk, and I have spent my only dollar to accomplish the object, and it has not quite done it. Ten cents' worth more of whiskey would just do it, and in this manner I should save the dollar already expended."

So a man who advertises at all must keep it up until the public know who and what he is, and what his business is, or else the money invested in advertising is lost.

Some men have a peculiar genius for writing a striking advertisement, one that will arrest the attention of the reader at first sight. This tact, of course, gives the advertiser a great advantage. Sometimes a man makes himself popular by a unique sign or a curious display in his window. Recently I observed a swing sign extending over the sidewalk in front of a store, on which was the inscription, in plain letters,

"DON'T READ THE OTHER SIDE."

Of course I did, and so did everybody else, and I learned that the man had made an independence by first attracting the public to his business in that way and then using his customers well afterwards.

Genin, the hatter, bought the first Jenny Lind ticket at auction for two hundred and twenty-five dollars, because he knew it would be a good advertisement for him. "Who is the bidder?" said the auctioneer, as he knocked down that ticket at Castle Garden. "Genin, the hatter," was the response. Here were thousands of people from the Fifth Avenue, and from distant cities in the highest stations of life. "Who is Genin, the hatter?" they exclaimed. They had never heard of him before. The next morning the newspapers and telegraph had circulated the facts from Maine to Texas, and from five to ten millions of people had read that the tickets sold at auction for Jenny Lind's first concert amounted to about twenty thousand dollars, and that a single ticket was sold at two hundred and twenty-five dollars, to "Genin, the hatter." Men throughout the country involuntarily took off their hats to see if they had a "Genin" hat on their heads. At a town in Iowa it was found that in the crowd around the Post Office, there was one man who had a "Genin" hat, and he showed it in triumph, although it was worn out and not worth two cents. "Why," one man exclaimed, "you have a real 'Genin' hat. What a lucky fellow you are!" Another man said, "Hang on to that hat, it will be a valuable heirloom in your family." Still another man in the crowd, who seemed to envy the possessor of this good fortune, said, "Come, give us all a chance; put it up at auction!" He did so, and it was sold as a keepsake for nine dollars and fifty cents! What was the consequence to Mr. Genin? He sold ten thousand extra hats per annum, the first six years. Nine-tenths of the purchasers bought of him, probably, out of curiosity, and many of them, finding that he gave them an equivalent for their money, became his regular customers. This novel advertisement first struck their attention, and then, as he made a good article, they came again.

Now, I don't say that everybody should advertise as Mr. Genin did. But I say if a man has got goods for sale, and he don't advertise them in some way, the chances are that some day the sheriff will do it for him. Nor do I say that everybody must advertise in a newspaper, or indeed use "printers' ink" at all. On the contrary, although that article is indispensable in the majority of cases, yet doctors and clergymen, and sometimes lawyers and some others can more effectually reach the public in some other manner. But it is obvious, they must be known in some way, else how could they be supported?

BE POLITE AND KIND TO YOUR CUSTOMERS. Politeness and civility are the best capital ever invested in business. Large stores, gilt signs, flaming advertisements, will all prove unavailing if you or your employees treat your patrons abruptly. The truth is, the more kind and liberal a man is, the more generous will be the patronage bestowed upon him. "Like begets like." The man who gives the greatest amount of goods of a corresponding quality for the least sum (still reserving to himself a profit) will generally succeed best in the long run. This brings us to the golden rule, "As ye would that men should do to you, do ye also to them," and they will do better by you than if you always treated them as if you wanted to get the most you could out of them for the least return. Men who drive sharp bargains with their customers, acting as if they never expected to see them again, will not be mistaken. They never will see them again as customers. People don't like to pay and get kicked also.

One of the ushers in my Museum once told me he intended to whip a man who was in the lecture room as soon as he came out.

"What for?" I inquired.

"Because he said I was no gentleman," replied the usher.

"Never mind," I replied, "he pays for that, and you will not convince him you are a gentleman by whipping him. I cannot afford to lose a customer. If you whip him, he will never visit the Museum again, and he will induce friends to go with him to other places of amusement instead of this, and thus, you see, I should be a serious loser."

"But he insulted me," muttered the usher.

"Exactly," I replied, "and if he owned the Museum, and you had paid him for the privilege of visiting it, and he had then insulted you, there might be some reason in your resenting it, but in this instance he is the man who pays, while we receive, and you must, therefore, put up with his bad manners."

My usher laughingly remarked, that this was undoubtedly the true policy, but he added that he should not object to an increase of salary if he was expected to be abused in order to promote my interests.

BE CHARITABLE. Of course men should be charitable, because it is a duty and a pleasure. But even as a matter of policy, if you possess no higher incentive, you will find that the liberal man will command patronage, while the sordid, uncharitable miser will be avoided.

Solomon says: "There is that scattereth, and yet increaseth; and there is that withholdeth more than is meet, but it tendeth to poverty." Of course the only true charity is that which is from the heart.

The best kind of charity is to help those who are willing to help themselves. Promiscuous almsgiving, without inquiring into the worthiness of the applicant, is bad in every sense. But to search out and quietly assist those who are struggling for themselves, is the kind that "scattereth and yet increaseth." But don't fall into the idea that some persons practice, of giving a prayer instead of a potato, and a benediction instead of bread, to the hungry. It is easier to make Christians with full stomachs than empty.

DON'T BLAB. Some men have a foolish habit of telling their business secrets. If they make money they like to tell their neighbors how it was done. Nothing is gained by this, and ofttimes much is lost. Say nothing about your profits, your hopes, your expectations, your intentions. And this should apply to letters as well as to conversation. Goethe makes Mephistopheles say: "Never write a letter nor destroy one." Business men must write letters, but they should be careful what they put in them. If you are losing money, be specially cautious and not tell of it, or you will lose your reputation.

PRESERVE YOUR INTEGRITY. It is more precious than diamonds or rubies. The old miser said to his sons: "Get money; get it honestly, if you can, but get money." This advice was not only atrociously wicked, but it was the very essence of stupidity. It was as much as to say, "If you find it difficult to obtain money honestly, you can easily get it dishonestly. Get it in that way." Poor fool, not to know that the most difficult thing in life is to make money dishonestly; not to know that our prisons are full of men who attempted to follow this advice; not to understand that no man can be dishonest without soon being found out, and that when his lack of principle is discovered, nearly every avenue to success is closed against him forever. The public very properly shun all whose integrity is doubted. No matter how polite and pleasant and accommodating a man may be, none of us dare to deal with him if we suspect "false weights and measures." Strict honesty not only lies at the foundation of all success in life financially, but in every other respect. Uncompromising integrity of character is invaluable. It secures to its possessor a peace and joy which cannot be attained without it—which no amount of money, or houses and lands can purchase. A man who is known to be strictly honest, may be ever so poor, but he has the purses of all the community at his disposal;—for all know that if he promises to return what he borrows, he will never disappoint them. As a mere matter of selfishness, therefore, if a man had no higher motive for being honest, all will find that the maxim of Dr. Franklin can never fail to be true, that "honesty is the best policy."

To get rich, is not always equivalent to being successful. "There are many rich poor men," while there are many others, honest and devout men and women, who have never possessed so much money as some rich persons squander in a week, but who are nevertheless really richer and happier than any man can ever be while he is a transgressor of the higher laws of his being.

The inordinate love of money, no doubt, may be and is "the root of all evil," but money itself, when properly used, is not only a "handy thing to have in the house," but affords the gratification of blessing our race by enabling its possessor to enlarge the scope of human happiness and human influence. The desire for wealth is nearly universal, and none can say it is not laudable, provided the possessor of it accepts its responsibilities, and uses it as a friend to humanity. The history of Money Getting, which is commerce, is a history of civilization, and wherever trade has flourished most, there, too, have art and science produced the noblest fruits. In fact, as a general thing, money-getters are the benefactors of our race. To them, in a great measure, are we indebted for our institutions of learning and of art, our academies, colleges, and churches. It is no argument against the desire for, or the possession of wealth, to say that there are sometimes misers who hoard money only for the sake of hoarding, and who have no higher aspiration than to grasp everything which comes within their reach. As we have sometimes hypocrites in religion, and demagogues in politics, so there are occasionally misers among money-getters. These, however, are only exceptions to the general rule. But when, in this country, we find such a nuisance and stumbling block as a miser, we remember with gratitude that in America we have no laws of primogeniture, and that in the due course of nature the time will come when the hoarded dust will be scattered for the benefit of mankind. To all men and women, therefore, do I conscientiously say, make money honestly, and not otherwise, for Shakespeare has truly said, "He that wants money, means, and content, is without three good friends."

—P.T. Barnum, 1869

16 | How to Barnumize Your Business

Should this be, as perhaps it may, my last communication to you, I wish to assure you of my unalterable esteem, affection, and trust in you, and to bestow a fatherly blessing upon one who is in every way so worthy to become my successor.

—P.T. Barnum, 1891, five days before he died

By the 1850s Barnum's fame was so great that any innovation in marketing was called a "Barnumism" and any well-promoted business was considered "Barnumized." Now that you've discovered Barnum's 10 rings of power for creating an empire, read an interview with Barnum, and studied his famous speech on money getting, you are ready to Barnumize your own business.

The following quick-start set of guidelines will help you brainstorm a marketing strategy that will get results. However, don't limit yourself to these steps. Use them to help you create your own map for Barnumizing your business. As you know by now, Barnum didn't limit himself to what had been done before. He created new, wild, imaginative ways to increase his business. You can, too. Here's how.

217

A Fresh Look at Barnum's Rings of Power

1. *Remember there's a customer born every minute.* And go after them. Ask yourself, "Where are my prospects, and who can I work with to turn more of them into customers?" Although many business gurus advise targeting your market, Barnum targeted the world. Decide who could benefit from your product or service and conceive of every way possible to reach this audience. Bear in mind that your audience changes every day: Some customers die, new ones are born, past customers develop new interests and needs, and still others will develop an interest in your product. You cannot stop marketing to your prospects because your world of prospects changes daily. They are a moving parade. And remember that you don't have to go after this market by yourself. You can create a successful cross-promotion campaign with another business by asking yourself three questions:

1. Who are my potential customers?
2. Who else wants to reach these same people?
3. How can we reach our potential customers more effectively?

2. *Fire off skyrockets.* What are you going to do to get attention in today's competitive marketplace? Be audacious. Often there isn't much difference between you and your competition. To stand out in the crowd, do something different. Hold an event. Sponsor a contest. Create the world's largest hot dog. Have a parade. Add some zing to your business. When doctors wanted to give shots to children, they created a campaign that made kids line up, smiling, eager to get poked with needles. Every child got to wear a badge that said "I was shot!" The media coverage was staggering.

When John Martin of Bold Creative Services wanted to get more printing business, he tied his service to the phone company's plan to give many businesses new area codes. Martin invented a Club 281 for business people in the new 281 area code. He explained that everyone in the new area code exchange would need new printing. As a result, he received newspaper, radio, and television coverage. All he did was dress up his service, add a little excitement to it, and tie it to the current news.

Keep in mind that getting attention may mean thinking of preposterous ideas—and actually doing them. Consider Houdini hanging from a building, wrapped in a straitjacket, squirming free of it before thousands of people—all to promote his performances. Consider Barnum looking for the world's smallest man or the world's biggest elephant, and then courageously displaying these curiosities to the world.

3. *Toot your own horn.* What can you do right now to give the media news while promoting your business? You won't get publicity if you don't tell the media. Barnum went out of his way to befriend editors and hire reporters. More than anything else, he knew the value of publicity. In the aforementioned examples, neither those doctors nor Martin would have gotten any media coverage if they had not informed the media. About 80 percent of what you see in the papers is planted by business people like yourself. Reach out and inform someone in power of what you are doing. It could easily put your business on the map.

A few days after the start of 1997, CNN broadcasted a story on British tycoon Richard Branson, head of Virgin Atlantic Airways. He was news because he was attempting to be the first person to fly around the world in a hot-air balloon. The media showed him at his launching pad with his balloon. What was plastered all over the balloon? Signs promoting his business. A Reuters news story said, "The balloon flight is the latest in a series of record-breaking attempts that have indulged Branson's taste for adventure while earning publicity for his businesses." How did the media know what he was planning to do? He told them, of course. That's Barnumizing a business.

4. *Advertise relentlessly.* Where can you advertise your business to reach the largest possible customer base, and what ads can you create to get their attention? When Jim "Mattress Mac" MacInvale came to Texas, he barely had enough money to feed his family, but he invested his funds into advertising. As a result, he is a millionaire, and his company gets visited by people every day.

I once wrote an ad for a company that was so successful they made a quarter of a million dollars in less than three months. Not bad for a startup business selling software. Good, persistent advertising can make you rich.

When Barnum took over the Scudder Museum, he invested virtually all the incoming money into advertising. Within two years, he was out of debt and his museum was famous (and so was Barnum).

5. *Throw a party!* How can you make your business more fun, something your customers will feel so good about that they tell all of their friends? Barnum transformed the circus from a sleazy but interesting place for amusement into a mesmerizing house of educational entertainment. He transformed the dime museums of his day into cultural art centers commanding great respect. Ask yourself, "How can I better serve our customers?" It may seem ridiculous to have to remind business people that good service will keep your customers happy and that happy customers will return again and again to your business, but you and I experience lousy service every day. Don't let it happen in your business. Keep your employees (and yourself) happy. Hire good people and keep them. Barnum employed hundreds of people, treated them with respect and paid them well. They in turn remained loyal to him, helping him create his own empire and running to his rescue when he went bankrupt.

6. *Utilize the power of the pen.* How can you begin writing your own ticket to success? Conceive materials to promote your product or service. Think of all the business people who have written or paid someone to write books. Consider how Barnum wrote letters to the editors, articles for the press, his own autobiography, biographical material on Tom Thumb and Jenny Lind (and even Jumbo). Find ways to use the power of the pen in your own business. Write a newsletter. Send out sales letters. Writing lives forever, while you may not. Barnum said a man's autobiography was the greatest gift. You may not be a Barnum, but you are bound to have a unique message, experiences, or insights to share. Put them in writing.

7. *Plug into your network.* Ask yourself, "Who do I know who can help me achieve my dreams?" Barnum was able to meet royalty because he obtained letters of introduction from people he already knew. Donna Fisher, author of *People Power*, says we are less than three people away from anyone we want to meet. Use your circle of contacts to meet new people to help you achieve your goals. Simply ask your friends, "Who do you know who can help me (fill in the blank)?" You will be amazed at how resourceful your network can be—if you only ask for their help. I've helped clients obtain testimonials from celebrities and legends. How? By asking the people we already know who *they* know who could help us. And with the arrival of the Internet, you can be in touch with virtually anyone else with simple e-mail. Barnum would have loved it.

8. *Negotiate fairly.* How can you make better deals with your employees, vendors, or customers, arrangements that respect them while helping you? Give people what they want and they will give you what you want. Barnum was a fair but shrewd negotiator. When he wanted to buy something, he made large offers based on what he felt he could earn back. When Ulysses S. Grant went bankrupt in 1884, Barnum offered to help by giving Grant $100,000 in cash, plus a percentage of profits, to display his war trophies. Though Grant had already sold his possessions (and died a few months later), Barnum's offer was fair and respectful. When Jenny Lind grew tired of singing in America and wanted out of her contract, Barnum let it end without a whimper. He had made a great deal of money and respected Lind's desires. Negotiate fairly and people—your customers as well as your employees—will remain happy. Lind remained friends with Barnum throughout her life.

9. *Speak and grow rich.* How can you begin speaking about your product or service? Start giving talks to breakfast, lunch, and dinner business meetings. Offer yourself to a speaking bureau. Create a speech based on real benefits to people and begin delivering it. You don't have to talk about your business, but it should be an aspect of your business. If you are a manufacturer of textile products, you might create an interesting talk titled 10 Surprising Facts About Textiles. The more you speak, the more you gain credibility and publicity for you and your business. It made Barnum famous. And Mark Twain. And business guru Tom Peters. And me. It can work for you, as well.

10. *Relax.* Where is your faith? Find your own creed. Discover how to live at a no-stress level of being, where business setbacks and challenges don't stop you. Barnum found his inner strength in his religion. You may find it there, or in support from family and friends, or by reading good books that remind you that faith moves mountains. You might also begin to use the experiences of your life to learn more about yourself. When you get angry, explore what pushed your button so you can disconnect that switch. At that point, business becomes a path of self-discovery. Although Barnum did not tend to deeply explore himself, he admitted many of his setbacks made him more aware of his personality, his shortcomings, and his gifts. Find faith and you can weather any storm while trucking forward to create the empire you desire.

You're Not Barnum?

"But I'm still not sure how to create Barnum-like ideas for my business," one of the early readers of this book told me.

"I'm not Barnum," he continued, sounding frustrated. "He was a creative genius. I'm just an executive trying to show a profit. How do I start seeing the marketing opportunities in my business—the big ones that my mind keeps missing?"

"Well, you can always hire me to train you in my Project Phineas marketing program," I said with a smile.

"Maybe so, but I want answers *right now*. I can read and marvel at Barnum's exploits, but how do I start to *think* like Barnum?"

My friend's comments bothered me. I suddenly realized that many people were going to read this book, find it entertaining and educational, but then not do anything because they didn't know exactly what to do. They may be so accustomed to their own mindset and way of doing things that trying to implement Barnum's rings of power in their business might seem unimaginable. This troubled me for several weeks.

Finally I decided to get help.

Wear the Head of Barnum!

Early one Monday morning I called Dr. Win Wenger, a man who teaches executives leading-edge techniques on how to increase their IQ, think like visionaries, and act like creative wizards. Wenger has written several books, including *The Einstein Factor* with Richard Poe, *Discovering the Obvious*, and *Beyond Teaching and Learning*. I knew he could help me. I got him on the line, told him my situation, and he immediately offered the following advice:

"I'd teach your readers how to Image Stream," he began. "Then I'd tell them how to put on the head of P.T. Barnum."

As strange as those suggestions may sound to you, keep in mind that Wenger has helped average people easily increase their IQs by 20 points after only 25 hours of using his methods; taught business people how to quickly generate hundreds of ideas, solutions, and inventions; and his methods are used by numerous schools, companies, and countries around the world. His techniques get results.

Beware of Cannibals Who Attack You

Image Streaming remains Wenger's cornerstone technique. It is his basic process for learning to be more creative by tapping into more of your brain.

"We each have huge masses of information, experience, data, understanding, and overall intelligence in every sense of the word," Wenger explains, "located throughout our brain but not directly linked into immediate verbal consciousness."

Wenger's Image Streaming process helps you tap into your stored intelligence and then verbalize it. He illustrates his theory by talking about Elias Howe, inventor of the sewing machine and a contemporary of P.T. Barnum:

> Imagine the astonishment and excitement Elias Howe must have felt as he emerged from the sweaty, breathless, dry-mouthed terrors of his nightmare, when he realized that those odd holes in the spearheads of the attacking cannibals in his nightmare were the key solution for the sewing machine he had been trying for so long to invent.

In his *Techniques of Original, Inspired Scientific Discovery*, Wenger writes, "Encephalographic (EEG) studies show that 80 percent of the area of the brain is involved with visual responses." He adds, ". . . less than 5 percent of the volume of the brain and less than 1 percent of the cells of the brain are involved in conscious experience—the rest is 'unconscious.'"

Consequently, you need a technique that relies on the visual and taps into the unconscious. That's why Wenger created Image Streaming. It is a proven tool to unlock your *entire* brain's potential.

How to Image Stream

First, ask yourself a question. It can be about Barnum, marketing, your business, or anything else on your mind. You name it.

Second, set aside 20 minutes where you do nothing but describe aloud the images you see in your mind. Wenger says you must describe the pictures you see, no matter what they are, in vivid detail, and out loud.

"By speaking audibly, you create a feedback loop to your brain," he says.

In short, words come out of your brain through your mouth and go back into your brain through your ears. This helps awaken more of your mental powers.

You don't need to know how this process operates for it to work. The images you see are coming from your subconscious mind and may not make any logical sense at first. That's fine. Don't try to control or direct what you see. Let the images stream out. As they do, describe them out loud.

Finally, determine how the images you see answer your question. In other words, assume the images are your answers. What are they trying to tell you?

During this process, the images may suddenly blossom into an obvious answer to your question. If so, great. Usually what happens, however, is that the images will make sense to you a day or so later. Whatever the case, jot down your insights or discuss them with a friend to help make them more concrete and to further your understanding of this process.

The Borrowed Genius Procedure

Wenger's other suggestion is for you to "put on the head of P.T. Barnum."

This is a powerful imagery exercise—very much like the one I described with Melissa Etheridge in Chapter 14—where you role-play what it might be like to actually *be* Barnum.

"Just create a genius to model in the same sense that tribesmen of the Bear Clan wore the heads of bears to better understand the wilderness where they had to survive," explains Wenger.

Because you now know Barnum's rings of power and have read his famous speech, your brain has collected more information on Barnum and his techniques than you might ever realize. As you were reading, skimming, and thinking about the ideas in this book, your brain stayed busy. You know more about Barnumizing your business than you may consciously grasp or admit. Using Wenger's Borrowed Genius technique will help you bring Barnum-like ideas into your life. Here's how the process works:

1. Decide what skills you want to acquire from Barnum (or any other genius you can imagine).
2. Breathe slowly . . . relax . . . and visualize yourself in a beautiful garden.
3. Describe—out loud—what you see in the garden. Let the images lead you.
4. Now see Barnum (or the genius you selected) come to you. Start describing this genius in rich sensory detail, and out loud.

5. At this point you are ready to become the genius. Just imagine lifting the head off Barnum's body and sliding it over your own head. Pretend this experience is like fitting a helmet or mask over your own head, and align the eyes, ear, and mouth so Barnum's head fits right over your own.

6. Now look out through Barnum's eyes, and describe whatever you see. If you are still in the garden, describe it. If you are somewhere else (because the images are allowed to change), describe this new place. Again, as with the image-stream process, let the images come and go and simply continue describing aloud whatever you see.

7. Now turn your thoughts to your business. Let Barnum look at your business. Describe what you see through his eyes. Do this for several minutes . . .

8. Let your mind drift to the defining moment in Barnum's life when he became a business genius with his own empire. Let your mind take you to whatever moment that may have been. (There is no one right answer.) Imagine what that must have been like for him. See it through his eyes. Describe it out loud.

9. You are now ready to separate from Barnum. Imagine a full length mirror in front of you. As you look through Barnum's eyes, you see his reflection in the mirror. Now let the mirror vanish. As it does, you are again separate from Barnum. He is standing before you, smiling.

10. Before you open your eyes and end this exercise, let Barnum tell you something important about your business. There is something he wants you to know. What is it? Allow yourself to be surprised by Barnum's advice.

When you have completed this process, immediately jot down your ideas, insights and reflections, or call a friend and discuss what occurred. You may be astonished by how you now perceive your business.

"The geniuses you encounter in the above exercise are, of course, nothing more than dissociated elements of your own mind," Wenger writes in *The Einstein Factor*. "Their mighty talents and subtle perceptions exist within you."

Barnum Tells Mark Twain His Key Secret

What was Barnum's key secret to success in business?

Barnum summed it up when he wrote Mark Twain in 1878, saying:

> I think it is conceded that I generally do pretty *big* things as a manager, am audacious in my outlays and risks, give *much* for *little* money, and make my shows worthy the support of the moral and refined classes.

For that reason, don't limit yourself to the rings of power you've learned here. Barnum would not. Were he alive today, he would continue to do "pretty *big* things," take audacious risks, give enormous value for a fair price, and make his offerings attractive to all people.

He would also be looking toward the future. He saw the railroad span the states and was one of the first to put his shows on the rails. He was one of the pioneers in using the telephone, telegraph, and electric lights. Edison recorded Barnum's clear New England–New York sounding voice on an early recording device. Matthew Brady took photographs of the famous showman. Barnum kept up with the times while looking ahead.

Barnum would be excitedly exploring new technology today, new opportunities, building a bigger and better business, looking for new products and services, and experimenting with new ways to get attention for his enterprises. He would be showing his zest for life by persistently looking for new ways to delight his customers: people everywhere. He knew "There's a customer born every minute."

Face it. Just as Barnum lived in the middle of explosive growth in the 1800s, we now live in a very similar situation with very similar opportunities. No one knows where our expanding technology will take

us. The Internet, new inventions, new ways of doing business, new products and services—the changes happen at speeds that can make us dizzy. As
we move into this new century, we stand at the biggest window of opportunity ever seen in history. The world and the wealth in it sits waiting for
the next P.T. Barnum. That person could very well be *you*.

Maybe the real question to ask yourself in your business is, "What
would Barnum do today?"

And whatever your answer, take a deep breath and *do it*.

Epilogue

Farewell by P.T. Barnum

To my Readers: Although I have reached the evening of life, my heart is young, and the sweetest music in my ears is the merry laughter of childhood. Before the parents of many of you were born, I entered upon my career as a manager of public exhibitions. I have catered to the instruction and amusement of generations. I have gathered from every point of the habitable globe the most marvelous curiosities in the realms of science and invention and the animal kingdom, and am still adding to my collection. I have expended millions in my efforts to educate, interest and amuse. I have appeared before presidents, kings, queens, emperors and rulers, and there are few if any places in the world where my name is unknown. Looking back through the long vista of years, it is a great satisfaction to know that my labors have been so well appreciated by those in whose behalf they were put forth.

P.T. Barnum died quietly in his home on April 7, 1891. He was 80 years old.

229

This way to the Egress . . .

Notes

Chapter 1 Presenting . . . the Greatest Marketeer of All Time—
P. T. Barnum!

When I had the conversation with the fellow on the plane, I had no idea it would become the basis for the first chapter in my book, so I no longer have his name or business card. All of the facts I told him are verified in all of the biographies of Barnum, with Saxon's biography being my primary source. The matchstick guitar can be seen in the October 1996 issue of *Acoustic Guitar* magazine. The description of the 1800s comes from Saxon, as well as from McCutcheon's *The Writer's Guide to Everyday Life in the 1800s*. Material on Barnum in this chapter and throughout the book comes from Saxon's biography, Kundardt's *P.T. Barnum: America's Greatest Showman*, and the George Bryan edition of Barnum's autobiography. The opening quote is from Barnum's letter to his partner, James Bailey: It and all other opening quotes come from letters in Saxon's published collection, *Selected Letters of P.T. Barnum*.

Chapter 2 P.T. Barnum's Amazing 10 Rings of Power for
Creating an Empire

The opening story about Tom Thumb meeting Lincoln comes from *The Autobiography of Mrs. Tom Thumb*. All of the stories and facts come from Saxon's biography, Kundardt's *P.T. Barnum: America's Greatest Showman*, and the George Bryan edition of Barnum's autobiography. They are supported by the Root and Wallace biographies.

231

**Chapter 3   Bonus: *Barnum's Rules for Success in Business*
                    by P.T. Barnum**

This 1852 article by Barnum was reprinted in his 1855 autobiography. I found it in the George Bryan edition of the autobiography. It's used here with Barnum's permission, because he released the copyright to his writing in 1884.

Chapter 4   P.T. Barnum's Amazing Mind-Set for Success

The opening material about famous misquotes is from the book *They Never Said It*. Facts about Barnum's imposters are in Saxon's biography, as well as in Bluford Adams's biography, *E Pluribus Barnum*. The story of the Cardiff giant comes from R.J. Brown, editor-in-chief of the Newspaper Collectors Society of America, and found online at http://www.serve.com/ephemera/library/refbarnum.html. Hoaxes by Poe, Twain, and others are from *The Big Book of Hoaxes*. "Irina" is in the March 1997 issue of *The Net* magazine. Stories about Ivy Island, the Fejee mermaid, the Jenny Lind auction, and the fire extinguisher are from Saxon's biography, Kundardt's *P.T. Barnum: America's Greatest Showman*, and the George Bryan edition of Barnum's autobiography.

**Chapter 5   Attention! What P.T. Barnum Learned When He Was
                    Almost Hanged**

Barnum's near-death experience is common knowledge to anyone who has read his autobiography or any good biography of him. The story about Mangin comes from Barnum's *The Humbugs of the World*. Barnum's attention-getting methods are in Kundardt's *P.T. Barnum: America's Greatest Showman*. The stories about merchants in the 1800s are in Presbrey's *The History and Development of Advertising*. Iranistan material is in the Saxon biography and Barnum's autobiography. The Brooklyn Bridge story is from Lennie Grimaldi's history of Bridgeport, and found in numerous other books. Houdini material is all from Silverman's *Houdini!!! The Career of Ehrich Weiss*. Stories about business people today are from *Promotional Feats*. Barnum shocking his staff and renaming musicians come from Kundardt and Saxon. Stories about W&B and S.T. 1860 X come from Presbrey. The Beacon story is from an article found by Allen D'Angelo. All material about Stanley Arnold is from his autobiography, *Tale of the Blue Horse*. Ending quote is from a letter in Saxon's book of selected letters.

Chapter 6 Barnum Knew People Would Spend Their Last Nickel on This One Thing

Barnum's museum and the African lungfish story are from Kundardt and Saxon. The Buffalo Hunt is told in several biographies and in Barnum's autobiography. The list of businesses that create fun are from material compiled by Allen D'Angelo. The fishing story comes direct from Blair Warren. Ending facts come from Saxon's biography.

Chapter 7 P.T. Barnum's Secret for Making Unknowns Famous and Himself Rich

Description of Lind comes from Shultz's *Jenny Lind: The Swedish Nightingale*. The Lind story is also told in Saxon's biography, Kundardt's *P.T. Barnum: America's Greatest Showman*, and the George Bryan edition of Barnum's autobiography. Elssler material is from Kundardt. Toilet-paper story is from Reichenbach's autobiography, *Phantom Fame*. Bernays material from his autobiography, *Biography of an Idea*. Pease story in Barnum's *The Humbugs of the World*. Barnum making news comes from Kundardt. Morabito quotes are from a private interview with the author. The blackmail story is in Barnum's autobiography and numerous biographies. The George Bush story is from a private interview with Linda Credeur and the author. Ending facts are from the sources stated in the chapter.

Chapter 8 The Shakespeare of Advertising's Rules for Jumbo Success

The ads I reviewed to draw my conclusions are found in the Bridgeport Public Library, Historical Collections, and at the Hertzberg Circus Collection and Museum, San Antonio Public Library. Some ads are in the Kundardt biography. The fact about 90 percent of white Americans could read came from Jonathan Hall's "The Man Who Invented Mass Marketing," *Audacity*, Fall, 1995. John Caples's statistic is from *Tested Advertising Methods*. The Go on Home story is from Fitz-Gibbon's *Macy's, Gimbels, and Me*. The Tody story about using adjectives is from Fellows's *This Way to the Big Show*. The ending quote is from the Root biography of Barnum.

Chapter 9   How an Unknown P.T. Barnum Met
Queen Victoria—and Got Rich

Barnum going overseas with Tom Thumb is from Saxon's biography, Kundardt's
P.T. Barnum: America's Greatest Showman, and the George Bryan edition of Barnum's autobiography. Barnum at the Great Exposition, and the Cary Salon story, is
from Kundardt. Dan's bake sale is from Limbaugh's *See, I Told You So*. Balloon flight
material is from Kundardt and Saxon books.

Chapter 10   How Barnum Purchased the Business of
His Dreams with No Money

The story of Barnum's negotiations is from Saxon's biography, Kundardt's *P.T.
Barnum*, and the George Bryan edition of Barnum's autobiography. The
Swedish bikini team story is from a private interview with Garis and the au-
thor. The Brooklyn Bridge story is from a private interview with Hartunian
and the author. Trump material is from his book, *The Art of the Deal*. The
Dallas story is in Freiberg's *Nuts! Southwest Airlines' Crazy Recipe for Business and
Personal Success*. "Friend Barnum" material is from Shultz's *Jenny Lind: The
Swedish Nightingale*. The ending Barnum material is from Saxon, Kundardt, and
Barnum.

Chapter 11   P.T. Barnum's Secret for Surviving Disasters
and Tragedies

Opening material about the times during which Barnum lived are from Saxon, as
well as from McCutcheon's *The Writer's Guide to Everyday Life in the 1800s*. Barnum's reactions to losses are in Saxon's biography, Kundardt's *P.T. Barnum: America's
Greatest Showman*, and the George Bryan edition of Barnum's autobiography. My
companion to Barnum's grave was Penny Perez, who still cannot believe we found
the graveside. Material from Barry Neil Kaufman and Mandy Evans is from their
books, as mentioned in the chapter. Barnum's small dollar book comes from his
book, *The King of the Animal Kingdom*. Facts about Tileston's book are printed on
that book's jacket cover. Barnum's ending quote is from a letter in Saxon's collection of selected letters.

Chapter 12   How P.T. Barnum Wrote His Own Ticket
                   to Success

Barnum's jail experience is described in numerous places, including Saxon's biography, Kundardt's *P.T. Barnum*, and the George Bryan edition of Barnum's autobiography. Facts about authors come from the August 1994 issue of *DBA* magazine. The Barnum-Twain material can be found in Saxon's biography. The ending material about Barnum releasing his copyright is in Saxon, Kundardt, and George Bryan.

Chapter 13   Bonus: My Exclusive Interview with P.T. Barnum

All answers are from Barnum's own writings, particularly the George Bryan edition of the autobiography, with some additional material from letters found in the Saxon collection.

Chapter 14   How P.T. Barnum Got Rich Right after
                   Going Broke

The Jerome Clock story can be found in every biography of Barnum, with the clearest and most accurate material in Saxon's biography. Description of Barnum as a speaker is from the Root biography. The Bergh story is in Saxon and Kundardt. The ending facts are from the George Bryan edition of Barnum's autobiography.

Chapter 15   Bonus: *The Art of Money Getting* by P.T. Barnum

Barnum's speech comes from his 1869 autobiography, as reprinted in the Bryan edition. It's used here with Barnum's permission, because he released the copyright to it in 1884.

Chapter 16   How to Barnumize Your Business

Opening facts about Barnumisms and Barnumizing are from Bluford Adams's well-researched book, *E Pluribus Barnum*. John Martin's 281 story is from a personal interview with Martin and the author. The Richard Branson story is from a Reuters news story, faxed to me by Blair Warren. MacInvale is a hero in Texas, where his story is common knowledge. Barnum's offer to Grant is in the Saxon biography. Material from Win Wenger, Ph.D., is from a private interview with Wenger and the author. Other quotes are from the sources mentioned in the chapter. Barnum's letter to Twain is in the Saxon published collection.

Epilogue: *Farewell* by P.T. Barnum

Barnum's ending words are from his handwritten introduction to his book, *The King of the Animal Kingdom*.

Bibliography

Abel, Alan. *The Confessions of a Hoaxer.* Toronto: Macmillan, 1970.

Abel, Alan. *The Great American Hoax.* New York: Trident Press, 1966.

Adams, Bluford. *E Pluribus Barnum: The Great Showman and the Making of U.S. Popular Culture.* Minneapolis: University of Minnesota Press, 1997.

Alderson, William. *Mermaids, Mummies, and Mastodons: The Emergence of the American Museum.* Washington, D.C.: American Association of Museums, 1992.

Allen, Robert. *Creating Wealth.* New York: Simon and Schuster, 1986.

Allen, Robert. *Nothing Down.* New York: Simon and Schuster, 1990.

Anderson, Kare. *Pocket Cross-Promotion.* New York: MasterMedia, 1996.

Anderson, Kare. *Walk Your Talk.* Sausalito, CA: Spiral Publishing, 1994.

Andronik, Catherine. *Prince of Humbugs: A Life of P.T. Barnum.* New York: Atheneum, 1994.

Arnold, Stanley. *Tale of the Blue Horse.* Englewood Cliffs, NJ: Prentice-Hall, 1968.

Barnum, P.T. *Dollars and Sense.* Chicago: People's Publishing, 1890.

Barnum, P.T. *Humbugs of the World.* New York: 1866.

Barnum, P.T. *The King of the Animal Kingdom.* Chicago: Peale Co., 1891.

Barnum, P.T. *Struggles and Triumphs; or, The Life of P.T. Barnum, Written by Himself.* Edited and introduced by George S. Bryan. Two volumes. New York: Knopf, 1927. (Author's Note: Barnum's famous autobiography was edited and updated by him over decades, and published and republished many times throughout his life in numerous editions and under different titles, beginning in 1854. Because Barnum put his writing in the public domain in 1884, letting anyone who had the urge print their own edition of his autobiography, there have been many versions, under different titles, of his book. Most scholars consider the Bryan edition the most complete and accurate, while unfortunately the hardest to obtain.)

Barnum, P.T. *Why I Am A Universalist.* Chicago: Universalist Publishing, 18-?.

Barton, Bruce. *What Can A Man Believe?* New York: Grosset & Dunlap, 1927.

Bernays, Edward L. *Biography of an Idea: Memoirs of Public Relations Counsel Edward L. Bernays.* New York: Simon & Schuster, 1965.

Bernays, Edward L. *Propaganda.* New York: Liveright Publishing, 1928.

Bly, Robert. *Targeted Public Relations.* New York: Holt, 1993.

Boese, Alex. *The Museum of Hoaxes: A Collection of Pranks, Stunts, Deceptions, and other Wonderful Stories Contrived for the Public from the Middle Ages to the New Millennium.* New York: Dutton, 2002.

Boller, Paul F. *They Never Said It: A Book of Fake Quotes, Misquotes and Misleading Attributions.* New York: Oxford University Press, 1989.

Bondeson, Jan. *The Feejee Mermaid, and Other Essays in Natural and Unnatural History.* London: Cornell University, 1999.

Borkowski, Mark. *Improperganda: The Art of the Publicity Stunt.* London: Vision On, 2000. Photos and brief stories compiled by a modern day Barnum.

Branson, Richard. *Losing My Virginity: The Autobiography.* London: Virgin, 1998.

Braudy, Leo. *The Frenzy of Renown: Fame and Its History.* New York: Vintage Books, 1997.

Brown, Stephen. *Free Gift Inside!* London: Capstone, 2003.

Brown, Stephen. *Marketing: The Retro Revolution.* London: Sage Publications, 2001.

Bulgatz, Joseph. *Ponzi Schemes, Invaders from Mars, and More Extraordinary Popular Delusions and the Madness of Crowds.* New York: Harmony, 1992.

Butts, Rick. *The Safari Adventure Company: Discovering the Three Treasures of Courage.* Houston: Coyote Creek Press, 1997.

Caples, John. *Tested Advertising Methods.* Englewood Cliffs, NJ: Prentice-Hall, 1974.

Castle, William. *Step Right Up! I'm Gonna Scare the Pants Off America.* New York: Pharos Press, 1976.

Cook, James. *The Arts of Deception: Playing with Fraud in the Age of Barnum.* Cambridge: Harvard University Press, 2001.

Cook, Fred. *Entertaining the World: P.T. Barnum.* Chicago: Britannica Books, 1962.

Crilley, Jeff. *Free Publicity: A TV Reporter Shares the Secrets for Getting Covered on the News.* Dallas: Charisma Press, 2003.

Cull, Nicholas; Culbert, David; Welch, David. *Propaganda and Mass Persuasion: A Historical Encyclopedia, 1500 to the Present.* Santa Barbara, CA: ABC-CLIO, Inc., 2003.

Cushman, Aaron. *A Passion for Winning: Fifty Years Promoting Legendary People and Products.* Pittsburgh: Lighthouse Point Press, 2004.

Cutlip, Scott. *The Unseen Power: Public Relations, a History.* Hillsdale, NJ: Lawrence Erlbaum Associates, 1994. A truly fascinating and complete history.

Debelak, Don. *Marketing Magic.* Holbrook, MA: Bob Adams, Inc., 1994.

Dennett, Andrea Stulman. *Weird and Wonderful: The Dime Museum in America.* New York: New York University Press, 1997.

Desmond, Alice Curtis. *Barnum Presents Tom Thumb.* New York: MacMillan, 1954.

Evans, Mandy. *Travelling Free: How to Recover from the Past by Changing Your Beliefs.* Desert Hot Springs, CA: Yes You Can Press (Box 337, Desert Hot Springs, CA 92240), 1990.

Ewen, Stuart. *PR! A Social History of Spin.* New York: Basic Books, 1996.

Falk, Edgar. *1,001 Ideas to Create Retail Excitement.* Englewood Cliffs, NJ: Prentice-Hall, 1994.

Fellows, Dexter. *This Way to the Big Show.* New York: Halcyon House, 1936.

Fisher, David. *The War Magician.* New York: Coward-McCann, 1983.

Fisher, Donna. *People Power: 12 Power Principles to Enrich Your Business, Career and Personal Networks.* Austin, TX: Bard & Stephen Publishers, 1995.

Fitz-Gibbon, Bernice. *Macy's, Gimbels, and Me.* New York: Simon & Schuster, 1951.

Fitzsimons, Raymund. *Barnum in London.* New York: St. Martin's Press, 1970.

Fleming, E. J. *The Fixers: Eddie Mannix, Howard Strickling and the MGM Publicity Machine.* Jefferson, NC: McFarland, 2005.

Fowler, Gene. *The Mighty Barnum: A Screen Play.* New York: Covici-Friede, 1934.

Freiberg, Kevin and Jackie. *Nuts! Southwest Airlines' Crazy Recipe for Business and Personal Success.* Austin, TX: Bard Press, 1996.

Froelich, Paula. *It! 9 Secrets of the Rich and Famous that Will Take You to the Top.* New York: Hyperion, 2005.

Gompertz, Rolf. *Publicity Advice & How-To Handbook.* N. Hollywood: Word Doctor Publications (PO Box 9761, N. Hollywood, CA 91609-1761), 1994.

Gregor, Jan. *Circus of the Scars: The True Inside Odyssey of a Modern Circus Sideshow.* Seattle, WA: Brennan Dalsgard, 1998.

Grimaldi, Lennie. *Only in Bridgeport: An Illustrated History of the Park City.* Bridgeport, CT: Harbor Publishing, 1993.

Hall, Jonathan. "The Man Who Invented Mass Marketing." *Audacity*, Fall 1995.

Harding, Les. *Elephant Story: Jumbo and P.T. Barnum Under the Big Top.* London: McFarland, 2000.

Harris, Monique. *How to Make Yourself Famous in 6 Months or Less.* Greenbelt, MD: Marketing Moguls (6007 Springfield Dr. #304, Greenbelt, MD 20770-3129), 1997.

Harris, Neil. *Humbug: The Art of P.T. Barnum.* Chicago: University of Chicago Press, 1973.

Harris, Thomas. *The Marketer's Guide to Public Relations: How Today's Top Companies Are Using the New PR to Gain a Competitive Edge.* New York: Wiley, 1991.

Hartunian, Paul. *How to Get $1 Million Worth of Publicity . . . Free.* Upper Montclair, NJ: Hartunian Publications (Box 43596, Upper Montclair, NJ 07043), 1994.

Hicks, Jerry and Esther. *The Science of Deliberate Creation.* San Antonio: Abraham-Hicks Publications (PO Box 690070, San Antonio, TX 78269), 1997.

Joyner, Mark. *The Irresistible Offer.* Hoboken, NJ: Wiley, 2005.

Kaplan, Fred. *The Singular Mark Twain.* New York: Doubleday, 2003.

Kaufman, Barry Neil. *Happiness Is A Choice.* New York: Fawcett Columbine, 1991.

Kundardt, Philip B. Jr., Philip B. III, and Peter W. *P.T. Barnum: America's Greatest Showman.* New York: Alfred A. Knopf, 1995. Excellent. A fabulously illustrated, giant sized biography of Barnum, used to make the 1995 television documentary of the same name. Clearly the most enjoyable book ever created on Barnum to date.

Leamer, Laurence. *Fantastic: The Life of Arnold Schwarzenegger.* New York: St. Martin's Press, 2005.

Levy, Mark. *Accidental Genius.* San Francisco: Berrett-Koehler, 2000.

Limbaugh, Rush. *See, I Told You So.* New York: Pocket Books, 1993.

Mackay, Charles. *Extraordinary Popular Delusions and the Madness of Crowds.* New York: Crown, 1980.

Magri, Countess M. Lavinia. *The Autobiography of Mrs. Tom Thumb.* Hamden, CT: Archon Books, 1979.

McBride, Robert M. *Great Hoaxes of All Time.* New York: McBride Co., 1956.

McCutcheon, Marc. *The Writer's Guide to Everyday Life in the 1800s.* Cincinnati: Writer's Digest Books, 1993.

Michaels, Nancy. *Off-the-Wall Marketing Ideas.* Holbrook, MA: Adams Media, 2000.

Nickell, Joe. *Secrets of the Sideshows.* Kentucky: University Press of Kentucky, 2005.

Nierenberg, Gerard. *The Art of Negotiating.* New York: Hawthorne, 1968.

O'Brien, Timothy. *TrumpNation: The Art of Being the Donald.* New York: Time Warner, 2005.

Ott, Richard. *Creating Demand: Powerful Tips and Tactics for Marketing Your Product or Service.* Homewood, IL: Business One Irwin, 1992.

Pearlstein, Leo. *Celebrity Stew: Food Publicity.* LA: Hollywood Circle Press, 2003.

Pond, Major J. B. *Eccentricities of Genius.* New York: Dillingham, 1900.

Powers, Ron. *Mark Twain: A Life.* New York: Free Press, 2005.

Poynter, Dan. *Parachuting: The Skydiver's Handbook.* Santa Barbara: Para Publishing, 1992.

Presbrey, Frank. *The History and Development of Advertising.* Garden City: Doubleday, Doran & Company, 1929.

Reichenbach, Harry. *Phantom Fame: The Anatomy of Ballyhoo.* New York: Simon & Schuster, 1931.

Reiss, Benjamin. *The Showman and the Slave: Race, Death, and Memory in Barnum's America.* Cambridge: Harvard University Press, 2001.

Root, Harvey. *The Unknown Barnum.* New York: Harper, 1927.

Salzman, Jason. *Making the News: A Guide for Nonprofits and Activists.* Boulder, CO: Westview, 1988.

Sampson, Henry. *History of Advertising.* London: Chatto and Windus, 1875. Fascinating tome said to have inspired Houdini.

Saxon, A. H. *Barnumiana: A Select, Annotated Bibliography of Works by or Relating to P.T. Barnum.* Fairfield, CT: Jumbo's Press (166 Orchard Hill Drive, Fairfield, CT 06430), 1995.

Saxon, A. H. *P.T. Barnum: The Legend and the Man.* New York: Columbia University, 1989.

Saxon, A. H. *Selected Letters of P.T. Barnum.* New York: Columbia University, 1983. The most scholarly biography of Barnum to date, illustrated, with an accurate chronology of Barnum's life and events, and appendixes with important information.

Schechter, Harold. *The Humbug: A Novel.* New York: Pocket Books, 2001.

Schmidt, Connie. *Cosmic Relief: Honoring and Celebrating the Global Paradigm Shaft.* Houston: Misguided Angel Press (Box 270896, Houston, TX 77277-0896), 1997.

Sennett, Robert. *Hollywood Hoopla: Creating Stars and Selling Movies in the Golden Age of Hollywood*. New York: Billboard Books, 1998.

Severn, Bill. *A Carnival of Sports: Spectacles, Stunts, Crazes, and Unusual Sports Events*. New York: David McKay Co., 1974.

Shultz, Gladys Denny. *Jenny Lind: The Swedish Nightingale*. New York: J.P. Lippincott, 1962.

Sifakis, Carl. *The Big Book of Hoaxes*. New York: Paradox Press, 1996.

Sifakis, Carl. *Hoaxes and Scams: A Compendium of Deceptions, Ruses and Swindles*. New York: Facts on File, 1993.

Silverman, Kenneth. *Houdini!!! The Career of Ehrich Weiss*. New York: HarperCollins, 1996.

Simon, Ray. *Mischief Marketing*. Chicago: Contemporary Books, 2000.

Slater, Robert. *No Such Thing As Over-Exposure: Inside the Life and Celebrity of Donald Trump*. NJ: Pearson/Prentice-Hall, 2005.

Slutsky, Jeff. *Streetfighter Marketing*. New York: Lexington Books, 1995.

Soares, Eric. *Promotional Feats*. Westport, CT: Quorum Books, 1991.

Stauber, John and Rampton, Sheldon. *Toxic Sludge Is Good For You: Lies, Damn Lies and the Public Relations Industry*. Monroe, ME: Common Courage Press, 1995.

Sutton, Felix. *Master of Ballyhoo: The Story of P.T. Barnum*. New York: G.P. Putnam's, 1968.

Tileston, Mary Wilder. *Daily Strength for Daily Needs*. Boston: Little, Brown, 1994.

Tompert, Ann. *The Greatest Showman on Earth: A Biography of P.T. Barnum*. New York: Dillon Press, 1987.

Trump, Donald. *The Art of the Deal*. New York: Warner Books, 1987.

Turner, E.S. *The Shocking History of Advertising*. New York: Ballantine, 1953.

Vitale, Joe. *The AMA Complete Guide to Small Business Advertising*. Chicago: NTC Business Books, 1995.

Vitale, Joe. *The Attractor Factor: 5 Easy Steps for Creating Wealth (or anything else) from the Inside Out*. Hoboken, NJ: Wiley, 2005.

Vitale, Joe. *CyberWriting: How to Promote Your Product or Service Online (without being flamed)*. New York: AMACOM, 1997.

Vitale, Joe. *Hypnotic Selling Secrets*. http://www.HypnoticMarketingStrategy.com. Dallas: Nitro Marketing, 2004.

Vitale, Joe. *The Power of Outrageous Marketing*. Audio program. Chicago: Nightingale-Conant, 1998.

Vitale, Joe. *The Seven Lost Secrets of Success*. Houston: Morgan James Publishing, 1992.

Vitale, Joe. *Turbocharge Your Writing!* Houston: Awareness Publications, 1988.

Wallace, Irving. *The Fabulous Showman: The Life and Times of P.T. Barnum.* New York: Knopf, 1959.

Wallace, Irving. *The Two: The Story of the Original Siamese Twins.* New York: Simon & Schuster, 1978.

Ware, W. Porter. *P.T. Barnum Presents Jenny Lind: The American Tour of the Swedish Nightingale.* Baton Rouge, LA: Louisiana State University Press, 1980.

Walters, Dottie. *Speak and Grow Rich.* Englewood Cliffs, NJ: Prentice-Hall, 1989.

Weiner, Richard. *Professional's Guide to Public Relations Services.* New York: AMA-COM, 1988.

Wenger, Win. *Beyond Teaching and Learning.* Gaithersburg, MD: Project Renaissance (Box 332, Gaithersburg, MD 20884-0332), 1992.

Wenger, Win. *Techniques of Original, Inspired Scientific Discovery.* Gaithersburg, MD: Project Renaissance (Box 332, Gaithersburg, MD 20884-0332), 1997.

Wenger, Win and Poe, Richard. *The Einstein Factor.* Rocklin, CA: Prima Publishing, 1996.

Werner, M. R. *Barnum.* New York: Harcourt Brace, 1923.

Willis, David. *In Search of Gold: A Guide for Using Stress-Free Prospecting to Find and Mine Customers.* Houston: Relationship Marketing (20202 Highway 59 North, Suite 162, Humble, TX 77338), 1997.

Resources

Barnum Museum, 820 Main St., Bridgeport, CT 06604. Phone: 203-331-9881.
Bridgeport Public Library, Historical Collections, 925 Broad St., Bridgeport, CT 06604. Phone: 203-576-7417.
Hertzberg Circus Collection and Museum, San Antonio Public Library, 210 Market St., San Antonio, TX 78205. Phone: 210-207-7819.

Web sites:

www.ptbarnum.org
http://www.barnum-museum.org/ (The Barnum Museum)
http://home.nycap.rr.com/useless/barnum/ (P.T. Barnum—How He Changed the English Language Forever)
http://en.wikipedia.org/wiki/P._T._Barnum
http://www.lostmuseum.cuny.edu/intro.html (The Lost Museum)
http://www.well.com/user/kafclown/barnum/ptlinks.html
http://www.historybuff.com/library/refbarnum.html
http://www.nytimes.com/learning/general/onthisday/bday/0705.html (Read P.T. Barnum's Obituary)
http://www.findagrave.com/cgi-bin/fg.cgi?page=gr&GRid=56 (View P.T. Barnum's Gravesite)
http://www.electricscotland.com/history/barnum/index.htm (Read Joel Benton's biography of Barnum online)
http://www.hti.umich.edu/cgi/t/text/text-idx?c=moa;idno=AFW8590 (Read P.T. Barnum's book, *Humbugs of the World*, online)

http://freepages.history.rootsweb.com/~dav4is/people/BRNM137.htm (P.T. Barnum Links—An extensive collection of links about Barnum by a distant relative of old Phineas (Rod Davis). Mr. Davis is a genealogical wiz, and is both a second cousin, four times removed, and a third cousin, five times removed of Barnum. From a different portion of his web site, one can also learn that Barnum and his star attraction, General Tom Thumb, were also distantly related!)

About the Author

Dr. Joe Vitale, president of Hypnotic Marketing, Inc., located outside Austin, Texas, is the author of too many books to list here. Here are just a few of them:

He wrote the #1 bestseller, *The Attractor Factor: 5 Easy Steps for Creating Wealth (or Anything Else) from the Inside Out*, the #3 bestseller *The Greatest Money-Making Secret in History*, and the #1 best-selling E-book *Hypnotic Writing*. His latest books are *Life's Missing Instruction Manual* and *Meet and Grow Rich*.

Besides all of his books, Dr. Vitale also recorded the #1 best-selling Nightingale-Conant audio program, *The Power of Outrageous Marketing*. In addition, he has a complete home-study course in marketing at www.HypnoticMarketingStrategy.com.

His corporate web site is at http://www.HypnoticMarketingInc.com. Sign up for his complimentary newsletter *News You Can Use!* at his main web site www.mrfire.com.

Index

Special P.T. Barnum Bonus!

Here's How You Can Obtain a Million Dollars of *Free* Publicity on the Internet Plus Stand Out Like a 10,273 Pound Circus Elephant in a Mailbox!

From the desk of Dr. Joe Vitale
Wimberley, Texas

Dear Reader,

I would like to personally thank you for purchasing *There's a Customer Born Every Minute.*

With over a million and a half books in print in the United States alone, I am honored that you somehow ended up with this one in your hands. Whether you found this book at your local book store or a friend recommended it to you, I can assure you that it wasn't by chance.

It was by publicity.

With the astonishing amount of books published every day, it truly takes creative marketing and uncommon publicity on and off the Internet to get noticed in today's mass-marketed world.

I can't help but wonder where marketing and publicity would be today if P.T. Barnum were alive and had access to the Internet. What cutting edge strategies would he use to stand out in an over-marketed society?

And what about you? *What will you do today that your potential customers will remember tomorrow?*

As a personal thank-you for reading my book, I'd like to extend an incredible offer to you. If you've been endlessly searching for ways that would literally force your product or service to stand out on the Internet, *I have your answer.*

In my brand new, limited edition special report, I'll share countless methods and ideas that you can start implementing right away to obtain over a million dollars of free publicity on the Internet. Believe me, you will be shocked by how quickly you will see the results!

Now, instead of doing what everyone else does, which is simply allowing you to download my report, I've taken P.T. Barnum's advice on this one. I'm actually going to physically mail you the report, plus an exclusive bonus!

Truly, I have a very limited number of copies that I will be mailing out. Now, I cannot promise you that these reports will become collectors' items because of their scarcity, but what I can promise you is that, if you do not order your free report and bonus today, they may not be here tomorrow.

To Order Your Free Report Plus The Exclusive Bonus, Go To:
www.barnumbonus.com

Go for it!

Joe Vitale

Dr. Joe Vitale